Revised Edition

ESL TEACHING
Principles for Success

Yvonne S. Freeman, David E. Freeman, Mary Soto, and Ann Ebe

HEINEMANN
Portsmouth, NH

Heinemann
361 Hanover Street
Portsmouth, NH 03801–3912
www.heinemann.com

Offices and agents throughout the world

Figure 8–2: We are grateful to TESOL Italy for permission to reproduce material from Luciano Mariani's article "Teacher Support and Teacher Challenge in Promoting Learner Autonomy," which was first published in *Perspectives: A Journal of TESOL Italy*, 1997, 23 (2). http://tesolitaly.org /new/perspectives/. This figure was adapted with permission and previously published in *English Learners, Academic Literacy, and Thinking* (2009) and *Scaffolding Language, Scaffolding Learning* (2015) by Pauline Gibbons. Published by Heinemann, Portsmouth, NH.

Library of Congress Cataloging-in-Publication Data
Names: Freeman, Yvonne S., author. | Freeman, David E., author. | Soto, Mary,
    author. | Ebe, Ann, author.
Title: ESL teaching : principles for success / Yvonne S. Freeman, David E.
    Freeman, Mary Soto, and Ann Ebe.
Other titles: ESL/EFL teaching
Description: Revised Edition. | Portsmouth, NH : Heinemann, 2016 |
    Previous title: ESL/EFL teaching, 1998.
Identifiers: LCCN 2015037775 | ISBN 9780325062495
Subjects: LCSH: Second language acquisition. | English language—Study and
    Teaching—Foreign speakers.
Classification: LCC P53 .F73 2016 | DDC 418.007—dc23

LC record available at http://lccn.loc.gov/2015037775

Editor: Holly Kim Price
Production: Vicki Kasabian *and* Hilary Goff
Cover design: Suzanne Heiser
Interior design: Shawn Girsberger
Typesetter: Shawn Girsberger
Manufacturing: Steve Bernier

Printed in the United States of America on acid-free paper

2 3 4 5 6 RWP 24 23 22 21 20

We dedicate this book to the caring and creative teachers of emergent bilinguals who give of themselves in order to meet their students' needs. We especially dedicate this book to the teachers working with the growing numbers of refugee emergent bilingual students who have suffered so much, and yet, come here to face more challenges. We hope this book will make a difference.

—*Yvonne and David Freeman*

I dedicate this book to my husband, Francisco, and children Romero and Maya, and to my emergent bilingual students, both past and present. Their struggles and their achievements have inspired me to strive to be the best educator possible.

—*Mary Soto*

I dedicate this book to the very committed and passionate teachers of emergent bilingual students in the United States and abroad and also to my husband, Christopher, and children Christiana and Alexander, who are acquiring their third language in our new home, Mexico City.

—*Ann Ebe*

Contents

Acknowledgments

This new edition of *ESL Teaching: Principles for Success* is a much-needed update. In the time since the previous publication of this book the number of emergent bilinguals has grown, and now all teachers need to know about effective methods, not just ESL and bilingual specialists. States have developed new standards for English language proficiency, and teachers are now charged with teaching both academic content and academic language. Despite all these changes, the principles for successful teaching have remained the same. Our goal in this book is to show how the principles we discuss are based on current research. We also include many new examples from talented teachers using these principles for success in classes with emergent bilinguals.

We wish to acknowledge the outstanding educators whose work we share in this book: Kay Armijo, Charlotte Brown, Jason Cain, Peter Chue, Bria Cianci, Charlene Klassen, Mike Lebsock, Choa Lor, Nou Lor, Connie Patton, Gregoria Rodriguez, Maria Rosario, Adriana Ruiz, Charene Santiago-Chapman, Nancy Solorio, Francisco Soto, Jenna-Marie Theofield, Rhoda Toews, and Natascha Yarussi.

In addition, we would like to thank our professional colleagues whose guidance and support have helped us develop a better understanding of effective practices for working with emergent bilinguals. Mary would like to acknowledge teacher educators with whom she has worked and from whom she has gained inspiration: Esther Larocco, Charles Zartman, Elizabeth Stevens, Nora McKay, and Lettie Ramirez. Ann would like to acknowledge Ofelia García and the CUNY-NYSIEB research team; Jenny Tuten, the Acting Dean of Education at Hunter College, as well as all of her literacy program colleagues at Hunter; and finally, Brian Collins, her bilingual program colleague, supporter, and friend.

We want to acknowledge the support and advice we received from our editor, Holly Kim Price. She read each chapter of our manuscript and encouraged us as we wrote and revised this book. The production team at Heinemann always does an outstanding job. Lauren Audet oversaw the figures and permissions for the book. Hilary Goff helped design the beautiful cover. We were fortunate to be able to work with Vicki Kasabian again, a friend and editor who is responsible for the overall book design. Thanks, too, to Sherry Day, who oversaw the back cover photos. Ann would also like to thank her photographer, Pallavi Kerjiwal. Finally, we would like to acknowledge Kim Cahill for her work in promoting this book.

Introduction

> We have a thirty-five-minute period each day where kids are supposed to get either enrichment or support. The teachers are supposed to monitor the students and decide what they need. We don't like the idea because it is separating the high and the low students. Teachers were not able to collaborate, monitor, and assess students, so now our vice principal says everyone is going to take a standardized reading test that is quick to administer. What are they gonna find out? That newcomers don't speak English? That long-term English learners struggle with reading? This proves two things: Our administration is clueless because they think that separating students is the best way to go. Second, that our teachers don't want to make the effort to get to know their students.

This description was sent as a text to Mary, a teacher educator in a program preparing future teachers to work with English learners or what we call *emergent bilingual students*. The author of the text is a new teacher working in a rural farming community in her first teaching job. This new teacher learned how to work with emergent bilingual students in her teacher preparation program, but, unfortunately, other teachers in her school have received very little training in how to work with students who come to school speaking languages other than English. Schools in the U.S. are growing more ethnically and linguistically diverse each year, and all educators, not just ESL or bilingual teachers, need to understand how to work with the changing populations of students (Goulah and Soltero 2015; Lucas, Villegas, and González 2008; Wiley et al. 2013).

We believe that educators want to do what is best for their students. Good teachers are open to knowledge and are the ones best suited to use that knowledge to provide effective instruction (Majumdar 2014). But with the growing changes in student demographics and the demands of standardized testing and curriculum, teachers like the teacher quoted earlier are not always supported in using current methods. A Teaching and Learning International Survey conducted by the

Organization for Economic Cooperation and Development (OECD) showed that American teachers face many more challenges than teachers in other developed countries (Majumdar 2014). They receive less helpful professional development and do not feel that their profession is valued by society. In contrast, in countries where teachers are respected and are given high-quality professional learning opportunities, teachers feel empowered "to make complex decisions and solve problems easily" (1). These teachers are able to connect theory and practice, and their students experience academic success.

Majumdar suggests that appropriate teacher development goals should include the integration of new knowledge and skills into practice, the connection of discipline knowledge with curriculum standards, the development of research-based practices, and the achievement of measurable school achievement in a complex school environment.

This book, *ESL Teaching: Principles for Success*, is written with these teacher development goals in mind. Although the principles in this book can be applied broadly to different contexts, the book and the examples are specific to the U.S. setting. We wrote this book to support administrators and teachers, both mainstream and ESL/bilingual, to work more effectively with emergent bilingual students in schools.

Emergent bilingual learners (EBLs) or emergent bilinguals (EBs) are students who come to school speaking languages other than English. Many different terms are used to describe these students, including English Language Learners (ELLs), English Learners (ELs), English as a Second Language (ESL) learners, English to Speakers of Other Languages (ESOL) students, culturally and linguistically diverse (CLD) learners, bilingual learners, English as an Additional Language (EALs) learners, Language Minority (LM), Limited English Speakers (LES), second language learners (L2), and a term used in government documents, Limited English Proficient students (LEPs). In early childhood a commonly used description of preschool English learners is dual language learners (DLLs), because educators understand that these young learners are developing the basics of their home language while they are learning their new language, English (E. Garcia 2012; O. García and Kleifgen 2010; Goldenberg et al. 2013; Severns 2012).

O. García, Kleifgen, and Flachi (2008) argue that *emergent bilingual* is a more appropriate way to refer to students who are learning English because it validates the language or languages students come to school speaking and acknowledges the fact that, as they learn English, they are becoming bilingual. They are not simply learning English, as the term *English learner* implies; they are emergent bilinguals. It is critical to consider the names we use to describe students. As O. García and Kleifgen (2010) explain

When officials and educators ignore the bilingualism that these students can and must develop through schooling in the United States, they perpetuate inequities in the education of these students. That is, they discount the home languages and the cultural understandings of these children and assume that their needs are the same as a monolingual child. (2)

In fact, many of these students learning English are becoming emergent multilinguals as they already speak more than one language before beginning to learn English. In this book, we use the term *emergent bilingual* as well as other commonly used terms to describe these students.

DEMOGRAPHIC CHANGES IN SCHOOLS

The number of children under the age of 17 living with immigrant parents grew 60 percent from 1990 to 2000 and another 33 percent from 2000 to 2012 to 17.4 million (Nwosu, Bartalova, and Auclai 2014). These demographics have important implications for schools. *Education Week* reported that in fall 2014 for the first time minority students became the numerical majority in schools in the U.S. The combined population of Latinos, African Americans, and Asian Americans represents 50.3 percent of the K–12 student population. This shift in the student population has not been accompanied by a corresponding shift in the teacher workforce. In the 2011–2012 school year, 82 percent of public school teachers were non-Hispanic white, 7 percent were non-Hispanic black, and 8 percent were Hispanic (Maxwell 2014b). These demographics have particular implications for those minority/majority students who are emergent bilinguals.

The number of students in U.S. schools who are emergent bilinguals has risen from 3.5 million in 1998 to more than 5 million. They represent a little over 10 percent of the school population overall and a much higher percent in some parts of the country (Bartalova and McHugh 2010). These numbers continue to grow as students arrive from different places for different reasons. Immigrants come into this country because of both push and pull factors. There are reasons immigrants feel pushed away from their home countries. Some come here fleeing extreme poverty, war, or religious or ethnic persecution. Others are escaping natural disasters, limited access to water, or famine. The U.S. pulls immigrants who are seeking education and job opportunities not available to them in their native countries. In addition, many immigrants come here to reunite with family members who have immigrated here earlier.

Immigrant families from across the globe are sometimes able to immigrate when other family members living here sponsor them, but oftentimes women and children come alone. It is estimated that almost two million Mexican and Central

American unaccompanied minor children are living in the U.S. Between 2011 and 2014, 137,000 minor children and family units with at least one parent arrived in the U.S. (Rosenblum 2015). In the fall of 2013 more than 55,000 family units and unaccompanied immigrant children fleeing violence, abuse, and poverty at home arrived in the U.S. (Maxwell 2014). These children, most of whom eventually reunite with some family members living in this country, have tenuous status.

In 2012 the Secretary of Homeland Security announced that certain unauthorized immigrants who entered the United States as children would be able to apply for deferred action, granting relief from deportation and receiving work authorization for two years. The Migration Policy Institute estimates that more than one half million of these Deferred Action for Childhood Arrival (DACA) immigrants have applied for deferred action (Batalova, Hooker, and Capps 2013; Nwosu, Bartalova, and Auclai 2014). Their cases need to be reviewed and, in the meantime, they can attend school while awaiting decisions from immigration judges about whether they may remain (Maxwell 2014). However, in August 2014, the House of Representatives voted not to renew DACA, leaving new arrivals in a limbo situation.

More recently, the tension between protection and enforcement of laws regarding unauthorized immigration of people not having valid humanitarian claims has initiated a new child and family court docket to speed up review of these immigrants. In addition, new cross agency coordination with Mexico and additional detention centers have stemmed the flow of these immigrants considerably (Rosenblum 2015). An investigative report by Nazario (2015) is an exposé of this cross agency coordination with Mexico. The report revealed that the U.S. government has spent "tens of millions of dollars" that has resulted in "a ferocious crackdown on refugees fleeing violence in Central America" (1). Nazario explains that many of these refugees are trying to escape escalated gang violence in Guatemala, El Salvador, and Honduras and provides examples from her interviews of the atrocities refugees face at home and in their journey to escape. Nazario concludes her report saying

> The United States should develop a system for these refugees, much like Europe is now doing for Syrians, to equitably allocate people who are fleeing harm throughout this continent—including sending them to safer countries in Latin America, to Canada and to the United States. (2)

Nazario reports that many refugees are killed, kidnapped, raped, and mistreated by Mexican gangs and some corrupt officials as they try to reach the U.S. for asylum. There is a good possibility the U.S. will provide even more money to Mexico to stem the tide of undocumented refugees entering the country. Even though Mexico is apprehending about 70 percent of Central Americans attempting to cross through Mexico, in September 2015 more than twice the number of unaccompanied children were caught and put into federal custody at the U.S. border than were caught the previous year.

Schools will continue to be impacted by these unaccompanied minors who have suffered and are real refugees. The students struggle with English as well as with psychological factors, including stress from their long and dangerous journeys and a feeling of abandonment by relatives they are living with now and those who left them behind in their home countries.

Some states, including California, Texas, Illinois, New York, New Jersey, and Florida, have had large numbers of emergent bilinguals for many years. However, other states have experienced rapid growth in recent years—Nevada, North Carolina, and Georgia have experienced an almost 400 percent growth in the last twenty years. Arkansas, Tennessee, Nebraska, South Carolina, Utah, Washington, and Alabama all experienced 200 percent or more growth in this same time period (Pandya, Bartalova, and McHugh 2011). Teachers in these states are often less well prepared to work with EBLs, and training for both preservice and inservice teachers is often more limited.

Teachers must be prepared to meet the needs of the many emergent bilingual students in schools; however, a recent report concerning how prepared teachers are tells us that

> While it is true that there are educational specialists, for example, English as a second language and bilingual teachers, who have expertise in supporting ELLs, many teachers do not. Yet the reality is that most, if not all teachers have or can expect to have ELL students in their classroom and therefore must be prepared to best support these children. In many cases, a general education teacher who knows the content and pedagogy to teach to the grade-level standards will also need specific knowledge and skills to help ELLs access the curricula. (Samson and Collins 2012, 1–2)

Our own work in professional development for inservice teachers in the last few years alone has taken us to several states with fast-growing emergent bilingual populations, including North Carolina, Tennessee, Utah, and Alabama. In addition, we have worked in other states, including Virginia, Mississippi, Nebraska, Wisconsin, and Iowa, where districts have experienced a sudden growth in the number of emergent bilinguals. As we talk to and with teachers, we are impressed by the diversity of the schools and students. At the same time, the needs of the teachers are quite similar. Both teachers and administrators need to understand second language acquisition, linguistics, second language teaching methods, and cross-cultural communication. In this book we focus on principles for effective teaching of emergent bilinguals. These principles are based on current understandings of second language acquisition, linguistics, and cross-cultural communication.

PRINCIPLES FOR EFFECTIVE TEACHING

In the first chapter of this book we review older ESL teaching methods up through the 1980s and the educational theories that influenced the development of these methods. We then discuss what educational organizations, researchers, and practitioners say constitutes best practices for emergent bilingual students. Next, we lay out seven principles for supporting the academic success of English learners in schools based on these reports as well as our own work with schools and individual teachers. Our goal is to take theory and research, explain it in a comprehensible way, and demonstrate to readers how to implement the principles. While all seven principles listed in Figure I–1 are interrelated and should be present in effective classrooms, we will explain each with specific examples in individual chapters.

The first principle, teaching should be learner centered, emphasizes the importance of knowing one's students. We describe different types of English learners and their needs. We lay out the general levels of progress that emergent bilinguals move through and what teachers should expect from students at different stages of their development of English. We provide examples of how teachers who understand their students' backgrounds have met the needs of students at different levels of English proficiency.

In our discussion of the second principle, teaching should go from whole to part, we provide a rationale for the development of thematic instruction or units of inquiry based on big questions. When emergent bilingual students understand the big picture of what they are studying, they can make better sense of the English language instruction. When teachers plan integrated units that seek to answer important questions, they support students in learning both language and subject area content.

As we discuss the third principle, teaching should develop academic language and content, we show how creative teachers develop both content and language objectives to meet the standards and support the development of academic language for their English learners. We provide examples from teachers who have carefully planned language and content objectives and have scaffolded instruction to help their students develop the academic language they need to access the curriculum. In addition, we discuss methods, such as CALLA, that have been developed to teach academic language and content.

1. Teaching should be learner centered.

2. Teaching should go from whole to part.

3. Teaching should develop academic language and content.

4. Teaching should be meaningful and purposeful.

5. Teaching should include interactions to develop both oral and written language.

6. Teaching should support students' languages and cultures.

7. Teaching and assessment should reflect faith in the learner.

FIGURE I–1 *Principles for Effective Teaching*

The fourth principle, teaching should be meaningful and purposeful, empha-sizes the need to provide learners with meaningful and purposeful activities that engage them in learning academic language and content. Students need to be interested in what they are learning, and teachers need to draw on students' back-grounds and interests so that they become actively involved in learning the content laid out by the standards.

The fifth principle is that teaching should include carefully planned interac-tions to develop both oral and written language. Students are often more engaged when they are interacting and learning with others. Emergent bilinguals need opportunities to use academic language, so teachers need to carefully plan activ-ities that encourage students to talk together, problem solve together, and com-pose together using their new language. Through involvement in carefully planned interactions emergent bilinguals develop both oral and written language.

In all classrooms, students' languages and cultures should be supported and promoted. For this reason, teaching should support students' languages and cul-tures, our sixth principle. Lessons should be based on language acquisition theory and research showing the importance of using students' first languages in teaching. As we discuss this principle, we review models of bilingual education and review the research showing the effectiveness of each model. We also discuss *translanguag-ing*, the use of students' home languages and English to negotiate meaning in the classroom. In addition, we show how teachers can support students' first languages even when they do not speak their languages.

In our final chapter, we explain the last principle, that teaching and assess-ment should reflect faith in the learner to expand student potential. Even students with low levels of English proficiency can and do learn when teachers organize curriculum in ways that help them develop the academic language of school as they learn the academic content.

EXAMPLES OF CLASSROOM PRACTICE

Our goal in this book is to help teachers understand these seven key principles by explaining them and showing how teachers have applied them. Throughout the book we will describe classrooms where the theory and research is brought to life. These classroom examples come from practicing teachers with years of experience working with emergent bilinguals as well as from new teachers who are working to understand how to translate theory and research into practice. The examples provided are from different grade levels and from urban, suburban, and rural schools. Emergent bilinguals speak different home languages and bring different educational, social, and economic backgrounds to school. It is our belief that when teachers follow the principles we outline in this book, they will be able to implement effective practices for all their students.

1
Methods of Teaching a Second or Foreign Language

A book on methods should include an understanding of the history of teaching ESL or a foreign language, so we begin with a background of the history of language teaching methods. In this chapter we describe methods that have been used to teach second and foreign languages. In his book, *25 Centuries of Language Teaching: 500 BC–1969*, Kelly (1969) reviews the history of language teaching. He comments:

> Throughout the history of language teaching, methods of presentation have varied according to the type of mastery required of the pupil. During the Middle Ages and the eighteenth and nineteenth centuries, languages were usually presented through the codifications of grammarians. It was expected that skill in using languages would follow from an intellectual knowledge of their formal analyses. However, during the classical era, the Renaissance, and the early twentieth century, it was intuitive command of the target languages that was required, formal knowledge being seen as a mere reinforcement of practical mastery. (7)

Kelly goes on to note that over time there has been an alternation between formal and informal approaches to language teaching. He adds that the approach to teaching the classical languages, Latin and Greek, has been more formal while the teaching of modern languages has been more informal. By *formal* Kelly means that there has been a focus on the grammatical forms of the language, what he terms "the codifications of grammarians" in the previous quote. By *informal* Kelly is referring to methods that focus on developing an "intuitive command" of the target language, with formal knowledge of grammar only being used to reinforce students' skill in using the language.

Kelly also states that methods of language teaching have varied "according to the type of mastery required of the pupil." Some methods are designed to help students learn to communicate in a new language. Other methods have the goal of

1

teaching students to translate classical literature into their native or home language as part of becoming better educated and increasing their cognitive abilities. As we describe different methods, it is important to keep in mind the goal for the students as well as the techniques the teacher uses. In this chapter we examine methods used from earliest times up to the 1980s. Then in Chapter 3 we examine more recent methods developed to teach both academic content and academic language.

EARLY METHODS OF LANGUAGE TEACHING

The quote from Kelly raises important questions in choosing a method for teaching ESL: What role should the instruction of grammar play? Should grammar be the focus of each lesson? Should it be used to reinforce the language being taught if it is used at all? In addition, should class activities be based on the grammatical forms of the language, such as a drill that requires students to use past tense forms? Or should the activities be based on the language functions students need, such as making introductions and apologies or asking how to find a restaurant? As we review the different methods that have been used to teach language, we will examine the role grammar plays and the techniques used to teach the lesson content. We begin by describing two early methods: Grammar-Translation and the Natural Method. Many aspects of these two approaches to teaching a second language form the basis of current methods.

Grammar-Translation

Grammar-Translation was originally the method used to teach Latin and Greek in schools. This approach to teaching classical languages followed from the goal of teaching students to translate great works of literature such as the *Illiad*, the Greek epic poem attributed to Homer, and the *Aeneid*, Virgil's epic poem from ancient Rome. Students were not expected to master the oral language when they studied Latin or Greek once these languages were no longer used in the society. Language instruction focused on the vocabulary and grammar of the written language. Students studied the complex grammar, including declensions involving the variation in the forms of nouns, pronouns, or adjectives. They learned that these variations determined the case, number, and gender of words they translated from the great works. They also studied verb paradigms.

Latin and Greek During the Renaissance

The Grammar-Translation method began when Latin was still a living language. Latin and Greek were taught in Europe during the Renaissance. This period began in 1453, after the end of the Byzantine Roman Empire when the Crusaders sacked Constantinople, and lasted up until the early-eighteenth century. Many scholars emigrated to Western Europe in this period, and they revived Greek and Roman studies. This led to Renaissance humanism and science. Europeans looked to the classics because they considered their Greek and Roman heritage to be the height of culture (Hay 1977).

Although most instruction during this Renaissance period was in Latin, teachers used the home language to explain grammar. Grammar was taught by providing examples and having students practice using grammatical forms. Grammar was taught deductively. Students were taught the rules in their home language and given examples to practice in the target language. In addition, they memorized vocabulary.

Classical Languages in Modern Times

Latin, a classical language, was often taught in U.S. schools until the 1960s when teaching a dead language fell out of favor. Interest in teaching Latin was revived somewhat in the 1970s and began picking up in the 1980s. Latin instruction has become popular in areas like New York. In 2008, 134,000 students took the National Latin Exam. The executive director of the American Philological Association, a society for classical studies, explains that studying Latin "builds vocabulary and grammar for higher SAT scores, appeals to college admissions officers as a sign of critical-thinking skills and fosters true intellectual passion" (retrieved from www.nytimes.com/2008/10/07/nyregion/07latin.html?pagewanted=all&_r=0; January 31, 2015).

Methods for the teaching of Latin and Greek were originally based on premises of faculty psychology, a theory which holds that different kinds of knowledge are located in separate sections of the brain—mathematics in one area, art in a different area, and language in yet another. By studying these different subjects, students were thought to be exercising the various parts of their brain. Thus, even if conjugating verbs in Greek might not be too useful, it was thought to provide good mental exercise.

Diller (1978) sums up the assumptions that guided the Grammar-Translation method.

> Learning a language means learning the grammar and the vocabulary.
>
> Learning a language expands one's intellect.
>
> Learning a foreign language enables one to translate great works of literature.
>
> Learning the grammar of a foreign language helps one learn the grammar of one's native language. (10)

The grammar students studied in Latin and Greek classes was traditional, like the grammar many of us studied in English class in elementary and high school. We divided sentences up into subjects and verbs. We underlined the nouns in a sentence. We also studied verb tenses and filled out worksheets on subject-verb agreement.

Grammar-Translation and Foreign Language Teaching

Some instructors of foreign languages follow the Grammar-Translation method today. Students might be asked to translate a passage from French into English or from English into French. They would also be given vocabulary to memorize. Each lesson would include a grammar point. The teacher might write the rule for forming the simple past tense on the board and give examples showing students how to form the past tense of verbs. After that, the teacher might give students a list of verbs and ask them to write a sentence in the target language with each one. The teacher would use the students' home language to explain the rule and answer questions, and students could ask questions using their home language (Larsen-Freeman 1986).

Very few ESL teachers use Grammar-Translation as it was used to teach classical Latin or Greek using classical literature, although they may incorporate some aspects of the method, especially the explicit teaching of grammar. Teachers have ESL students memorize vocabulary. Students often read simplified texts in English and answer comprehension questions. However, all instruction is usually in English, and teachers do not use the students' home language to teach the grammar. Instead, they use English.

The Natural Method

Although Grammar-Translation was the primary method used to teach classical languages, modern languages have been taught from the earliest times using methods based on the observation of how children acquire their first language. Comenius (1592–1670) was an educator, philosopher, and theologian whose ideas on education form the basis of our current educational systems. Arguing that learning in schools should follow a natural progression, he promoted the following ideas for teaching and learning a second language: (1) learning foreign languages through the vernacular; (2) obtaining ideas through objects rather than words; (3) starting with objects most familiar to the child to introduce him to the new language; (4) giving the child a comprehensive knowledge of his environment, physical and social, as well as instruction in religious, moral, and classical subjects; (5) making this acquisition of a compendium of knowledge a pleasure rather than a task; and (6) making instruction universal (Kelly 1969).

In addition to promoting the use of the first language along with objects and actions to convey meaning, Comenius introduced the use of pictures in language texts. By using pictures, Comenius could teach ideas that would be difficult to convey with objects or actions. His best-known book, *Orbis sensualium pictus* (1728), included pictures with numbers. The book looked much like modern-day manuals for assembling furniture or putting together toys. For example, two facing pages show a knight in a field with all the parts of his armor as well as his sword numbered. The key at the bottom is in Latin, German, Hungarian, and Czech. Each two-page spread shows a scene like this. Teachers could use the individual pages as lessons.

Comenius (in Kelly 1969) listed the following steps for teaching a language using an illustrated book.

1. The pupils were to familiarize themselves with the book itself.
2. They were to make sure they knew the vernacular names of everything depicted in the book.
3. If possible, the teacher was to show them the real thing.
4. The pupils were to copy the illustrations.
5. Finally, they were to color in their own copies, and even the etchings, in the book.

Comenius' writings influenced other areas including reading. His *Orbus pictus* was one of the first picture books for children to be published in English. *Orbis pictus* provided teachers with a useful resource for teaching vocabulary, but because of the cost of producing the illustrations, the book was used by only a few followers of Comenius. In fact, illustrations were not widely used in texts for the next two centuries, although charts and picture dictionaries were developed.

In the area of language teaching Comenius' ideas helped form the basis of the Natural Method because of his connection of pictures to words and concepts as well as his de-emphasis on teaching language through grammar. One difference between Comenius and other proponents of a natural approach to language learning was that he advocated for the use of students' home languages in learning a second language while others, partly in reaction to the Grammar-Translation method's use of the vernacular, stated that no translation should be allowed in the second language classroom.

Lamy (1645–1715), for example, argued that a second language should be learned the same way as a first language. He called this approach the Natural Method. He pointed out that children learn language by associating sounds with objects and actions, not through instruction in grammar. Many other language educators also argued for taking a natural approach to language teaching. Lemare (1819, in Kelly 1969) explains:

When for the first time a child hears the sentence: 'Shut the door,' if he does not see a gesture accompanying the order, if he does not see it carried out immediately, he will not know what it means . . . But if a voice from somewhere shouts, 'Shut the door,' and someone rushes up to close it . . . he perceives the sense of the expression he has heard. (6)

No translation was used in the Natural Method. Instead, teachers relied on objects and gestures or actions to convey meaning in a new language. In classrooms using this method, the teacher was always active. Students observed the teacher and then imitated the language associated with the actions. In some classes, such as those following the ideas of Pestalozzi, the students imitated the actions as well as the words of the teacher. In the late 1860s Sauveur opened a language school in Boston using the Natural Method. Students were taught a foreign language without translation; instead, the teacher demonstrated words and phrases and also used objects and gestures to convey meanings.

The Series Method

All the variations of the Natural Method followed the same basic principles with the goal of teaching the second language naturally, the same way children learn their first language. However, implementation of the Natural Method varied. In 1880 in France François Gouin wrote an influential book, *The Art of Learning and Studying Foreign Languages*. In it he introduced one variation on the Natural Method that he called the Series Method. To explain this method, Gouin described his own experience of trying to learn German by memorizing words and studying the grammar. He moved from France to Germany and lived in Hamburg for one year. During this time, he stayed in his apartment and memorized a book in German and also memorized a list of 248 irregular German verbs. Feeling confident, he tested his knowledge by attending a class at the local university. However, he quickly left when he realized he could not understand anything the people around him were saying.

He tried harder. He memorized 30,000 words from a German dictionary and translated books from German to French. But he still could not understand Germans when he tried to speak with them, so he returned to France. There he realized that while he was gone his three-year-old nephew had become very competent in speaking French. The boy had done this naturally and without any instruction.

Thus, based on these observations of his nephew, Gouin developed his Series Method, a version of the Natural Method. It reflected the insights Lemare had recorded much earlier when he criticized the teaching of language through discrete parts because it was not the way children acquired language. In the Series Method, the teacher performs a series of related actions while at the same time stating what he is doing in the target language. Students learn the vocabulary and grammar through observation of the actions. Grammar is taught implicitly. A sample series, then, might look like the following:

> I stand up.
>
> I walk to the window.
>
> I reach out my hand.
>
> I pull up the shade.
>
> I turn the handle
>
> I open the window.

[handwritten note: Series of tasks through repetition]

Students listen to the teacher and then begin to repeat the words they hear. They may also perform the actions. They understand the new language because it is contextualized in a series of related actions. At the beginning stages, the home language is used to help translate some key vocabulary. The exercises that follow the demonstration all build on the language the teacher introduced. Gouin used some reading and writing. He would write the sentences leaving out words and have students fill in missing words. He observed that students could remember whole sentences in a series if he simply listed the verbs. The limitation of the method was that it could only be used to demonstrate actions, and students did not learn to express judgments, such as "good" or "bad," or abstract concepts (Brown 2007).

During the eighteenth and nineteenth centuries many versions of the Natural Method developed. While they varied in some ways, all were based on teaching a second language in the same way a first language is acquired naturally. Teachers used strategies to make the target language understandable through the use of objects, actions, and pictures.

METHODS WITH AN EMPIRICIST ORIENTATION

Methods of teaching language are based on the orientation a teacher takes. An orientation is a set of assumptions or beliefs about how people learn generally and how they learn language specifically. Advances in psychology and linguistics have influenced changes in orientations toward language teaching and learning. Two orientations toward language teaching are the empiricist orientation and the rationalist orientation. Empiricists believe that knowledge comes primarily from sensory experience and evidence based on observation. The Natural Method would be consistent with empiricist assumptions. Diller (1978) sums up the key principles of methods with an empiricist orientation:

1. The native language should not be used in the classroom.
2. Students should make direct associations between the target language and the meaning.
3. Language is primarily speech, but reading and writing should be taught from the beginning.
4. Learning a language involves learning about the culture. (14)

The Direct Method

The Direct Method was based on Gouin's Series Method. Both the Direct Method and the Series Method were based on the assumption that direct experience with the target language was the key to language acquisition, and for this reason these methods could be classified as having an empiricist orientation. Supporters of the Direct Method, like proponents of the earlier Natural Method, held that a second language is learned the same way as a first language.

The Direct Method gets its name from the fact that students are encouraged to make direct associations between objects or concepts and the corresponding words in the target language. In 1884 German scholar and psychologist F. Franke provided a theoretical justification for the method by writing about the direct association between forms and meanings in the target language (Richards and Rodgers 1986).

He argued that rather than explaining, teachers should use the language actively in the classroom. All instruction in the Direct Method is given in the target language, even at the beginning. No translation is allowed. Instead, new target language words or phrases are introduced through objects or realia, real things or pictures and pantomime. Abstract concepts, like *love* or *honesty*, are taught by acting out scenes or by associating ideas, such as associating *honesty* with an honest person like Abraham Lincoln. Teachers demonstrate, rather than translate, to answer questions. A goal of the method is to get students to think in the target language.

Direct Method lessons are organized around topics, such as body parts, food, and clothing. As students become more proficient, the topics include many of the cultural aspects of the countries where the target language is spoken. Students learn about the geography, history, and customs of the target culture. In this process, vocabulary is emphasized and grammar is only taught inductively. Students figure out rules through the linguistic input they receive. The students and teacher work together. Teachers ask students questions and students ask one another questions. Teachers work on pronunciation and standard grammatical form, but they help students to self-correct rather than correcting directly. Some natural conversation is included in the lessons, but students are asked to use full sentences, which is not characteristic of natural conversation, to improve vocabulary and sentence structure.

The focus of lessons is on the spoken language. However, even though speaking and listening skills are emphasized, reading and writing are also taught from the beginning. Teachers create situations in which students can communicate for real purposes using common, everyday speech in the target language. Students are evaluated through actual use of the target language with activities such as oral interviews and assigned written paragraphs.

Larsen-Freeman (1986) lists several activities that are commonly used in a Direct Method class. Students read aloud, they engage in question-and-answer exercises, they are encouraged to self-correct, they practice conversations on different topics, and they complete fill-in-the-blank exercises. In a Direct Method class the teacher dictates in the target language, and the students listen and then write down the dictation. Students also draw maps and complete other exercises as they learn about the target language culture, and then they write paragraphs on topics related to the target culture. For example, they might write about the capital city of a country where the language is spoken.

In 1878, around the same time Gouin was developing the Series Method, Maximilian Berlitz popularized the Direct Method, calling it the Berlitz Method. Berlitz is the most widely known application of the Direct Method, with 550 Berlitz language schools today in 70 countries around the world (retrieved from www.berlitz.com /Careers/33/).

Although the founder, Maximilian Berlitz, referred to the method as the Berlitz Method, the principles applied have been, and continue to be, those of the Direct Method. Berlitz classes are generally for highly motivated adults needing language for business purposes. Although many techniques developed for the Direct Method have also been used in other methods, applying the Direct Method in noncommercial schools fell out of favor as early as 1920 (Richards and Rodgers 1986).

ADDITIONAL METHODS WITH AN EMPIRICIST ORIENTATION

Although there were some attempts to teach language communicatively in public schools in the U.S. using the Natural Method and the Direct Method, most language teaching continued to be done through Grammar-Translation in the first half of the twentieth century. The entry of the U.S. into World War II brought significant changes to language teaching methodology because it soon became clear that the Grammar-Translation methodology used in universities did not produce people who could use languages for real purposes. Even those with Ph.D.s in foreign languages could not serve as code assistants, translators, or, especially, spies! The launching of Russia's Sputnik into space in 1957 brought concerns that the U.S. was behind. The following year the National Defense Education Act was passed to provide monies to increase the numbers of college graduates, especially in mathematics, engineering, and foreign languages. The government pressured universities to develop foreign language programs in which students would develop conversational proficiency. This renewed emphasis on communication at the university level brought about the development of several new communicative methods.

These newer methods were based on behaviorist psychology and structural linguistics. At the time these methods were developed, psychologists viewed all learning as a process of forming stimulus-response bonds (Skinner 1957). During this same period, linguists analyzed language as consisting of certain structural patterns (Fries 1945). These insights from psychology and linguistics came together and led to the following set of premises about language and language teaching.

1. Language is speech, not writing.
2. A language is a set of habits.
3. Teach the language, not about the language.
4. A language is what its native speakers say, not what someone thinks they ought to say.
5. Languages are different. (Diller 1978, 19)

Language Is Speech, Not Writing

Linguists analyzed the structure of oral language. They argued that written language was a secondary form of language based on the oral language and that language teaching should emphasize oral language. For this reason, the communicative methods introduce aspects of language following the natural order of children learning a first language. Students first listen, then speak, and only later read and write.

A Language Is a Set of Habits

Behavioral psychologists claimed that learning involved forming habits, and they considered that learning a language was a process of learning a set of habits. In classes using empiricist methods students formed good language habits by engaging in role plays, drills, and exercises. While meaning was not central, classes were designed to help students comprehend the target language through repetitious drilling and produce the language correctly with good pronunciation by following the teacher modeling.

Teach the Language, Not About the Language

In Grammar-Translation classes, students learned grammatical rules for forming correct sentences and then tried to apply those rules in translating works of literature.

However, this method did not enable students to communicate with speakers of the target language. Students who studied in Grammar-Translation classes learned about the language, but they didn't learn the language.

Widdowson (1978) captured the difference between grammatical and communicative teaching methodologies with his terms *usage* and *use*. For example, a student might develop the grammatical competence needed to produce a sentence such as *I like to eat hamburgers*. This sentence shows the student's mastery of usage. We would judge such a sentence in isolation as being formed correctly. On the other hand, if a speaker produced a sentence such as *I like eat hamburger*, we would judge this usage to be incorrect.

A mastery of usage, as Widdowson argues, is not the same as a mastery of use. If I ask you, *What is your name?* and you tell me your name, that would be proper "use" of the language. But if you answer with *I like to eat hamburgers* or *I like eat hamburger*, neither answer reflects proper "use," although the first response contains grammatically correct usage. In communicative methods the focus is on "use," not "usage."

A Language Is What Its Native Speakers Say, Not What Someone Thinks They Ought to Say

Structural linguists use a descriptive approach to language analysis. They base their descriptions on recordings of what native speakers say. Often textbooks or teachers prescribe a set of rules for students to master. Thus, for English learners, a rule might be "descriptive adjectives precede the noun." Rather than have students memorize such prescriptive rules, teachers using empiricist-oriented methods have students learn dialogues that include natural, colloquial speech based on current descriptions of how language is used. So students working in pairs would repeat a dialogue with descriptive adjectives.

> Do you like fast or slow cars?
> I prefer fast cars.

They would then substitute other descriptive adjectives into substitution drills. The teacher might say "small-large." Students would then produce the following:

> Do you like small or large cars?
> I prefer small cars.

Languages Are Different

As linguists in this period analyzed a variety of languages, they realized that there were considerable differences between many of the European languages and languages spoken by Native Americans and other non-European groups. They conducted contrastive analyses to show how languages differed in syntax, morphology, and phonology. It followed logically that when a teacher taught English to a Spanish speaker, for example, she should be aware of the language contrasts and teach the parts that differed. So in Spanish, for example, descriptive adjectives usually follow nouns as in *¿Le gustan los carros grandes o pequeños?* Here *big* and *small*, *grandes* and *pequeños,* follow the noun *carros.* In English *big* and *small* would precede *cars.*

Two communicative methods that follow an empiricist orientation are the Audiolingual Method (ALM) and Suggestopedia. ALM is still used in the teaching of second and foreign languages, although it fell out of favor after Rivers critiqued the method (Rivers and Temperley 1978) and Chomsky critiqued structural linguistics and behaviorism (Chomsky 1959). Suggestopedia is a somewhat exotic method that has attracted attention in academic circles. We also include in this section a brief description of the notional-functional approach. Notional-functional is not really a method; rather, we see this communicative approach as essentially a variation on ALM with a different grammatical base. We include it because a great many textbook series for both ESL and EFL teaching reflect a notional-functional approach.

Audiolingual Method (ALM)

The audiolingual method was developed in response to the psychological and linguistic advances described earlier. In a typical ALM lesson, students begin with a dialogue designed to include a particular structural pattern. The exercises and drills that follow are all based on the dialogue. They give students more practice with the structure being studied. The teacher only speaks in the target language and, as with the Direct Method, conveys meaning using nonverbal cues, pictures, and realia. In addition, lessons teach about the target culture in that they reflect the daily life of people. In many respects, ALM is similar to Direct Method but is more clearly based on the linguistic and psychological theories that were accepted at the time ALM was developed.

In an ALM class, the emphasis is on development of the oral language. Accordingly, most of the class time is spent repeating the dialogue or doing role plays and drills. ALM teachers act like drill sergeants or cheerleaders as they lead the whole class, groups within the class, or individual students. Various types of drills have been developed. For example, in a single slot substitution drill, the teacher might hold up a pencil while saying, "This is a pencil." Then the teacher would cue the class with the word *pen,* and students then chorus, "This is a pen." A more complicated drill would require filling two slots. After hearing the sentence "Bob is a teacher" and the cues "Betty, dentist," the students would be expected to produce "Betty is a dentist." One problem with such drills is that students may repeat the phrase without understanding it. However, the emphasis in ALM is on learning the syntactic patterns rather than on constructing meaning. A good deal of attention is also paid to correct pronunciation.

Following behaviorist psychology, ALM lessons are designed to give students intense practice with the language in order to form good habits in the target language. The theory holds that with sufficient practice, the language structure will be internalized and come automatically. Correct answers are positively reinforced, and errors are corrected immediately to avoid the formation of bad habits. Lessons are based on the structures of the target language and on differences between the phonology, morphology, and syntax of the home language and the target language. These differences were identified by linguists using contrastive analysis. For example, a Spanish speaker learning English would work on the vowel plus *r* sound in words like *girl*, a sound that is present in English but lacking in Spanish.

ALM was touted as a scientific approach to language teaching because it was developed by linguists and psychologists. Publishers were quick to produce a number of ALM textbook series, especially for languages commonly taught in high school and college. Although successful in intensive language institutes with highly motivated students, the Audiolingual Method has generally not produced fluent communicators. A frequently told joke about the method goes like this:

> A student who had studied four years of Spanish using audiolingual materials took a trip to Mexico. Upon her return, she was asked how she did speaking Spanish. Her reply was, "Not very well. I kept waiting to speak Spanish, but no one ever gave me the first line of a dialogue!"

The story is perhaps an exaggeration, but the point is clear: Even though ALM has not been shown to be effective, this method and features of the method continue to be used in both ESL and EFL settings.

Notional-Functional Approach

ALM is based on the patterns and contrasts that structural linguists identified. In the 1970s, a number of linguists analyzed how languages express notions, such as time or space, and functions, such as greetings or apologies (Wilkins 1976). This approach to the study of language led to the publication of language teaching texts that include the same kinds of dialogues, role plays, and drills found in ALM texts. However, a notional-functional textbook differs from an ALM textbook in the way language is presented. The difference would be that in the ALM lesson, the dialogue might be written to help students practice the present continuous tense, and in the notional-functional lesson, the dialogue would be written to give students practice with introductions.

A typical notional-functional lesson for high school and adult learners might include a dialogue containing introductions. Students would listen to the dialogue, repeat it, and then try out the forms in class by going up to classmates and saying "Nice to meet you." The correct response, "Nice to meet you too," would come back even if the two students knew one another before the practice with introductions. Later students might be asked to perform introductions using forms such as "Tony, this is Maria." Notional-functional lessons often include brief writing activities that are meant to be practice for real-life functions, such as completing a registration form or creating an ad for selling a car.

Notional-functional texts have been widely used in both ESL and EFL settings, especially with adult learners. Lessons focus on practical use of both oral and written language. The content of the lessons is different from the content of ALM lessons, but the beliefs about how people learn language are essentially the same as the beliefs that underlie ALM.

SUGGESTOPEDIA

Suggestopedia (suggestion+pedagogy) was developed by Bulgarian psychiatrist-educator Lozanov (1982), who wanted to eliminate the psychological barriers that people have to learning. Stevick (1976) summarizes Lozanov's view of learning into three principles: (1) People are able to learn at rates many times greater than what is commonly assumed; (2) learning is a "global" event and involves the entire person; and (3) learners respond to various influences, many of them nonrational and nonconscious.

Suggestopedia uses drama, art, physical exercise, and desuggestive-suggestive communicative psychotherapy. The teacher "desuggests" that students have any limitations in what they can learn and "suggests" that they are able to learn well. Later developments of Suggestopedia focused on desuggestion as an important component. Lozanov believed that adults could learn more if they believed they were capable, so an important role of the teacher is to use desuggestion to help students feel confident.

Class meetings are called "sessions." In these sessions instruction is made pleasant and students' aesthetic interests are aroused through the use of music and art. Lozanov's (1982) goal is that "new material to be learned will be assimilated and become automatic and creatively processed without strain and fatigue" (157). Students take on a new persona, so a student learning Spanish might be called Francisco and might wear a special hat or other piece of clothing to become this competent Spanish speaker.

Several characteristics of Suggestopedia distinguish it from other second language teaching methods. First, the physical setting is extremely important. Classes are small and students sit in comfortable armchairs in a semicircle. On the walls of the room hang posters from countries where the target language is spoken as well as posters with grammatical information such as verb conjugations.

Lessons begin with the teacher speaking in the students' first language. The teacher tells the students about the successful and enjoyable experience they are going to have. Students are told they will choose a new identity and a new name in the language they are learning. Baroque music is played as students close their eyes and do yoga breathing exercises to relax. The students and teacher then read the lesson to the beat of the music. Then students listen to the lesson and music with their eyes closed.

The lessons are based on lengthy dialogues. In the first part of the lesson, the teacher reads the dialogue aloud, matching her voice with the rhythm of the Baroque music. The students follow along on their copies of the dialogue. They can check the translation as needed along with some notes on the grammar and vocabulary. Then the teacher reads the dialogue a second time at normal speed while the students relax and listen. For homework, they read the dialogue before going to sleep and again when they wake up.

In subsequent lessons, students do role plays, sing songs, play different games, and make up skits to work with the material in the dialogue. Lozanov (1982) claims that Suggestopedia has had great success because students can assimilate a great deal of vocabulary, they can put the vocabulary to use, they can read, they can communicate, and they are not afraid to use their new language. Lozanov attributes the success of Suggestopedia to the use of many modalities. Besides listening, speaking, reading, and writing, students listen to music, relax using techniques based on yoga, and perform role plays.

In Suggestopedia the teacher decides which material to present, leads all activities, and is the center of instruction. According to Lozanov, students learn better when they see the teacher as a strong authority figure. In some respects Suggestopedia could be seen as an enhanced version of ALM. There are still dialogues, but they are presented artistically by teachers specially trained in presentation skills. Students do follow-up activities to practice the language presented in the dialogue, but they do this through games and role plays. Unlike ALM, in Suggestopedia classes teachers take into account the physical and emotional needs of students so they can learn more efficiently. Despite these advances over ALM, Suggestopedia has not been widely adopted in the West. It is impractical for large language classes with limited resources. In addition, it would be difficult, in most places, to find textbooks or other materials designed for Suggestopedia or to find teachers trained in its specialized techniques.

Suggestopedia differs from other methods with an empirical orientation. Unlike the Direct Method and ALM, teachers in Suggestopedia classes use the students' native language to help students relax and feel confident and to explain the dialogue. As students become more proficient, the home language is used less often. Further, although most grammar is taught inductively, Suggestopedia teachers do some explicit grammar instruction. Suggestopedia classes are also different from Direct Method or ALM classes because they emphasize a relaxed and playful atmosphere as well as the use of drama. Finally, while errors are quickly corrected in ALM classes, in Suggestopedia classes errors are not corrected since students would feel that they could not learn easily. Instead, the teacher uses the correct form later in the lesson. Despite these differences, Suggestopedia is largely based on empiricist principles.

RATIONALIST ORIENTATION METHODS

New insights in psychology and linguistics prompted a shift from the empiricist orientation to a rationalist orientation. Methods that align with a rationalist orientation put less emphasis on sensory experience and more emphasis on cognition and reason. Chomsky (1959) argued convincingly in his review of Skinner's *Verbal Learning* that behaviorist psychology could not account for language learning. Behaviorism, which emphasized the influence of external stimuli on the learner, was gradually replaced by cognitive theories of psychology, which stress the importance of the activity of the learner. Research in cognitive psychology showed that learning results equally from how the learner acts on the environment and how the environment acts on the learner. From a behaviorist perspective, people are simply blank slates. A cognitive perspective, on the other hand, recognizes the many innate abilities humans have.

Chomsky developed a new approach to linguistics called transformational-generative grammar. Structural linguists described patterns in oral language. Chomsky argued that an analysis of what people say or write is not adequate. Instead, he showed that underlying the large number of patterns found in speech or writing, which he called the surface structure of language, was a smaller number of patterns at a more abstract or deep level and that these patterns could be transformed into the different surface structures.

Chomsky also claimed that language ability is innate. Humans are born with knowledge of those aspects of grammar common to all languages, a Universal

Grammar, so learning a language consists of determining which aspects of the Universal Grammar are present in the particular language people around us speak. This process is carried out subconsciously.

Learning a language is a natural process that involves developing deep structures and also the ability to transform them into the different surface structures. Thus, for Chomsky, questions and statements follow the same pattern at deep level. For example, the statement, "Today is Wednesday" can be transformed by moving the verb to the front to produce, "Is today Wednesday?"

These new insights in linguistics and psychology led to a new set of assumptions about language learning that shaped the rationalist orientation:

1. A living language is characterized by rule-governed creativity.
2. The rules of grammar are psychologically real.
3. People are especially equipped to learn language.
4. A living language is a language in which we can think. (Diller 1978, 21)

A Living Language Has Rule-Governed Creativity

When linguists say that languages are "rule governed," they refer to an innate ability, the knowledge that a sentence "sounds right" rather than the knowledge of the kinds of grammar rules taught in school. Thus, native English speakers know that "big red balloon" sounds right, but "red big balloon" is somehow wrong. From Chomsky's perspective, native speakers of a language can determine whether or not an utterance is grammatical in the speaker's dialect. They can do this even though they may not be able to state the rule. These grammaticality judgments are different from knowing the difference between using "who" or "whom" in standard or conventional written language. Further, using their innate knowledge of rules, native speakers can create new sentences that they have never heard before.

The Rules of a Language Are Psychologically Real

Chomsky claims that innate rules are psychologically real. Just as a physical theory can be physically real, a theory about language can be psychologically real. Chomsky explains that something is psychologically real if it is psychological in nature. The innate rules of language are psychological because we can use them to judge whether something sounds "right" in a language we have acquired. For a theory to be true, it should be the best explanation of observed phenomena. Our ability to make judgments about whether or not something spoken in our native language sounds right is a phenomenon best explained by saying we have acquired subconscious rules that govern the language.

Language Is Innate

Chomsky goes on to say that humans don't imitate or repeat what they have heard. Instead, they use the rules they have internalized to create new sentences. Humans can do this because much of this ability is innate. That's why all normally functioning humans develop language proficiency even though all of us don't learn other things, like math or science or social studies. We have what Chomsky first called a Language Acquisition Device and later called Universal Grammar.

Humans Can Think in Their Language

The final assumption of a rationalist orientation toward language is that we can think in a living language, one we have acquired. We have not simply memorized words or phrases that we are repeating, and we have not simply formed good language habits. When we use language we are doing so meaningfully and creatively.

Chomsky and other linguists based their claims about language acquisition on the development of a person's primary language. Several methods of language teaching based on a rationalist orientation apply these insights from linguistics and psychology to learning or acquiring additional languages, including the Silent Way, Community Language Learning, Problem Posing, Total Physical Response, and the Natural Approach.

The Silent Way

The Silent Way, developed by Gattegno, gets its name from the fact that in this approach to teaching language the teacher is usually silent. Gattegno says the Silent Way is not a method but a general approach to teaching and learning, and one of the key principles is that teaching should be subordinated to learning (Larsen-Freeman 1986). By remaining largely silent, the teacher makes students responsible for their own learning and encourages learners to become independent. The Silent Way has a rationalist orientation because the teacher draws heavily on the students' ability to reason rather than providing them with language experiences through drills, role plays, and other language exercises. Silent Way classes are conducted very differently from Audiolingual or Direct Method classes.

During Silent Way lessons, teachers model an expression only once, or they point to objects or charts, and then students are responsible for producing the target language. The goal of lessons is that students will take responsibility for learning and develop their own internal understanding of the language they are studying. Beginners are initially taught the sounds of their new language from color-coded sound charts. These charts are divided with the vowels at the top and the consonants underneath. There is a colored square for each phoneme in the target language. The teacher points to the chart and produces the sound just once. Then she guides the students as they try to reproduce the sound. The teacher starts with the vowels and then adds consonants. Beginning lessons focus on sounds similar to sounds in the home language. The teacher may use hand gestures to indicate that a sound should be longer or shorter. Once students learn a few individual sounds, the teacher points to several sounds in succession, and students combine the sounds to produce words.

In later lessons, teachers use colored rods called Cuisenaire rods. Students learn phrases like "a green rod" or "a blue rod." Then, they learn to "pick up a green rod" or "pass the red rod." Students are encouraged to help one another. The rods may also be used to visually represent parts of words and sentences. For example, for a noun plural, such as *boys*, a long white rod could represent the base, *boy*, and a short blue rod could represent the inflectional affix *s*. As students begin to understand more of the language, they are taught stories using the rods as props. For instance, in a story about a little girl walking her dog near a park bench, the teacher might use a red rod to represent the little girl, a green rod for her dog, and a yellow rod for the park bench. At all stages, the teacher models as little as possible, and students try to repeat after careful listening and with help from each other. The teacher leads them toward correct responses with nods or negative head shakes along with brief explanations in the students' home language.

Teachers also use a series of word charts to teach 500 common words in the target language. The teacher points to a word and says it once, and then the students work to learn the words. In addition, the teacher uses eight charts, called *Fidel charts*, that show possible spellings of each sound to help students learn to read and write the target language. In addition to the rods and charts, there are books and pictures that Silent Way teachers use to help students gain proficiency in the language. The teacher makes occasional use of the home language to explain concepts or procedures but generally speaks in the target language. The home language is also used at the end of the lesson when the teacher conducts a short session in which they invite students to offer feedback on the lesson. The teacher uses what the students say to develop subsequent lessons.

The Silent Way has been used successfully, especially with adult learners. It is fairly complex and requires students to learn how the system of teaching with the charts and rods works and how they need to take charge of their own learning. This can cause problems in an adult education setting where students do not attend consistently or where new students enter at various times during the year. The Silent Way is also difficult for teachers who are used to talking as they direct class activities. It is hard for most teachers to remain silent most of the time. The idea of shifting responsibility for learning to the student is a good one, but some students may become confused and frustrated by the complex system and the silent teacher. The Silent Way has seldom been used in K–12 classes.

Community Language Learning

Community Language Learning (CLL) is a method for teaching a second language that was developed by psychologist Charles Curran, who based his method on Rogers' (1951) principles of humanistic psychology. Curran saw learners as a group in need of counseling. He created Community Language Learning as a kind of positive therapy. He used a counseling–learning, whole-person approach (Larsen-Freeman 1986). In CLL, teachers serve as language counselors charged with facilitating learning by taking into account the fears of adult students as they learn a new language. Teachers join together with students to form a learning community characterized by an accepting atmosphere. The goal of the method is to lower students' defenses, which encourages open communication.

Like Suggestopedia, also developed by a psychologist, CLL takes into consideration the affective factors in language learning. In both methods, teachers work to help students overcome their fear of looking foolish as they learn a new language. However, the two methods are very different. In a Suggestopedia class, the teacher is the leader and center of attention, the one who directs all activities. In a Community Language Learning class, the teacher is a supportive counselor who facilitates learning. As with other rationalist-oriented methods, both the Silent Way and CLL emphasize student activity with teacher guidance; in contrast, empiricist-oriented methods involve teachers being more active in leading the class and providing students with experiences with the language.

In a typical beginning CLL lesson, students who have previously come to know each other sit in a small circle. The teacher explains in the home language what they will do and how long this will take. Then the teacher/facilitator stands behind one of the students. This student makes a statement or asks a question in his or her native language. In a gentle, supportive voice the teacher translates what the student said from the student's native language to the language being learned. The student repeats what the teacher says until he or she is comfortable enough to record the new phrase or sentence on a tape recorder. This procedure is repeated with others in the circle until a short conversation has been recorded. Then students listen to their conversation, and the teacher writes it on the board using a kind of language experience approach. What the teacher writes becomes the text for the lesson. Students often copy the written conversation from the board to take home and study.

What is done with the language after it is written down is important. Often, this language is analyzed using the home language for grammar study or vocabulary clarification. For example, if students use the verb *to be* in an early lesson, the teacher might isolate this verb for the students to conjugate and then compare with a regular verb such as *walk*. In other words, once the conversation is completed, it may become the basis for direct instruction in grammar. In addition, the students may practice pronouncing specific words or phrases from the transcript.

At the end of a lesson or an activity within a lesson, the teacher may stop and, using the students' home language, discuss how the students feel about the lesson and about how they are progressing as learners. These times give students a chance to express their feelings and to reflect on their learning. This activity is much like the structured feedback that students give after Silent Way classes. The difference is that in the Silent Way, feedback is designed to help the teacher plan future lessons, and in CLL the feedback helps students express their concerns and feelings.

In later lessons, students work in small groups to practice the language they are learning. They use words or phrases from the transcript to create new sentences, which they share with the class. Another activity in CLL classes is that the teacher becomes a "human computer" who repeats words or phrases that a student wants to practice. The student says the word or phrase, and the teacher repeats it until the student feels that she is pronouncing it correctly. The goal here is self-correction, and it is the student who initiates and directs the activity.

The curriculum in a CLL class comes from the students, so the curriculum is restricted by the fact that it *only* comes from the students with the teacher as a resource. Teachers expand lessons by using a variety of other resources including books, magazines, realia, and media.

When deciding whether or not to implement CLL, there are several considerations. This method is designed for adults rather than younger students. There must be a low student-teacher ratio. In large classes, students would not get many opportunities to participate actively. The teacher needs to be bilingual or multilingual and must have training in the role of a language counselor. The students must all speak the same home language. These restrictions may make CLL impractical in most K–12 settings.

Problem Posing

Problem Posing is based on the work of Paulo Freire (Freire 1970; Freire and Macedo 1987). Freire was working with illiterate peasants in Brazil, and he wanted to find ways to empower them through literacy. There are three phases in Problem Posing: listening, dialogue, and action. First, the teacher listens to students to discover problems they have that they wish to solve. Then the teacher engages with the students through dialogue to discover solutions to the problem. Finally, the students take action.

An example of where Problem Posing could be implemented might be that students are living in substandard housing. Using Problem Posing, the teacher first listens to the students and assesses their situation to help them determine the things that truly concern them. The teacher then chooses what Freire calls a *code*. This could be a picture, a story, or a song. The code is presented to the students to help them take an objective look at their personal experiences and concerns, the problems they have posed earlier. For example, the teacher might show students a snapshot that depicts the substandard housing in the neighborhood where they live. Next, the students meet in small groups that Freire calls *culture circles* to discuss the picture. In the process, they identify or "pose" what they perceive as a problem. Through their collective dialogue in the culture circles, they plan for social action to improve their situation.

In discussing their situation and planning social action, students learning a second language use the target language to solve a real problem. Younger students might deal with a problem such as lack of playground space or graffiti in the neighborhood. Middle or high school students might tackle the problems presented by drug dealers on campus. Adult students could consider the effects welfare programs have on members of their community.

Auerbach and Wallerstein (2004) adapted Problem Posing for ESL classes. The content of the curriculum comes from students' problems. For example, new immigrants often have problems in the workplace. In their book *Problem-Posing at Work: English for Action* Auerbach and Wallerstein include units on finding a job, health and safety issues, negotiating their rights, and union activity. In the process of discussing these topics, students develop the English they need to solve their problems.

For each unit the authors include a number of activities to build students' English proficiency. Lessons often start with a series of pictures and a dialogue. For example, the first lesson begins with introductions. Students develop the English needed to engage in the activities through various techniques, such as role play, language experience, and skits using puppets. All of these are techniques that emphasize building language through social interaction. Many of these techniques are used in other ESL methods. The difference between other methods and Problem Posing is the overall structure of the lessons. In Problem Posing the curriculum is organized around problems that students often encounter in their new country.

The problems the teacher identifies become the source for the curriculum in a Problem-Posing class. Creative teachers have been able to use Problem Posing, even with beginners, but this method is used more often with intermediate or advanced students because of the language that is often needed to adequately discuss problems. Problem Posing is similar to Notional-Functional teaching in that students learn the grammatical forms of a language as they learn to use language for different functions, such as making introductions or arguing a point. While Problem Posing could be used with younger students, it has been developed primarily for adults.

Total Physical Response

Many methods of teaching a second or foreign language require students to speak from the beginning. However, when children acquire their first language, they go through a period of listening before they begin to speak. Total Physical Response (TPR), developed by Asher (1979), begins by having students develop listening comprehension. Asher conducted research that suggests that we learn language better when our muscles are involved as well as our mind. He also believed that learning happens when we are stress free. For that reason, students in TPR first respond to commands by the teacher to demonstrate comprehension. They do not need to speak, which lowers their stress.

At the beginning, the teacher uses the home language to explain that students should listen to him and then do as he does. He calls three or four students to come and sit at the front of the class. Then he gives the students a simple command, such as "Raise your right hand." As the teacher gives the command, he raises his hand and motions the students to raise their hands. He repeats this procedure with other commands. When students seem to understand the process, the teacher has the students return to their seats and continues the lesson with the whole class (Larsen-Freeman 1986).

As students progress through TPR lessons, the commands become more complex. For example, "If you are wearing a blue shirt, scratch your nose" might be one combination command. In addition, the teacher may give the commands in a series, as in "Stand up. Walk to the door. Open the door." As students become more advanced, they begin to speak, and they give the commands to their teacher and classmates.

TPR is similar to Gouin's Series Method. However, the Series Method did not use commands. Instead, the teacher modeled as he spoke, as in "I walk to the desk."

At the end of a lesson, the teacher writes the commands on the board, and students copy the writing or follow commands that are written. The sequence that is generally followed begins first with listening and then speaking, with reading and writing coming after students have developed some oral language proficiency.

Commands are used as the basis of TPR for two reasons. In the first place, reliance on commands ensures the active involvement of students. Second, in English, the verb forms used for commands are in the uninflected imperative form. Students don't have to consider tense changes or more complex verb forms as long as they are responding to or giving commands.

A textbook for teaching TPR, developed by Segal (1983), *Teaching English Through Action* emphasizes the acquisition of oral language. In her rationale for the book, Segal explains that reading and writing "come easily and naturally after considerable exposure to listening and practice in speaking" (1). Although Segal does provide some context for commands by organizing them in series around different topics to develop semantically related vocabulary, she doesn't specify exactly what constitutes "considerable exposure." In fact, in her book of 102 lessons, there is no reading or writing at all.

Another textbook for teaching TPR, written by Romijn and Seely (1979), also presents commands in a contextualized series. Their book, *Live Action English*, includes reading and writing much sooner. The following is a typical sequence taken from *Live Action English*:

Candle

1. Put the candle in the candle holder.
2. Take out your matches.
3. Tear out a match.
4. Light the match.
5. Light the candle.
6. Blow out the match.
7. Throw it away.
8. Put the matches away.
9. Look at the candle.
10. Smell it.
11. Blow it out. (2)

A *Live Action English* lesson begins by having the teacher set out the props, perhaps talking about them while doing so. Then the teacher goes through the steps in the sequence, acting each one out and repeating the words as the students watch and listen. When students are familiar with the sequence, they perform the actions along with the teacher, but they are still silent. Then the students are shown a written version of the sequence and may be asked to copy it. In the next step, the teacher performs the actions without speaking, and the students provide the dialogue. The teacher may stop at any point to work on students' pronunciation. Once students are able to repeat the sequence, they read the commands and the teacher performs the actions. Finally, students go through the sequence in pairs, one student reading the commands and the other student acting them out.

In a later book, *TPR Is More Than Commands at All Levels* (Romjin and Seely 2006), the authors expand the uses of TPR to include dialogues, role play, and storytelling. They provide a number of examples to show how teachers with students at different levels can use these extensions of TPR to provide comprehensible input. They include specific ideas on teaching verb tenses, grammatical features such as count and noncount nouns, and idioms. One benefit of TPR is that it allows students time to develop an understanding of the target language before they are asked to speak it. Students also enjoy the gamelike atmosphere involved in acting out commands. However, for most teachers TPR is used with beginning students as one technique rather than as a complete method.

The Natural Approach

One of the most widely used methods of teaching a second or foreign language is the Natural Approach, developed by Krashen and Terrell (1983). This method is similar to the earlier Natural Method and Direct Method. All of these methods attempt to model second language acquisition on first language acquisition. Unlike the earlier methods, the Natural Approach is clearly based on Krashen's (1982) theory of second language acquisition and is based on Chomsky's theory of generative grammar. This theory emphasizes the importance of *comprehensible input*, messages that are understood. Krashen claims that students acquire a second language when they receive comprehensible input. He posits that acquisition occurs in a natural order for any language. Some aspects of the language are acquired earlier than others. Students acquire languages when their *affective filter* is low—that is, when they are not nervous or bored and when they are motivated to learn. Krashen also proposes that learners use an internal monitor for their output based on their knowledge of learned rules about the target language. However, only a limited amount of grammar is taught. Class time is primarily focused on providing comprehensible input, and grammar may be assigned as homework.

At beginning stages the Natural Approach emphasizes listening. The teacher uses a number of techniques, including TPR, for making oral input comprehensible. At later stages, reading and writing are introduced. Krashen believes that reading is a key to language acquisition. In fact, after developing the Natural Approach, he began writing extensively about the value of free voluntary reading (Krashen 2004). Krashen claims it provides even greater amounts of input than oral language does. The written input from reading is also important because students can begin to acquire the academic language of texts.

Krashen and Terrell identified stages learners typically go through as they acquire a second or foreign language. The following scenarios come from a promotional booklet from *The Rainbow Collection* (Martini et al. 1984). These Natural Approach materials were produced to be used in elementary school. Each scenario in the booklet is presented in cartoon form to show how a teacher would conduct a typical lesson and how students would be expected to respond in that stage of the Natural Approach.

Scenario 1: Preproduction—First Stage

In the first scenario for this *preproduction* stage, the teacher is talking about the color of her eyes as she points to them. She also talks about the color of the students' eyes and has the students point to their eyes as well as other body parts. Students are then asked to point to one of the other students who has brown eyes, for instance, or to name students who are pointing to parts of their body. So the teacher might ask, "Who has brown eyes? Who is pointing to his nose?" Finally, the teacher asks some yes/no questions about body parts, such as "Is this my nose?" In preproduction, students do not have to talk except to name other students or answer yes or no. They are encouraged to communicate with gestures and actions. Lessons focus on listening comprehension and build receptive vocabulary. TPR is often used as a strategy during this preproduction stage.

Scenario 2: Early Production—About a Month Later

In the pictures for the second stage, *early production*, the teacher is holding a plant and talking about the flowers and leaves. When she asks, "Do any of you like to smell flowers?" students answer with responses like "I do" and "Yes." As the lesson continues, students answer questions about the color of the leaves (*green*) and what we use our noses for (to *smell*). In this stage students use one or two words or short phrases. Often teachers use either/or questions such as "Is the plant green or brown?" The vocabulary required to answer the question is contained in the question. The lessons at this stage expand the learners' receptive vocabulary. Activities are designed to motivate students to produce vocabulary they already understand.

Scenario 3: Speech Emergence—Some Time Later

In the example for the third stage, *speech emergence*, the teacher is holding a picture of a boy smelling a flower. When she asks what the boy is doing, students answer, "Smells flower" and "He smelling flower." As the lesson continues the teacher explores the students' understanding of their senses by asking, "What do our eyes and hands tell us about the flower in the picture?" Students answer, "It's white and yellow," "Leaves are green," "It feel smooth." The teacher may model correct structures in her response by saying, for example, "Yes, it feels smooth." However, the teacher responds to the message and does not overtly correct the grammar. In the speech emergence stage, students are speaking in longer phrases and complete sentences. Lessons continue to expand students' receptive vocabulary. The activities are designed to develop higher levels of language use.

Scenario 4: Intermediate Fluency—Still Later

In the fourth stage, *intermediate fluency*, the teacher is discussing several pictures that are related to the senses. When the teacher asks, "How do our senses help us?" one student answers, "We can know if something is hot or cold." When asked how our senses could tell us about the orange in a picture she is holding, students explain, "I smell it," "I can see it. It's round and orange," and "You could taste it." At the end of the discussion, the students and teacher write a story together about their senses. At this stage, students engage in conversation and produce connected narrative. They continue to expand their receptive vocabulary. The activities are designed to develop higher levels of language use in content areas, and reading and writing activities are incorporated.

It should be noted that methods such as the Natural Approach were developed to counter the emphasis that traditional methods, such as ALM, put on early production. In many second language classes, students were expected to produce the target language by repeating words or phrases from the very first day. By delaying production, methods such as the Natural Approach lower what Krashen calls the affective filter by allowing students to relax and understand what they are hearing, before being forced to produce the new language.

The Natural Approach has a well-articulated theoretical base and has been widely used, especially in public schools. Unlike some other methods, it does not require special materials or extensive teacher training. It can be used with large classes. Teachers do need to learn ways to make input comprehensible, and they also need to learn about the stages that students naturally progress through. This method can easily be adapted to teach academic content and academic language.

SUMMARY OF METHODS

People have studied second or foreign languages for hundreds of years. Some people study language to be able to communicate with others when they move or travel to a new country. Others study languages as part of their general education. The purpose of the learner has helped shape methods of language teaching.

Methods vary depending on the view of grammar they take. In some methods grammar is taught explicitly while in others it is taught implicitly or not at all. Methods also vary in their use of students' home languages. Some methods exclude the home language from second language teaching while other methods make some use of students' first languages to help them learn a second language.

Assumptions about language learning shape orientations toward language teaching. Two orientations are the empiricist orientation and the rationalist orientation. Different methods align with these orientations. Empiricist-oriented methods include the Direct Method, the Series Method, the Audiolingual Method, and Suggestopedia. The Silent Way, Community Language Learning, Problem Posing, Total Physical Response, and the Natural Approach are rationalist-oriented methods.

Figure 1–1 summarizes key aspects of the methods we have reviewed. Other than Grammar Translation, which involves students' learning the grammar of a language to translate great works of literature, all the methods have as their goal helping students acquire the language for communicative purposes along with some knowledge of the culture of the country where the language is spoken. Grammar Translation focuses on reading and writing while the other methods emphasize oral language and add written language instruction gradually. The figure lists typical activities carried out in class sessions. We describe the role of grammar, the consideration for students' feelings, the use of the home language, and the teacher's response to student errors. This is only a brief summary of key components of each method.

RESEARCH AND BEST PRACTICES FOR ENGLISH LEARNERS

We have reviewed methods that have been used and, in many cases, are still being used to teach emergent bilinguals. Many of the strategies and techniques that were promoted a long time ago are still being used today. In this section, we review some recent resources, including briefs and research reports that provide useful guides for educators as they decide how best to serve the needs of their emergent bilingual students. We then connect the findings from these reports with the principles we listed and briefly explained in the Introduction. In subsequent chapters, we discuss each research-based principle in more detail and give classroom examples showing how teachers can apply the principle with emergent bilinguals.

New York State Department of Education

The U.S. Department of Education, national education associations, state departments of education, university research groups, and school districts across the country recognize that there is a need to promote effective classroom and schoolwide practices for English learners. These organizations have published resources to help support educators as they work with the growing emergent bilingual population. Resources that list research-based approaches and strategies are readily available on the Internet.

One example is the New York State Department of Education's "Blueprint for English Language Learners' Success" (Bilingual Education 2014). In this short document, principles for administrators, policy makers, and practitioners working from prekindergarten through high school are laid out. These guidelines promote the

Method	Typical activities	Grammar	Student affect	Use of home language	Response to errors
Grammar-Translation	Students learn to translate from one language to the other. They study the vocabulary and grammar of the TL.	Grammar is taught explicitly. Students memorize rules, declensions, and paradigms.	Student affect is not considered.	The home language is used to explain grammar rules. The class is conducted using the home language.	Errors in grammar rules and vocabulary are corrected so that students learn to translate accurately.
Series Method	The teacher performs a series of related actions while stating what he is doing. Students listen and repeat. They may also perform the actions.	Grammar is not taught explicitly, although students do some written exercises to fill in missing words in a sentence.	Student affect is not considered.	The home language is used in beginning lessons to translate key concepts but is not used later.	The teacher may repeat actions if the students have difficulty learning the sequence, but there is no direct correction.
Direct Method	The teacher uses objects, actions, and realia to help students learn vocabulary and sentence structure.	Grammar is not taught explicitly. It is taught implicitly through written exercises.	Student affect is not considered.	The home language is not used at any time.	The teacher uses different strategies to help students self-correct.
ALM	The teacher engages students in dialogues and drills to form good habits in the TL.	Grammar is taught implicitly. Dialogues and drills are based on specific language structures.	Student affect is not considered.	The home language is not used at any time.	Errors are corrected immediately to avoid formation of bad language habits.
Suggestopedia	The teacher reads a dialogue twice. Students read the dialogue as homework. Follow-up activities include games and role plays to practice the language in the dialogue.	Grammar posters are placed around the room and the teacher gives brief grammar explanations.	Teachers use a number of desuggestive techniques, including music, to help students relax and become receptive to the TL in a comfortable setting.	Home language translation is used to make the dialogue clear. The teacher also uses the home language in some early classes.	Errors are not corrected immediately, but the teacher models correct forms in the class.

FIGURE 1–1 *Key Features of ESL Methods*

Method	Typical activities	Grammar	Student affect	Use of home language	Response to errors
The Silent Way	The teacher begins with sounds and uses charts, rods, and gestures to convey meaning. The teacher is silent and guides students to take responsibility for learning.	Grammar is taught implicitly through working with progressively complex sentence structures.	The teacher observes students carefully and uses different techniques to ensure that students feel confident.	The home language may be used for explanations when necessary. It is also used to debrief after a lesson.	The teacher attempts to get students to self-correct. He may use gestures and extra practice with students who make errors.
Community Language Learning	The teacher translates what students want to say and uses a recording of the conversation as a text for the class.	The grammar of the texts students create is used. The teacher chooses structures from the text and teaches the grammar explicitly.	Teachers act as language counselors to help students gain confidence in using the TL.	Students use the home language and the teacher translates. Some directions are given in the home language.	In a nonthreatening manner, the teacher may repeat correctly what the student has said incorrectly.
Problem Posing	The teacher listens to students, identifies a problem, and helps students develop the language they need to address the problem.	Grammar is taught as needed to help students develop the language they need to solve problems.	Students' problems are the content being studied, so students are motivated.	The home language is used to help identify problems.	Teachers correct errors if they impede communication.
Total Physical Response	The teacher gives commands for the students to follow.	Lessons may be designed to teach specific grammatical features inductively.	Students are not expected to speak in early stages, and the physical activities can help them feel relaxed. Teachers promote stress-free learning.	The home language is used at first to explain the basic procedures to be followed in the class, and then is seldom used.	The teacher may repeat a command if the student responds incorrectly. Students can self-correct.

FIGURE 1–1 *Continues*

Method	Typical activities	Grammar	Student affect	Use of home language	Response to errors
Natural Approach	The teacher uses a variety of strategies to make the input comprehensible. Students respond verbally or nonverbally.	A limited amount of grammar may be taught or assigned as homework.	The teacher attempts to lower the affective filter by making the input comprehensible.	The home language is not used.	Students progress through natural stages, moving toward correct language use. Teachers respond to a student's meaning and may model a correct response.

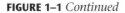

FIGURE 1–1 *Continued*

idea that all teachers are teachers of English language learners and should integrate language and content, purposefully scaffolding language as they teach.

The authors of the document explain that school boards and district leaders should ensure that all school leaders are trained to meet the needs of ELLs, including ELLs with disabilities. Instruction for ELLs should be grade-appropriate, academically rigorous, and aligned to the state Common Core standards. A key point is that schools should promote bilingualism and biliteracy and view both as assets. Parents and families of ELLs should be seen as partners in the education of their children. Schools should draw on the expertise of specialist bilingual, ESL, and LOTE (Languages Other Than English) teachers and encourage all teachers to participate in professional development that addresses the needs of ELLs. Finally, the guidelines suggest that diagnostic tools and formative assessments that are appropriate for ELLs, including those given in students' home languages, should be used to inform instruction and demonstrate growth of English learners.

The Blueprint was based in part on a research project the New York State Department of Education funded to improve the education of emergent bilinguals. The research was carried out by RISLUS (Research Institute for the Study of Language in Urban Society) and the Ph.D Program of the Graduate Center of CUNY (City University of New York). The researchers published "Supporting Emergent Bilinguals in New York: Understanding Successful School Practices" (Sánchez, Espinet, and Seltzer 2014). They reported on their study of ten schools that had a significant number of emergent bilingual students and were rated by the New York State Report Card as schools of "good standing." The researchers conducted surveys, interviews, and observations. They concluded that the schools all had certain characteristics in common, including (1) collaboration with others, (2) strong leadership, (3) using bilingualism as a resource, (4) curriculum and instruction that put emergent bilinguals at the center, (5) organic professional development, and (6) partnering with families (40). While the schools were all different, they all displayed the six characteristics, and the report includes rich examples of each characteristic including photographs and samples of activities and student work for each school. Reports like this have been published by organizations across the country, showing that there is a growing awareness that schools should make the needs of emergent bilinguals central in planning instruction.

Council of Great Schools

The Council of Great Schools is composed of sixty-seven large school districts in the U.S. These schools have "1.2 million English Language Learners or 26 percent of the nation's total." The organization has produced reports and studies on how urban schools can improve the academic achievement of ELLs.

In an early study on ELLs (Horwitz et al. 2009), the Council identified promising practices for ELLs. These practices are similar to those listed by the New York report. Schools should focus on support for academic language development so that ELLs have access to complex content and on preparing all teachers, not only ESL and bilingual teachers, to work with English learners.

Like other documents, the 2009 report proposed that school districts "ensure that all teachers of ELLs have access to high-quality professional development" so that they could implement differentiated instructional strategies, use student assessment data to inform instruction, and develop an understanding of second-language acquisition (5). Professional development should be provided for school administrators and other instructional leaders. In addition, assessment data on ELLs should include multiple measures and should inform instruction.

A 2014 Great Schools document (Walters et al. 2014) calls for focused language study (FLS) for emergent bilinguals to help them understand how English works. This would be what districts often call English language development (ELD) or ESL instruction. In addition, and key to the success of ELLs, is discipline-specific academic language expansion (DALE), in which all teachers in all academic subject areas help students develop the academic language of their specific disciplines.

The authors of the report explain that effective instructional practice depends on a number of factors including "high-quality, rigorous instruction materials" aligned to the demands of the standards; "provisions of scaffolding and other supports" to provide comprehensible input for emergent bilinguals; "supportive school structures, including instructional coaches, professional learning communities, and extended learning (before/after school, tutorials); leadership development"; and "quality professional development that is timely, effective, sustained, and designed to build district- and school-level capacity" (7).

Californians Together

Other groups have also produced important documents to support educators as they work with emergent bilinguals. Californians Together is an organization committed to equal access to a quality education for all children (http://californians together.org). This group has promoted the California Campaign for Biliteracy and the granting of the Seal of Biliteracy, an award given by a school, district, or county office of education in recognition of students who have studied and attained proficiency in two or more languages by high school graduation. Following California's lead, the seal has been adopted in New York, Illinois, Minnesota, New Mexico, Texas, Louisiana, and Washington. Several other states are in the process of adopting the seal of biliteracy.

In addition, the organization produces documents that outline effective education for English learners. Two key documents, a policy brief, "Essential Elements of Effective Practices for English Learners" (Kaplan, Lavandez, and Armas 2011) and a research and policy report, "Reparable Harm: Fulfilling the Unkept Promise of Educational Opportunity for California's Long Term English Learners" (Olsen 2010b), have helped educators in California and across the country serve emergent bilinguals.

In the 2011 policy brief the authors point out that, "Research indicates that instruction of ELs should be designed to maximize the development of English while also maximizing their development of core curricular knowledge and skills" (2). They list key features of "rigorous and relevant instructional practices for ELs." These include (1) bridging connections to instruction by drawing on students' prior knowledge and experiences and first language resources, (2) ensuring instruction is comprehensible using supports such as visuals, graphic organizers, manipulatives, and questioning strategies, (3) providing multiple opportunities for interaction with flexible grouping and collaborative routines that engage students in talking meaningfully about content, and (4) modeling types of academic language in the different genres of the content areas as well as encouraging students to use academic language in their reading, writing, and speaking.

Olsen's (2010b) research report focused specifically on long-term English learners (LTELs), English learners who have been in schools in this country for six or more years and are still struggling academically. While these students develop conversational English, their English proficiency is limited to basic communication. They struggle with expressing complex thoughts and with reading and writing academically. Olsen found that in California, "The majority (59%) of secondary school English Learners are 'Long Term English Learners'" (1). Her findings, based on research with forty school districts and representing more than 175,000 English learners, mirror what is happening in other states.

Olsen reports that many English learners do not receive appropriate language development support, and when they reach high school they are not prepared to meet rigorous academic standards. Her research shows that too often the curriculum and materials used with emergent bilinguals are not appropriate for them and that there is often no coherence or consistency in the programs English learners experience. In an in-depth look at forty-eight LTELs, Olsen found that three out of four students spend at least two years of their schooling "in 'no services' or in mainstream placements, and that 12% of the Long Term English learners may have spent their entire schooling in mainstream classes with no services" (14). It is important for educators who promote submersion into English for immigrant children to understand that these students do need ESL supports. Lindholm-Leary and Genesee (2010) point out that emergent bilinguals placed in mainstream settings in elementary school with no support services are the lowest achievers in middle and high school and are more likely to drop out.

Olsen's report lists design principles for schools with long-term English learners. She suggests that schools should have programs that target their specific needs. For example, these students should not be placed with newcomer students who cannot speak, read, or write even basic English yet. Programs for LTELs should include strategies that support literacy as well as oral language development. Language development should be rigorous and should focus on developing the academic language of the content areas. Students should be encouraged to draw on their first language resources and background experiences as they learn. Instruction should allow students to be active participants in their learning. They should be integrated into school life and not isolated from mainstream students. Finally, especially because these students have been largely ignored and poorly served, administrators, counselors, and teachers should show long-term English learners that they are important and matter and that others care about their success.

In a more recent report, Olsen (2014) provides additional information about how schools across the nation can identify and successfully teach long term English learners. She begins by pointing out:

The large population of Long Term English Language Learners (LTELs) is the starkest evidence of a school system still too unaware, ill prepared, and inadequately focused on the needs of English Language Learners. It is particularly striking that this group of students has remained unnoticed and their needs unaddressed in a time of strong accountability measures, intense scrutiny of student achievement, and major school improvement initiatives designed to meet the needs of "all students." (3)

One reason that many LTELs have remained unnoticed is that most states don't have clear definitions of LTELs, and schools do not keep data on their progress as a separate group. In this 2014 report, Olsen estimates that between one quarter and one half of all English learners who begin school in the primary grades in the U.S. become LTELs, and nearly 60 percent of all English learners in grades six to twelve are LTELs.

Olsen explains why many English learners become long-term English learners. They may be mainstreamed and not given the support they need, they may be put in classes with beginning English learners, or they may be put in classes for struggling readers. None of these approaches works, and most schools do not have programs specially designed for LTELs.

Olsen concludes her report by listing seven basic principles for meeting the needs of long term English learners. These include:

1. Focus urgently on accelerating LTEL progress towards attaining English proficiency and closing academic gaps.
2. Recognize that the needs of LTELs are distinct and cannot adequately be addressed within a "struggling reader" paradigm or a generic "English Language Learner" approach, but require an explicit LTEL approach.
3. Provide LTELs with language development, literacy development, and a program that addresses the academic gaps they have accrued.
4. Affirm the crucial role of home language in a student's life and learning, and provide home language development whenever possible.
5. Provide LTELs with rigorous and relevant curriculum and relationships with supportive adults (along with the supports to succeed).
6. End the ESL ghetto, cease the sink-or-swim approach, and provide maximum integration without sacrificing access to LTEL supports.
7. Invite, support, and insist that LTELs become active participants in their own education. (18–19)

Olsen concludes by listing components of effective school programs, the characteristics of educators who work effectively with long term English learners, and action steps for policymakers. This report effectively summarizes what we know about LTELs and outlines what is needed to help this group of English learners succeed.

PreK Through Third-Grade Education

While Olsen's reports suggest practices for older emergent bilinguals, Espinosa (2013) has identified the needs of PreK–third-grade emergent bilingual students. Her report is an action brief for PreK–third-grade education, "a national movement of schools, districts, educators, and universities seeking to improve how children from ages 3 to 8 learn and develop in schools" (2). Early childhood educators refer to "young children who speak a language other than English in the home and are not fully fluent in English" as dual language learners (DLLs) (3). Because DLLs often struggle with English and have low academic achievement, early childhood educators and researchers have seen an "urgent need to design and implement instructional approaches" (3) that will help these students become proficient in English and succeed in school.

Espinosa's report dispels seven common myths about dual language learners, including (1) learning two languages during the early childhood years will overwhelm, confuse, and/or delay acquisition of English, (2) the language development of dual language learners looks the same as monolingual language development, (3) total English immersion from prekindergarten through third grade is the best way for a young dual language learner to acquire English, (4) because schools don't have the capacity to provide instruction in all the languages represented in DLL children, programs should provide instruction in one common language—English, (5) Spanish-speaking Latinos show social as well as academic delays when entering kindergarten, (6) native English speakers may experience academic and language delays in dual language programs, and (7) if the instruction in your program is delivered primarily in English, you need not worry about DLL children's progress in their home language.

Espinosa addresses each of the myths and concludes that young DLL children are capable of learning academic content in two languages and actually benefit cognitively from learning in two or more languages. When students are immersed into all English from the beginning or transitioned into English too soon, they may lose their first languages and become long-term English learners. She concludes that students should develop their home languages and home language literacy as they are developing English. When teachers don't speak their students' first languages, they should look for strategies to support those non-English languages. The cultural and family backgrounds of children's families should be valued and incorporated into the curriculum. Professional development should be provided to early childhood educators so that they can implement appropriate instructional strategies for DLLs that are culturally and linguistically appropriate and that promote English language development.

Specific English language development instructional strategies suggested by Espinosa help dispel myths and are similar to those in the other reports we have summarized. They include meeting with students' families to learn critical information about the child and the child's background, having visual displays around the room that represent the languages and cultures of the children, providing books and other materials that are authentic and represent the languages and cultures of the students, introducing and using key vocabulary in the students' home languages to bridge into English, and using pictures and realia to make learning comprehensible.

REPORTS ON RESEARCH WITH EMERGENT BILINGUALS

University researchers have reviewed research studies of effective teaching practices for English learners, both young dual language learners and the general English learner population. Goldenberg, Hicks, and Lit (2013) and Goldenberg, Nemeth, and colleagues (Goldenberg et al. 2013) reported on research focused on early childhood dual language learners. They came to many of the same conclusions that Espinosa did, although they temper their conclusions by explaining that there is little research available on effective instruction for this English learner population.

In general, these researchers conclude that the research on young dual language learners suggests that helpful strategies for emergent bilinguals include (1) some explicit teaching or explanations of features of the English language, (2) language scaffolding with sentence frames, (3) connecting the home language to English, (4) engaging the whole body in learning, (5) learning and practicing rhymes, poems, and songs, (6) pairing DLLs with children of different proficiency levels, (7) providing classroom spaces where dual language learners do not have to use language and other spaces where they can interact in small groups, (8) using manipulatives, pictures, and gestures, (9) retelling and dramatizing familiar stories, and (10) providing culturally relevant bilingual materials and a bilingual listening center (Goldenberg et al. 2013).

Goldenberg, Hicks, and Lit discuss the research on home language use for DLLs and conclude that

> Preschool studies tend to find that at best, instruction in the home language contributes to growth in both English and home language skills; at worst, there is no difference in English achievement but an advantage in home language achievement. (27)

The researchers conclude that while more research is needed on young dual language learners, educators should use the home language when possible, employ strategies that help students with English language development, and build bridges with families to help them support their children's learning.

Saunders, Goldenberg, and Marcelletti (2013) review research specific to English Language Development (ELD) instruction, "instruction that focuses specifically on helping English learners develop English language skills and that is delivered in a portion of the school day separate from the academic content that students need to learn" (13). The researchers note that not all the research reviewed is limited to K–12 classrooms, but because of the limited available research, "we have chosen to review them [syntheses that include studies of university and adult students] and interpret them as best we can for the relevance to the K–12 ELD instruction" (15).

The researchers present several important conclusions. First, studies show that providing ELD instruction—that is, a time dedicated to language development for emergent bilinguals—is better than not providing it. Secondly, ELD instruction should be provided until students achieve advanced English language ability. Saunders and his colleagues point out that as emergent bilinguals move through the grades, the gap between ELs and native speakers increases. It takes from four to six years for students to develop advanced proficiency as measured by different measurements of English learner progress, and "while progress in acquiring English from beginning to middle levels of proficiency is fairly rapid, progress from middle to upper levels of proficiency slows considerably" (16).

A third conclusion is that ELD programs prove to be more successful when schools and districts make ELD a priority. Studies of high-achieving schools with high numbers of ELs found that these schools had a schoolwide focus on ELD and shared high expectations for emergent bilinguals. The ELD instruction that helped students succeed emphasized academic language, not just conversational language, and incorporated all four domains: speaking, listening, reading, and writing. Instruction on language was meaningful, but teachers also directed students' attention to forms and functions of the language.

In their conclusion, Saunders and his colleagues provide some specific guidelines for ELD instruction. They suggest that ELD instruction should be planned and delivered with specific language objectives in mind. While the use of English should be maximized, the primary language should be used strategically. ELD instruction should be interactive, and activities should be carefully planned and implemented. Finally, they propose that instructors might provide corrective feedback on language forms, but at the same time be sure that language is seen as communication.

Goldenberg conducted an additional review of research that he subtitled "What we know and don't yet know about effective instruction for English learners" (Goldenberg 2013). He comments that despite the great number of reports, books, and articles on the topic, "there is surprisingly little research on common practices or recommendations for practice with the more than 5 million ELs in our nation's schools" (4). Based on his review of the available research, Goldenberg provides readers with three basic principles to follow.

1. Generally, effective practices are likely to be effective with ELs.
2. ELs require additional instructional supports.
3. The home language can be used to promote academic development. (5)

In his discussion of generally effective practices he cites, among others, clear goals and objectives; appropriate materials that are challenging; well-designed instruction and routines; clear instructions; effective modeling of skills, strategies, and procedures; active student involvement; timely and appropriate feedback; application of new learning; and structured interactions with other students.

Goldenberg also lists ways to support emergent bilinguals during specific instruction for them. These include familiar suggestions such as building on students' past experiences and knowledge as new concepts are introduced; providing background knowledge; using graphic organizers, visuals, realia, and hands-on activities; providing extra time; designating language and content objectives; using sentence frames and models as students read and discuss academic content; and differentiating instruction.

Specific instructional supports for use of the home language suggested by Goldenberg include the use of cognates, brief explanations in the home language, a preview and review of lessons in the home language, and strategy instruction in the home language and applied to learning in English. Goldenberg concludes his article by calling for teachers to look at goals and standards and determine what they mean for their classrooms, and then analyze and evaluate student work with colleagues to help determine what is working and what is not.

PRINCIPLES FOR EFFECTIVE TEACHING

In this chapter we have described methods for second and foreign language teaching. We have also summarized some key reports and research reviews that can guide educators as they plan programs and instruction for emergent bilinguals. In addition, we have worked with outstanding teachers and visited schools with effective programs in many parts of the U.S.

Drawing on our review of the literature and our work in schools, we have developed seven key principles for the effective teaching of emergent bilinguals. These principles will serve as the basis for the chapters in the rest of this book. Each chapter will focus on one principle. For each principle, we will provide theory and research that supports it and describe lessons or units that show the principle in action. In the introduction we briefly discussed each of the principles; they are repeated here as Figure 1–2.

1. Teaching should be learner centered.
2. Teaching should go from whole to part.
3. Teaching should develop academic language and content.
4. Teaching should be meaningful and purposeful.
5. Teaching should include interactions to develop oral and written language.
6. Teaching should support students' languages and cultures.
7. Teaching and assessment should reflect faith in the learner.

FIGURE 1–2 *Principles for Effective Teaching*

APPLICATIONS

1. We have discussed methods used over a long period of time. Make a timeline showing when the different methods were introduced.
2. Think back to your own study of a second or foreign language. What method or combination of methods did your teacher use? Did your teacher use any strategies you found especially helpful? Did your teacher follow the practices we described for the method(s) in this chapter, and, if not, what changes did he or she make?
3. Many people consider the teaching of grammar to be essential for language learning. What is your view? How were you taught grammar in school? In a second language? In your home language?
4. Choose one method we described in this chapter to research more fully. Prepare a report to share with your classmates.
5. In the review of research, what findings were consistent? What findings surprised you?
6. We reviewed recent reports and research summaries in this chapter. Find additional research on the topic of effective practices for teaching emergent bilinguals and bring them to class to share.

2

Teaching Should Be Learner Centered

A LEARNER-CENTERED FIRST-GRADE UNIT

Alicia teaches first grade in a mid-sized city along the Texas–Mexico border. Most of her students speak Spanish as their home language, and many have family from Mexico or still living in Mexico. Some have one parent who is a native English speaker and another who is from Mexico and dominant in Spanish. Alicia's students are living between the worlds of the country on the U.S. side of the border with its customs and traditions and those of the neighboring country to the south. Alicia wants her students to be proud of both languages and cultures. She decides to begin her year with a theme on family organized around the big question, "How are our families the same and how are they different?"

Alicia teaches in a district that promotes instruction in English using all English materials, many of which are not culturally relevant for her students. However, while English is encouraged, Spanish is not prohibited. Alicia, once an immigrant child herself, is bilingual and tries to find ways that allow her students to draw on their first language as they are learning in English. She finds resources that support her students' lived experiences and their first language.

She begins her unit by reading *In My Family/En mi familia* (Garza 1996), a book describing experiences of Mexican American families living in the United States. Each page has a picture of a family activity and a passage in which the author writes her memories of the experience in English and also in Spanish. Alicia reads a page of the book in English, and then asks student to brainstorm a special word they remember from the story using Ada's "Building a Word Treasury" activity (Ada 2003). As children list words, Alicia writes them on a sheet to be kept hung up around the room. She allows children to respond in either English or Spanish. As children dictate words, all the children remember parts of the reading where they heard the words. Later in the day during guided reading, Alicia reads and discusses the same page of the book in Spanish to a group of students less proficient in English.

The children and the teacher read other books together about families including another Garza book, *Family Pictures/ Cuadros de familia* (1990), *Mi familia/My Family* (Ancona 2004), *We Are Cousins/Somos primos* (Bertrand 2007), and *Tortillas and Lullabies/Tortillas y cancioncitas* (Reiser 1998). Each of these books leads the students to talk about their own families. For instance, in *Tortillas and Lullabies*, four different generations of women share their traditions with food and family, and in *We Are Cousins*, González shows how cousins are friends and sometimes argue but, in the end, they are family. The teacher also reads *Celebrations/Celebraciones: Holidays of the United States and Mexico/Días feriados de los Estados Unidos y México* (Grande-Tabor 2004). Alicia has each student interview one of their relatives about family traditions and asks them to collect a favorite recipe.

Several of the children cross the border on weekends and visit *abuelos* (grandparents), *tíos* (uncles and aunts), and *primos* (cousins), and they interview one of their Mexican relatives. Other students interview relatives living nearby in the United States. With the results from the interviews, the teacher and students create a Venn diagram showing similarities and differences in traditions between the two cultures. They also gather the recipes and make an illustrated class recipe book.

A favorite class activity is writing together a letter to a favorite author/illustrator, Anthony Browne. They read and discuss *My Dad* (Browne 2000), *My Mom* (Browne 2005b) and *My Brother* (Browne 2007b), books Alicia also has in Spanish *Mi papá* (Browne 2002), *Mi mamá* (Browne 2005a), *and Mi hermano* (Browne 2007a). Browne's books are very popular with the children because they are humorous and have such imaginative illustrations. Alicia's students eagerly share their favorite parts of the stories and favorite illustrations as the class composes the letter to the author/illustrator.

Alicia culminates the unit by reading two books that reflect some of the experiences of her students, *René Has Two Last Names/René tiene dos apellidos* (Colato Lainez 2009) and *Marisol McDonald Doesn't Match: Marisol McDonald no combina* (Browne 2011). In the first book, René is confused when he first attends school in the U.S. because in school only one of his last names, his father's, is used. René feels part of his identity is missing because the custom in Spanish-speaking countries is to have children use both the mother's and father's last names.

In the second book, Marisol, who is a Peruvian, Scottish American bicultural girl, shows her bicultural preferences as she eats peanut butter and jelly burritos or plays soccer. When she tries to conform to U.S. culture, she is unhappy and loses her creativity. After brainstorming how they are alike and different from René and

Marisol, students list how they are the same as and different from one another. They then make their own "I Am Me" books. These books include their full names, describe how they look, what they like to eat, what they like to do, and who the members of their families are. Alicia's students begin their year engaged in reading about topics that they are interested in and that draw on their background experiences. They talk and write about things that are important to them.

The activities for the unit meet state standards for grade 1. For example, one standard asks that students describe the importance of family customs and traditions. Another requires that students learn the correct style for writing a formal letter, including where to place the date and how to choose an appropriate salutation and closing. In addition, grade 1 standards ask that students make personal connections to their readings and work on vocabulary building. The books they read connect to the unit content and reinforce both literacy and vocabulary development. See Figure 2–1 for a bibliography of the books Alicia used. Throughout the unit, Alicia's students are involved in well-planned activities that support their learning and their acquisition of English.

Ancona, George. 2004. *Mi familia: My Family*. New York: Children's Press.

Bertrand, Diane. 2007. *Somos primos: We Are Cousins*. Houston, TX: Piñata Books.

Browne, Anthony. 2000. *My Dad*. London, UK: Doubleday.

Browne, Anthony. 2002. *Mi papá*. México, D.F.: Fondo de Cultura Econóica.

Browne, Anthony. 2005a. *Mi mamá*. México, D.F.: Fondo de Cultura Económica.

Browne, Anthony. 2005b. *My Mom*. London, UK: Doubleday.

Browne, Anthony. 2007a. *Mi hermano*. México, D.F.: Fondo de Cultura Económica.

Browne, Anthony. 2007b. *My Brother*. London, UK: Doubleday.

Browne, Mónica. 2011. *Marisol McDonald Doesn't Match: Marisol McDonald no combina*. New York: Children's Book Press.

Colato Lainez, R. 2009. *René Has Two Last Names/ René tiene dos apellidos*. Houston, TX: Arte Público.

Garza, Carmen Lomas. 1990. *Family Pictures: Cuadros de familia*. San Francisco: Children's Book Press.

Garza, Carmen Lomas. 1996. *In My Family: En mi familia*. San Francisco: Children's Book Press.

Grande-Tabor, Nancy María. 2004. *Celebrations/ Celebraciones: Holidays of the United States and Mexico/Días feriado de los Estados Unidos y México*. Watertown, MA: Charlesbridge.

Reiser, Lynn. 1998. *Tortillas and Lullabies/Tortillas y cancioncitas*. New York: Greenwillow Books.

FIGURE 2–1 *Family Unit Books*

Family Unit for Older Students

Alicia's unit was developed for first-grade students, but the topic is also appropriate for ESL middle, secondary, and adult students. Teachers might begin the year with a family unit to get to know their students and to help students get to know one another. A family theme draws on older students' backgrounds, experiences, and interests and provides opportunities for English language development. In Figure 2–2 we provide various suggestions that teachers of middle, high school, or adult English learners could use to support their language development. The ideas include reading and writing activities that emergent bilinguals would find engaging and interesting. In addition, suggestions for activities that would allow teachers to evaluate students' growth are listed.

LEARNER CENTERED, NOT TEACHER CENTERED

Bill Keane, a cartoonist who drew Family Circus cartoons for over fifty years, often showed in one cartoon what teacher educators have researched for years. A favorite cartoon of ours is one in which Billy leads his younger sister, Dolly, into the house after school explaining to their mother, "Dolly's school would be better if they didn't have that lady up front talkin' all the time." Billy understood a key problem in many classrooms: the teacher, not the students, was the center of learning. In Alicia's classroom it is the students who are at the center, not the teacher. The books she chose and the activities she planned for the students were based on her knowledge of their backgrounds. The suggestions for older students also are meant to engage them and draw on their interests and experiences.

The idea of the teacher as the source of all knowledge standing up front and delivering instruction follows from commonsense assumptions of how teachers should teach. With English language learners, the temptation to have a teacher-centered classroom arises because the perception is that the teacher has the English proficiency the students need, and therefore all knowledge must come from the teacher. However, it is important to remember that English language learners are not deficient just because they do not speak English. They bring a rich and varied background of experiences and talent to the classroom. Teachers who understand principles for effective teaching find ways to use their students' knowledge, including their first language and culture, even when the students do not speak English. They ensure that their instruction is learner centered, not teacher centered.

The reports and research reviews we summarized in Chapter 1 emphasize the need for students to engage in meaningful social interaction. In effective classes for emergent bilinguals, students work in pairs and small groups. They engage in

Activities for Reading, Writing, and Oral Language Development

Conduct a "Find someone who . . . " with directions like "Find someone who has more than eight cousins."

Bring in family photographs or use pictures on phones, blogs, or Facebook pages to discuss families in groups.

Draw and discuss family trees.

Interview each other about families to report back to the class.

Survey members of the class about family characteristics to chart.

Read society pages in a magazine or newspaper in L1 or in English to summarize and discuss in English.

Look at marriage and birth sections of the newspaper.

Compare and contrast marriage and birth customs in the U.S. and other countries.

Discuss birth order in families.

Discuss naming customs in countries.

Discuss family hierarchy, both traditional and present day.

Ask students to keep a diary about family events and personalities.

Make "My Family and Me" posters using photos, drawings, and pictures from magazines to tell the story.

Materials

Family photos, pictures on phones, blogs, Facebook pages

Books about families

Newspaper and magazine article columns related to family relations

Evaluation

Diary entries about family members

Family trees (oral presentation and written diagram)

Interview summaries

FIGURE 2–2 *Family Unit Adaptations for Middle, Secondary, and Adult Learners*

hands-on learning as they complete projects and present what they have learned to classmates. The teacher plans and directs student activity, but the focus should be on the students, not the teacher.

The materials used in the classroom are also important. In this era of standards-based instruction and high-stakes testing, educators across the country are paying attention to the needs of emergent bilinguals. In the Great Schools 2014 report on meeting the needs of English learners (Walter et al. 2014), criteria for appropriate materials for these students are laid out. Besides providing a wide variety of rigorous materials that align with both content and language standards, the report calls for materials that "offer a wide variety of culturally relevant texts, organized in appropriate themes/topics." The authors also explain, "texts must acknowledge students' life experiences, and social and emotional development" (22). They point out, "Texts provided in Spanish (or any other language) should be authentic, high quality, and should help students meet standards" (23). Certainly, the books Alicia used for her family unit meet these criteria.

TYPES OF ENGLISH LANGUAGE LEARNERS

Alicia's students were all first graders. Most were emergent bilinguals. However, her English learners were not all at the same level of English proficiency, and their background experiences varied a great deal. For example, Felipe was born in Mexico City, and his parents, both physicians, made sure that he attended a private preschool and kindergarten there before entering Alicia's classroom. Salvador, on the other hand, came from a rural village in southern Mexico where there was no preschool or kindergarten. His indigenous parents did not have the advantage of an education beyond second grade and the first language of the home is Mixteco. Salvador can communicate in Spanish, but is more proficient in Mixteco. Norma was born in the U.S. and attended preschool and kindergarten in the same school where she is now in first grade. Her parents immigrated when they were in elementary school. They are bilingual and use both Spanish and English in the home. Norma's older siblings are dominant English speakers and use English at home, so Norma came to school more proficient in English than Spanish.

Students, like those in Alicia's classroom, come to school with diverse language histories and varied academic background knowledge. Yet some teachers view all English learners as the same. As we have worked with teachers across the country, we have heard comments like the following:

> "Ji-woo, Azad, and Francisco are newcomers and are learning to read and write English very well, better than English learners who have been here since kindergarten!"

> "What do I do with these new refugee students from Nigeria? I don't think they have been to school at all!"

"My new students from Pakistan seem to be doing very well. Some even speak some English already!"

These comments and questions are typical of those we hear from teachers across the country. ELLs enter classes at different ages. Some do very well while many struggle. Teaching these diverse students is complex.

In a review of the research on concerns about English learners, G. García (2000) points out that "There is no typical LEP child" (3). It is important that teachers consider some basic differences among English learners as they plan instruction for them, including differences in their academic background and their academic language proficiency. For teachers to plan and implement learner-centered instruction, they must understand differences among the types of English learners. In the following sections we describe four types of emergent bilinguals: newly arrived with adequate schooling, newly arrived with limited or interrupted formal schooling, long-term English learners, and students at risk of becoming long-term English learners. We provide specific examples of each type of English learner.

Newly Arrived with Adequate Schooling

Students like Felipe who are newly arrived with adequate schooling have come to the U.S. within the last five years. When they arrive, these students bring with them the schooling experiences of their native country. They are literate in their first language and their content knowledge is at or near grade level. These students usually catch up academically fairly quickly, and teachers are impressed with their academic progress, especially when compared with other emergent bilinguals who have been in school in this country for the same amount of time. However, students with adequate formal schooling still struggle with standardized tests and exit exams because they have not fully developed their English skills. In addition, there may be gaps in their understanding and knowledge because tests are written assuming all students have the background of native English speakers.

Recent arrivals with adequate schooling may or may not adjust well socially. The school and community factors that influence them are extremely important. The economic situation their families find themselves in also makes a difference as to whether they succeed academically. Looking at two examples helps us understand these students and better assess their chances for achieving academic success.

Marisa

Marisa and her family immigrated to the United States from Mexico City when she was in the seventh grade. Her parents, concerned about the frequent kidnappings and the gang violence in different parts of Mexico and El Salvador, Guatemala, and

Honduras to the south, moved to Houston, Texas. They are both professionals and had the financial resources to move to the U.S. and start a business of their own.

In Mexico City, Marisa attended a private school from PreK to seventh grade where she had English classes twice a week. Her parents also provided once-a-week private English lessons for her on Saturdays. When she arrived in Houston, she was placed in a large middle school. She was overwhelmed with the amount of English she had to read, write, and understand, as well as the differences in the way teachers and students interacted with one another in school compared with her private school in Mexico City. Marisa's parents found her an English tutor. The family also connected with other families from Mexico City, and soon Marisa had a network of friends at school and outside of school. In addition, she joined a local Latino organization focused on supporting Latinos' academic progress.

Within a year, Marisa was doing very well in all her classes, although she still worried about the state standardized tests in reading, math, and writing. Marisa is now a junior in high school. She is on a college preparatory track and wants to study engineering. With the encouragement of her parents and school counselors, she has attended local and state conferences for Hispanics interested in STEM (science, technology, engineering, and mathematics). She is applying for admission and scholarships at several universities.

Marisa is a clear example of an adequate formal schooling student. Her parents, who themselves were well educated, were able to provide her with a good private school education in Mexico and with tutoring resources when in this country. She also has home and school support as she explores career options for her future. Marisa's future looks bright.

Ahmed

Ahmed, a fifth grader, is another example of a newly arrived student with adequate schooling. Like Marisa, he attended a private school and arrived in this country with grade-level literacy and academic content knowledge in Arabic. Because his parents were well educated and spoke good English, they were recruited to help the United States forces when they were in Iraq. However, when the U.S. withdrew they received threats and decided the family needed to move.

Although his academic background is similar to that of Marisa, Ahmed lacks the kinds of supports she had. His family moved to a city in the Midwest. While there were government agencies there to help Iraqi refugees, there were few community groups other than members of the local mosque that supported Iraqi or other Arabic-speaking Muslim refugees. In addition, his parents, highly educated professionals, had to accept jobs for which they were overqualified. These jobs provided some money, but the family still struggles financially.

Ahmed's friends are other refugee children. He faces racism from some Americans both inside and outside of school. As tensions from Muslim terrorist groups escalate around the world, Ahmed and his Muslim friends feel the distrust and dislike of some peers. They also feel that some of their teachers are uncomfortable around them. Ahmed does not believe some teachers want to help him when he asks for help. He remains quiet in class and seldom participates.

Ahmed's parents, though academically prepared, are not emotionally ready to help him in school because they are busy establishing themselves economically in the U.S. In sum, Ahmed's academic background may ultimately enable him to succeed, but he lacks family, school, and community support. Even with his strong home language academic background, Ahmed may find it difficult to succeed in school due to these out-of-school factors.

Newly Arrived with Limited or Interrupted Formal Schooling

A second type of emergent bilingual is the recent arrival with limited or interrupted formal schooling. Students in this group are also referred to as students with interrupted formal education (SIFE) because of their inconsistent schooling. These students face all the problems of any new immigrants, but they are much less prepared academically than students like Marisa and Ahmed. When they arrive, they have either had little or no schooling or schooling that was so often interrupted that they are significantly behind their peers in literacy development and academic content knowledge.

Limited formal schooling students have limited or no native language literacy to draw on as they learn to read and write in English. Sometimes teachers can tell if a newcomer is a limited formal schooling student either by the student's poorly developed handwriting or by the student's inability to do even basic math computation, such as addition or subtraction. Because of their limited experiences in school, they lack basic concepts in the different subject areas and are often at least two to three years below grade level in the content areas (Freeman and Freeman 2011).

These students must develop both conversational and academic English, become literate in English, and acquire the academic knowledge and skills they need to compete with native English speakers. Because they do not have the academic background to draw on in their home languages, they have difficulty with coursework in English and do poorly on standardized tests. These students struggle more than students like Marisa and Ahmed as they try to adjust to school. Since they have attended school infrequently, they do not understand how schools are organized and how students are expected to act in schools. Many of these students arrive as refugees or as unaccompanied minors, alone with no resources. Once they arrive, they struggle socially as they try to adjust to living and learning in a new culture.

Fazilah

Fazilah, originally from the Sudan, moved first to Chicago when she was twelve. Her parents decided to leave inner-city Chicago and moved to Portland, Maine, when Fazilah was fourteen. She and her family joined a large group of Sudanese that chose Portland as a refuge from the political turmoil, civil unrest, and poverty of their homeland. Portland, Maine, has the reputation among Sudanese refugees as a small town with a secure and healthy environment despite unrest and clashes with police at times (MacQuarrie 2009).

The official languages of the Sudan are Arabic and English. Access to education, especially for girls, is limited because of the violence and instability in the country. While boys, including her brothers, did go to school in Sudan, Fazilah, like most girls, was seldom allowed out of her house. As a result, Fazilah only attended school sporadically before coming to this country. Because of this, she was identified at the beginning level according to the state English language proficiency (WIDA) standards when she arrived in Portland. While she could speak Arabic, her reading and writing was not at grade level, and she spoke English only in phrases and short sentences. Although she had some basic communication ability in English, she was often confused when spoken to in English even about everyday things and had trouble expressing her ideas.

High school was difficult for Fazilah. She was in an ESL class for two periods a day and needed ESL support in her content classes. She felt isolated during her content classes as her English was limited, and she looked different from the other students. She and the other Muslim girls wore their *hijab*, head scarf, and usually also wore the *jilbab*, a fitted cloak often practical in the cold Maine weather although certainly different from the parkas and jeans worn by their U.S. counterparts. Fazilah's only friends were other Muslim girls and a few other girls from other countries in her ESL class. Fazilah felt desperate in her new setting and wondered if she would ever learn English and fit into this society.

Daniel

Fourteen-year-old Daniel traveled more than 1,000 miles to the United States from his small village in Honduras through Guatemala and Mexico without his family. The journey took him several months, and was full of hardships and often extremely dangerous. Daniel was assaulted by gang members, rode the infamous *tren de la muerte* (death train) or *La Bestia* (The Beast), and crossed over into the United States illegally only to be caught by immigration authorities.

Daniel's story is not unlike Enrique's story told by journalist Sonia Nazario in *Enrique's Journey* (Nazario 2014). The number of unaccompanied minors who made this trip, like Daniel, is daunting. For example, between September and August

2014, 55,000 unaccompanied minors arrived in the U.S. (Maxwell 2014). Many attempt the trip several times before finally making it. Many never make it. It is estimated that 200 to 300 die annually, and many more are seriously injured in their attempts to make this journey. As explained earlier, this journey has become more difficult and dangerous due to the Mexican crackdown on immigrants crossing Mexico, which is supported by U.S. dollars (Nazario 2015).

Among unaccompanied minors, Daniel's story is a familiar one. Daniel's mother left him with his grandmother when he was five years old. She found jobs as a housekeeper or in restaurants and sent money for clothes, birthday and Christmas gifts, and school supplies. Her telephone calls to Daniel were frequent at first with promises to return home to get him. But as the years went by the calls became less frequent. Daniel's grandmother had no control over him, and he frequently skipped school. Even when he did attend, the rural school offered little. There were no real supplies, and the poorly trained teachers either lacked control over their classrooms or punished students severely when they misbehaved. Several of his friends dropped out of school, were recruited into gangs, and turned to drugs.

Like many of the other unaccompanied children, Daniel became desperate to reunite with his mother. When his grandmother died, he knew he had to leave. He did not get along with his aunt or younger cousins and felt like a burden living with them. He heard stories of others who had gone north, and believed he could too. With only the clothes on his back and a package of food, he set out for *el norte*.

After Daniel was detained by immigration, he was kept in a detention center near Brownsville, Texas, for several weeks. Immigration located his mother, now married with two children born in the United States. She traveled from San Jose, California, to pick him up. He went to live with his mother and her new family. Their house was small and cramped. Although everyone spoke Spanish, he had difficulty adjusting to life with his mother, his new father, and siblings.

On top of these challenges, school was difficult for Daniel. He had to adjust to a new culture after an extremely traumatic experience. He attended a large, modern middle school. He was placed in a beginning-level ESL class for a block of two periods, but he was completely lost in his content area classes taught in English. The textbooks were hard to understand not only because they were in English but also because he lacked background in science, social studies, and math. Daniel wanted to succeed, but he felt completely overwhelmed.

Long-Term English Learners

Long-term English learners (LTELs) are increasingly attracting attention from educators across the country. The 2000 census reveals that over half of the LEP secondary school children were U.S. born (Fix and Capps 2005). This is disturbing because LTELs are students who have been attending school in this country for six or more years yet still cannot pass English language proficiency tests and be redesignated as fluent English proficient.

These students are generally misunderstood or overlooked. Horwitz and her colleagues (2009), in a Council of Great City Schools report on large urban school districts across the country, state:

> Leaders and staff in each district were quick to point out the specialized needs of adolescent, newcomer students, yet they acknowledge that a majority of the students falling through the cracks are long-term ELLs who have been in the system for years. (29)

Olsen's report (2010b) about the long-term English learners in California has been referred to as "a wake-up call to California educators and policymakers." Olsen expresses concern that so many secondary students, despite many years in California schools and "despite being close to the age in which they should be able to graduate, are still not English proficient and have indeed incurred major academic deficits" (iii). Other states have also expressed concern in different reports about this population of students. For example, in studies of English learners in Texas researchers found that high numbers of struggling Latino students who drop out do not meet eleventh-grade standards in math and reading (McNeil, Coppola, and Radigan 2008; Flores, Bartalova, and Fix 2012).

Menken and colleagues (Menken, Kleyn, and Chae 2012) have studied long-term English learners with colleagues in New York City. They have identified common characteristics of this student population. LTELs are typically found in grades 6–12, speak different languages, and come from different countries. They are often orally bilingual and speak English like a native speaker, but they have limited literacy skills in English and in their native languages. These students perform below grade level in reading and writing and, as a result, struggle with their content-area classes. Usually, these students have low grades, often they have been retained at some point, and they are at high risk of dropping out.

Like Olsen, Menken and Kleyn (2009) report a lack of understanding of these students. They explain that needs of these students are different from those of secondary newcomer ELLs, "yet the language programming at the secondary level is typically for new arrivals [because] most educators are unfamiliar with the specialized needs of this population" (2).

Olsen (2010a) has given specific guidelines for districts to properly identify and then develop appropriate programs for LTELs. Some districts have begun to respond to the guidelines. Los Angeles Unified School District's 2012 Master Plan (LAUSD 2012), for example, has specific guidelines to identify and set up programs to meet the needs of long-term English learners, but there are still few school districts across the country where these students are identified and provided with programs specific to their needs.

Because there are so many of these long-term English learners, researchers have divided them into subcategories. Menken, Kleyn, and Chae (2007) have listed two main types: (1) transnational students, and (2) students with inconsistent and/or subtractive U.S. schooling. We will discuss each type briefly and provide an example of each.

Vaivén *Transnational Students*

The first group is sometimes referred to as the *vaivén* students because, as the label indicates when translated from Spanish, they "go and come." *Vaivén* students, although primarily U.S. educated, move back and forth between the U.S. and their country of origin. Many of these students also fit into the students with interrupted formal education (SIFE) designation since their schooling is interrupted as they move back and forth.

Carlos is a good example of this type of student. He lives near the Mexico–Texas border. He grew up in Mexico with his mother, Lydia, a single parent. Carlos began school in Matamorros, Mexico. When he was eight, his mother met a Mexican man who had legal residency in the U.S. and lived across the border in Brownsville, Texas. When she got pregnant with his baby, he wanted to get married and have the baby born and educated in the U.S. Carlos and his mother moved to Brownsville, and Carlos started second grade in Texas.

Carlos moved back to Matamorros twice to live with relatives. Once he attended school, but the other time he did not. He says he hates schools in the U.S. and doesn't like his stepfather. Although he tries to impress Mexican friends and relatives with his fluent oral English, he struggles academically in English. At sixteen Carlos is back in Mexico for the third time. He isn't attending school there, and his relatives struggle to support him in hard economic times. He will probably return to Brownsville soon, but one wonders if he will attend school there or not (Freeman and Freeman 2011).

Inconsistent/Subtractive Schooling LTELs

A second type of LTEL is the English language learner with inconsistent and/or subtractive schooling. These students may receive some bilingual instruction, some ESL instruction, or they may have a combination of different services. Often, the supports they receive, even within one district, are not well articulated. Guillermo is a good example of a student who received subtractive/inconsistent schooling.

Guillermo was born in the United States. His parents crossed the border when they were in middle school, but both dropped out of school when they were juniors in high school to get married. His mother is now a waitress and his father is a mechanic. While both of his parents speak English, the language of Guillermo's home before he started school was Spanish.

He started school as a monolingual Spanish speaker in a rural district in southeastern Texas when he was in preschool. The district where he first attended school provided bilingual education until third grade, so he started school with first language support. However, district policies changed so that when Guillermo entered first grade he was mainstreamed into an all-English classroom. He was provided with some ESL support in first grade during an ESL period. In second grade he was pulled out for ESL twice a week, and by third grade he stopped receiving any kind of language support services. Throughout the rest of his elementary and middle school years his instruction was in English only. Spanish was often his social language at home and with his friends.

Now, in ninth grade, Guillermo speaks English and Spanish but he cannot discuss complex ideas or read or write either language at grade level. Teachers are concerned that he might not be able to pass state-mandated exams or the high school exit exam. Guillermo is a typical example of an LTEL who has conversational English but struggles in academic reading and writing. As a result of his inconsistent, subtractive schooling, he has not developed age-appropriate language abilities in his home language or in English. He is not literate in Spanish and has limited English literacy.

Students at Risk of Becoming Long-Term English Learners

Children who begin the primary grades (PreK through third grade) speaking a language other than English don't fit into the first two categories of recent arrivals with adequate schooling or recent arrivals with limited schooling simply because they are just beginning their education and have had little or no previous schooling. They have not been in U.S. schools long enough to be classified as long-term English learners, but these students may be considered as potential long-term English learners. To reduce the number of long-term English learners, it is crucial to identify students at risk of becoming long-term English learners at an early stage in their academic careers and then provide them with the education they need to acquire academic English and academic content knowledge.

For example, if they are placed in a bilingual program, they can build on their first language skills as they learn English. Students in long-term bilingual programs with well-qualified teachers and appropriate materials have much more potential for academic success in English than students in other kinds of programs. On the other hand, if they are placed in a class taught only in English, they are likely to fall behind. In addition, if they attend schools that are crowded, underfunded, and poorly staffed, their chances for academic success are significantly diminished.

Another factor that influences the success of young English learners is the family situation. If their parents are well educated, financially successful, and socially stable, emergent bilinguals have a good chance of doing well. On the other hand, if children come from families with low levels of education and who struggle economically, they are more likely to become long-term English learners. Schools can work with parents and provide parent education programs. Community and religious organizations can also provide support and services that immigrant families need.

Amira, a Nigerian refugee entering kindergarten in a school on the outskirts of Los Angeles, is a good example of a potential long-term English learner. Her family recently came to California sponsored by a church group. Although English is a language used in school in Nigeria, she never attended school there. Amira only speaks Hausa. There is no support in her first language offered by the school as she is one of only two Hausa speakers in her large elementary school. Amira is having difficulty adjusting to life the U.S. Her parents are still coping with the violence they experienced in Nigeria and are overwhelmed as they go through culture shock and try to adjust to living in a new country. Although the church and refugee services offer some help, the family is not stable financially. Even with excellent support from caring teachers, Amira is a potential long-term English learner.

Virginia teaches second grade in an inner-city neighborhood of Houston, Texas. Many of her students are potential long-term English learners. Although Virginia is bilingual in Spanish and English, she has a class with students who speak five different languages, including Spanish, Nepali, Vietnamese, Mandarin, and Urdu. The families of her students all struggle economically and many have limited educational backgrounds themselves. While the parents want to help, they either do not have the time or the understanding to support their children's academic work.

Virginia has studied second language acquisition and knows that first language support is important, so she tries to draw on her students' first languages and cultures whenever possible. She looks for culturally relevant materials, invites parents to share their culture and language, and tries to employ strategies to make the English input for her students comprehensible. However, she struggles with demands of her administrator to prepare students for the tests and give them frequent benchmark exercises that only frustrate and confuse her students. The ESL pullout teacher tries to support what Virginia is teaching, but it is difficult to plan together and there is never enough time. Despite her efforts, Virginia's students are at risk of becoming long-term English learners.

Although schools are now beginning to develop programs for long-term English learners, there has not been a consistent set of criteria for identifying this group of students or for reporting their academic progress. Instead, data on LTELs is combined with data on other ELLs. However, recently, state departments of education have begun to require districts to collect data on how many LTELs they serve and on their academic progress.

In California, for example, an LTEL is defined as an English learner who is enrolled in any of grades 6 to 12, has been enrolled in schools in the United States for six years or more, has remained at the same English language proficiency level for two or more consecutive prior years, or has regressed to a lower English language proficiency level, and, for a pupil in any of grades 6 to 9, inclusive, who scored far below basic or below basic on the state English language arts achievement test.

In addition, California defines students at risk of becoming long-term English learners as an English learner who is enrolled in any of grades 3 to 12 in schools in the United States for four to five years, who has scored at the intermediate level or below on the state English language development test, and, for a pupil in any of grades 3 to 9, who scored in the fourth or fifth year at the below basic or far below basic level on the state English language arts achievement test (adapted from proposed Senate Bill 75). The state education department requires districts to collect and post the number of long-term English learners and students at risk of becoming long-term English learners each year.

This move to identify long-term English learners and to monitor their progress should prompt school districts to establish programs that meet the needs of this group of English learners. In addition, by identifying students at risk of becoming long-term English learners, schools can implement early programs to prevent these students from falling further behind in developing English proficiency and academic competence.

We have described four types of English learners. Figure 2–3 summarizes the characteristics of each type.

Language Proficiency of Emergent Bilinguals

In learner-centered classes teachers understand the many factors that influence the academic success of their students. One of these is their academic language proficiency. It was Cummins who first helped educators of emergent bilinguals understand that there are different kinds of language proficiency, conversational language and academic language (Cummins 1979, 1981). We devote a chapter later in this book to academic language development, but it is important for teachers to understand that the language students need to read, write, understand, and talk about the content they study in school is different from the language they use in everyday conversation to communicate in different social contexts.

Newly arrived with adequate schooling	• Recent arrivals (fewer than five years in U.S.) • Typically in grades 2–12 • Adequate schooling in their home country • Literate in their home language • Soon catch up academically • May still score low on standardized tests given in English • Social and economic factors can influence them positively or negatively
Newly arrived with limited formal schooling	• Recent arrivals (fewer than five years in U.S.) • Typically in grades 2–12 • Interrupted or limited schooling in home country • Limited home language literacy • Below grade level in math • Poor academic achievement • Social and economic factors can influence them positively or negatively
Long-term English learners	• Six or more years in the U.S. • Typically in grades 6–12 • Limited literacy in both home language and English • Some may get adequate grades but score low on tests • Struggle with content classes • Often have been retained and are at risk of dropping out • Are transnational students or students with inconsistent/subtractive schooling • Have had ESL or bilingual instruction but no consistent program
Students at risk of becoming long-term English learners	• Students in grades 3–12 who scored intermediate or below on state ELD tests after four to five years • Parents have low levels of education • Parents struggle financially and/or socially

FIGURE 2–3 *Types of English Learners*

Emergent bilinguals usually acquire conversational English fairly quickly. They learn how to ask for things they need, ask where things are, and tell people what they like or need. Cummins conducted research showing it takes about two years to develop conversational language. However, the language emergent bilinguals need to read, write about, and discuss concepts in science, social studies, language arts, and math requires academic language proficiency. Different research studies have concluded that it can take from five to seven years to develop grade-level academic language (Cummins 1981; Collier 1989).

The different types of learners we described vary in their conversational language proficiency. They all have some conversational proficiency in their home language.

Students with adequate schooling have academic language proficiency in their home language as well. However, all English learners are faced with the challenge of developing academic language proficiency in English. Figure 2–4 shows the language proficiency of most students in each group. An × means students have proficiency, an (×) means they may have proficiency, and a 0 means they lack proficiency.

Adequate formal schooling students come to school with both conversational and academic language proficiency in their home languages. They are at grade level in content-area subjects and can read, write, understand, and talk about math, science, social studies, and literature in their home language. While this background is very helpful as they are learning English, these students still need to acquire both conversational English and academic English. Some adequate schooling students studied English before beginning school in this country. For this reason, we put the × in parentheses on the chart. This gives these students a head start with conversational English, but there is usually a great deal they don't understand or cannot say despite that English instruction.

Many well-educated international students we have taught tell us they cannot believe how little they could understand or how uncomfortable they were speaking English even after having studied English many years in their country. Krashen (personal communication) commented that he had reached the intermediate level of proficiency in French when he first went to France. To his disappointment French people don't speak at the intermediate level.

However, despite the frustrations that come from learning to communicate and study in a new language, adequate formal schooling students usually catch up quickly and do better academically than the other types of students. These students have had a *de facto* bilingual education, because they have content knowledge and academic language in their home language that they can transfer to what they are learning in English (Krashen 1999). They know how school works and, although there are differences in schools in different countries, they adapt fairly soon. Despite the success that many adequate schooling students experience, they still need several years to score at grade level on standardized tests of reading in English.

	Conversational Language		Academic Language	
	English	L1	English	L1
Adequate formal schooling	(×)	×	0	×
Limited formal schooling	0	×	0	0
Long term	(×)	(×)	0	0
Potential long term	0	×	0	0

FIGURE 2–4 *Language Proficiency of Types of Learners*

Limited formal schooling students have the conversational proficiency they need for social situations in their home language, but they lack the important background knowledge provided by academic study. These newcomer students need to acquire conversational English, academic English, and academic content knowledge without the academic content background knowledge in their L_1 that adequate formal schooling students have. As a result, the task these students face is much greater. When limited formal schooling students can be provided content instruction in their home language while they learn English, they have a much better chance of success. However, this resource is not always available.

Long-term English learners usually have conversational language in both their home language and their second language. They often speak their first language at home or with peers in informal situations. Sometimes they lose the first language almost completely. For that reason, we put the × in parentheses under conversational language in the home language column for long-term English learners.

LTELs often speak English and their native languages without any kind of accent, and they appear to have oral control of the language. However, when asked to discuss a complex idea, even about their own lives, their vocabulary is limited and they struggle to explain their ideas clearly. For this reason we also put the × in parentheses under English in the chart. More important, they lack grade-level academic language proficiency in both their home language and in English. They have difficulty reading content texts or discussing academic concepts, and they cannot write even simple summaries clearly.

Students at risk of becoming long-term English learners have age-appropriate conversational language proficiency in their home language. However, they are not proficient in conversational English when they start school and, as a result, they are usually behind their native English-speaking classmates in both academic content knowledge and academic English by the time they develop conversational English. These younger students have time to develop proficiency in English and their home language, but school officials must ensure that they are provided with programs and teachers that can support their learning and help them develop their home language as they learn English.

LEARNER-CENTERED TEACHING

The first principle for effective teaching is that teaching should be learner centered. Understanding the differences among types of English learners and their conversational and academic language proficiency as well as their academic content knowledge is an important first step. Teachers we have worked with use different strategies for finding out about their students. Sometimes teachers give students questionnaires asking them how they feel about reading and writing in English and what their strengths and challenges are. Other times they ask students to interview each other about past schooling experiences and then report back. Teachers also gain important information about their students by reading with them and also by examining writing samples and then conferencing with students. In addition, teachers carefully observe students as they work independently or in small groups. Learner-centered teachers become what Goodman refers to as "kid watchers" (Goodman 1985). They base their instruction on their deep understanding of their students. The more information teachers can gather, the better they are able to help students succeed in school.

Mary's "Sense of Self" Unit

We began this chapter by describing the learner-centered family unit that Alicia, an elementary ESL teacher, developed. We end this chapter with another learner-centered unit. Mary, now a bilingual teacher educator, taught this unit when she was teaching ESL and English in a rural high school in the central valley of California. The school had a large Spanish-speaking population as well as some ESL students who spoke Punjabi or Tagalog. Mary taught one beginning ESL class of newcomers, a second-year ESL class, and regular ninth-grade English classes that included both proficient English speakers and long-term English learners.

Mary had these different classes, the year she taught this unit. She needed to plan in such a way that she could meet the standards for her grade level, challenge her students academically, and involve them in many different reading and writing activities. She had to do this without becoming completely overwhelmed in her planning. Therefore, she organized all her classes around the same basic theme, offering all her students the same kinds of challenging activities while still differentiating instruction to meet the varying language needs of her students. She scaffolded in different ways, supporting newcomers by reading to and with them, doing a preview in Spanish for Spanish speakers, and having students do most work in pairs and groups. She modified the scaffolds for her second-year students. She modeled activities and then had them work in pairs or small groups. She continued to do some preview in Spanish for her Spanish speakers. She found that in her regular English classes many students were long-term English learners, so the careful scaffolds, including many collaborative and hands-on activities she engaged them in, helped these students as well.

Mary created a unit of inquiry called "Developing a Sense of Self" to help her high school students answer the big question, "Who am I?" High school students are interested in each other. Emergent bilinguals need to understand themselves and their peers and appreciate strengths and differences. Mary based her unit on the state language arts writing standards that called for students to write biographical and autobiographical narratives, to relate a sequence of events and communicate the significance of the events, to locate scenes and incidents in specific places, and to make use of descriptions of appearance, images, and sensory details.

Her theme study, which she taught at the beginning of the year, served other important purposes: it helped Mary's students to set goals for themselves, and it helped Mary get to know her students. As students talked and wrote about themselves and classmates and laid out their goals, Mary gained insight into their lives and their academic strengths and weaknesses. Mary found her students enjoyed this learner-centered theme because the activities focused on them.

Goal Setting

First, Mary asked the students to think about three goals for her class. Mary and the students talked about what goals were, and they brainstormed together what some appropriate goals might be. For each goal, students filled out a sheet answering the questions, "What is your goal?" "What do you need to do to reach this goal?" and "Who can help you?" At the bottom of the sheet, students answered one last question, "What have you done so far this year that relates to your goals?"

José, one of Mary's newcomer ELs, listed his three goals as "finish school," "learnd more english," and "be a nice people." He listed "do my homework," "pay attention," and "come to school" as some of the things he needed to do to accomplish his goals. José put "teacher" and "parents" as people who could help him reach his goals. For the question about what he had done so far, he wrote, "I do my homework. started to work hard and be myself."

Personal Information Interview

After the students completed their goals sheets, Mary had them work in pairs to interview each other. Mary gave them the following questions as an interview guide:

> What is your name?
>
> Where were you born?
>
> How many brothers and sisters do you have?
>
> What do you do for fun?
>
> What is your favorite sport? Favorite team?

What is your favorite food?

What is your favorite book?

What is your favorite movie and or TV show?

When you think of English class, what do you think of?

What are your plans for the future?

What is something interesting/unique about you?

The students wrote down their partner's answers and then used this information to introduce their partner to the class.

Coat of Arms

After students had set goals and started to learn about their classmates, Mary organized activities to help them to think about how they were like others and yet were unique. One activity that helped students think about themselves and value their individuality was making a coat of arms. Students drew an empty coat of arms with five quadrants to fill in. In each quadrant they drew a picture that revealed something about themselves. For example, one quadrant was to show "something you do well," another "your greatest success," another "some special place you like to be," another "your favorite musical group," and still another "your dream for your future." After students finished drawing their personal coats of arms, they shared them in pairs. The students showed their coat of arms to their partner and asked the partner to guess what the drawings represented. Then they explained each one. After this, students worked in groups to make a cumulative coat of arms that they shared with the whole class.

Some students in Mary's ESL 1 classes simply drew pictures while others cut out pictures and labeled them. These pictures represented student responses to questions like those above but slightly modified; they included "things I love to do," "my favorite book," "what I want to do in the future," "where I want to live in the future," and "what I like to eat." Students with higher levels of English proficiency also drew but they wrote more in each section rather than simply labeling them. This coat of arms activity provided a scaffold for students, giving them opportunities to use language as they shared how they were the same as or different from their peers. It also provided the background and built vocabulary for other activities requiring more reading and writing in English. Throughout the year students referred back to the coat of arms as a starting point for writing assignments.

"I Am" Poem

Mary followed these introductory projects with a series of other related activities. To help her students prepare to write an autobiographical piece, Mary introduced two activities, an "I Am" poem and an Autobiopoem. Both activities were designed to help students expand their vocabularies by describing sensory details and images. The "I Am" activity asked students to write a poem by completing sentences about themselves (see Figure 2–5). Students only needed to put one or two words to complete each line. For example, the first line has the words "I am" and directs the writer to add two of their characteristics.

Autobiopoem

An extension that builds on this "I Am" poem is the Autobiopoem activity. Students wrote another poem about themselves that included more details than the "I Am" poem. On the second line, for instance, students were asked to list four of their traits and the third line asked for names of family members. Several templates for an Autobiopoem are available on various Internet sites. The one Mary used is shown in Figure 2–6.

I Am

I am (two characteristics you have)
I wonder (something you are curious about)
I hear (something you often hear)
I see (something/someone you see regularly)
I want
I am (repeat first line of poem)

I pretend
I feel (an emotion you feel sometimes)
I worry
I cry (something that makes you sad)
I am (repeat first line of poem)

I believe
I dream
I try
I hope
I am (repeat first line of poem)

FIGURE 2–5 *"I Am"*

Mary found that her students enjoyed writing and illustrating both their "I Am" poems and their Autobiopoems. Although students in her ESL classes had some difficulty understanding all the categories and their English was not always standard, they did an excellent job of describing themselves, their wants, and their interests. They were engaged in these projects and wanted to know the English words to describe themselves. They also learned new vocabulary from each other as they shared their poems. They developed both oral and written English as they wrote their poems, discussed them with classmates, and read other students' poems.

Here's Looking at You

To involve her students in writing longer prose pieces, Mary next had her students do another, more complex interview. In this case, as they worked in pairs, they

---

Autobiopoem

Follow the directions and you will discover that you are a poet. Write only what is indicated on each line.

Line 1: Your first name

Line 2: Four traits (adjectives) that describe you

Line 3: Son/daughter of . . . or . . . Brother/sister of

Line 4: Who loves (3 people, ideas, or a combination)

Line 5: Who feels (3 sensations)

Line 6: Who finds happiness in (3 items)

Line 7: Who needs (3 items)

Line 8: Who gives (3 items)

Line 9: Who fears (3 items)

Line 10: Who would like to see (3 items)

Line 11: Who enjoys (3 items)

Line 12: Who likes to wear (3 colors or items)

Line 13: Resident of (your city, street, or road name)

Line 14: Your last name

FIGURE 2–6 *Autobiopoem*

filled out a form called "Here's Looking at You" (see Figure 2–7). It includes questions asking for more details from the students' lives, such as "What five words would you use to describe yourself?" "What five words would your mother (father, teacher) use to describe you?" "Tell me about your friends: What do you do? Where do you go?" and "What are your favorite classes? What types of activities do you enjoy?"

Mary's English learners found this activity much more challenging than the previous ones. To help her students succeed, Mary first talked with them about each question to be sure they understood them. Then she had them work in small groups to talk about how they would answer their questions. Finally, she told them that instead of five descriptive words, they could write two or three for now. Then she had students work in pairs to conduct the interviews and write down the answers.

Positive–Negative Graph

One final activity that challenged her students and gave them topics for writing autobiography was the positive–negative graph. To start this activity and to build

Here's Looking at You

1. What five words would you use to describe yourself?

2. What five words would your mother (father, teacher) use to describe you?

3. How do teachers see you (include one who likes you and one who does not, if applicable)?

4. What five words would you use to describe school? Tell me about your experiences in school.

5. Tell me about your friends: What do you do? Where do you go?

6. In school what are some of your strongest abilities?

7. Out of school what are your strongest abilities?

8. What are your favorite classes? What types of activities do you enjoy?

9. What abilities do your parents admire most about you?

10. Describe how you get along with others at school and at home.

11. If you had a chance to be part of a group or to be an individual, which would you choose and why?

12. What is your greatest accomplishment at this time?

FIGURE 2–7 *Here's Looking at You*

upon the interviews students had conducted, Mary had students list ten important events in their lives. She found students needed some support with this activity, so she listed ten events in her life. She then demonstrated how she would place these events on a positive–negative graph. She drew a vertical line on the white-board and divided it by an intersecting horizontal line. On the horizontal line she marked approximate ages when the events in her life took place. On the vertical line she numbered from plus-one to plus-five from the middle to the top. Next, she numbered from minus-one to minus-five numbering down. She then wrote in key events in her life from her list and evaluated how positive or how negative each was. For example, she marked her move to Mexico City as minus-3 because there was a definite adjustment she had to make. Her wedding day was marked as a plus-five.

Following Mary's modeling, her students made their own list of ten important events in their lives and then placed them on a positive–negative graph of their own. Needing to make a judgment about how positive or negative an event was encouraged students to really think about their lives and the events that had influenced them. Figure 2–8 is a sample positive–negative graph from one of Mary's students. For this student, "Passed 9th" was quite high, but "grandma passed away" was low.

After this, Mary asked them to write two paragraphs about themselves using the information from their previous projects: the interviews, the coat of arms, the "I Am" poem and "Autobiopoem," the "Here's Looking at You" activity, and the positive–negative graph. Even Mary's beginning ESL students could write something about themselves, a task that would not have been possible without the earlier activities.

Areli wrote the following description. Although this piece has some errors, Areli tells readers some important things about herself:

> My name is Areli Alonso. I am very happy and romantic. My mother says that I am beauty and responsable. I have a lot of friends but my best friends name is Carmen. My other importants friends are my mother and my sister. My ability out of school is to be friendly. My parents tell me I am intelligent.
>
> In school I have the ability of understand easy. I like my school because the people are very kind. My favorite classes are Biology, Geography and sometimes English. I want to learn this year too much.

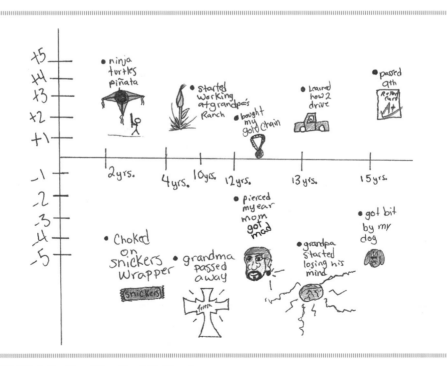

FIGURE 2–8 *Positive–Negative Life Graph*

Areli's writing showed that she was developing proficiency in English. Mary knew that it was important to help her students move toward standard English, but she recognized that it was also important not to overwhelm them. Mary asked her students to look at only one or two items for each piece they wrote. For example, Areli makes nouns and adjectives agree (importants friends); this shows a transfer from Spanish. She also capitalizes names of school subjects, such as biology, again a transfer from Spanish. Mary might do a minilesson on these two points and ask students to look for these two kinds of errors in their writing. She has students keep track of the errors they make and list them in a notebook along with the correct form. Before students begin the next writing piece, they review what they have corrected before to help them avoid making the same kinds of writing errors again.

English learners gain confidence in their abilities to write when they can produce extended text after a very short time in the U.S. The various activities Mary engaged the students in served as scaffolds for Mary's newcomer students and gave them the vocabulary and skills they needed to write a short composition in their new language. Mary's native English speakers and more advanced ESL students also benefited from these kinds of activities. Their paragraphs were full of rich details.

Mary followed up these activities with relevant readings and further discussions and writing, so students continued to increase their academic English proficiency. By the end of the unit they could all write an autobiography, although there were clear differences among the newcomers, the second-year ESL students, and the mainstream English students.

CONCLUSION

The first principle for effective teaching for emergent bilinguals is that teaching should be learner centered. The key for making lessons learner centered is to know your students. By reviewing students' cumulative folders, as well as through observations, surveys and interviews, and reading and writing conferences, teachers can learn a great deal about their students. This is easier when teachers have a self-contained classroom and more difficult when a teacher works with five classes a day; but in either case, over time teachers can get to know their students. Alicia worked with one group of students while Mary worked with five classes each day. Both teachers designed activities that would help them learn more about their students and would help their students learn more about each other.

Getting to know emergent bilinguals includes assessing their conversational and academic English and their subject matter knowledge in both their home language and English. This information can be used to plan lessons and find materials and texts that connect with students' backgrounds so that they can build new knowledge on their existing knowledge. During lessons, students work independently, in pairs, and in small groups. They engage in projects, conduct research, and share the results with the class. They often become the experts on a topic. In a learner-centered class, both the teacher and the students have important ideas and knowledge to share. Figure 2–9 lists the characteristics of a teacher in a learner-centered class.

In a learner-centered class the teacher:

- Uses a number of sources and activities to learn about her students, including their previous schooling and home language literacy.
- Learns about students' families, cultural background, and experiences.
- Plans units and lessons that draw on student's backgrounds, including their languages and cultures.
- Helps students make connections between the academic content and their own experiences.
- Engages students in collaborative activities, projects, and research so that students can become experts in the subject being studied.
- Has students share their work in pairs, small groups, or with the whole class to help them learn and show that they are the experts.

FIGURE 2–9 *The Teacher's Role in a Learner-Centered Classroom*

APPLICATIONS

1. Alicia's first-grade unit on families and Mary's high school unit on sense of self were both learner centered. Make a list of specific ways the units centered on the students.
2. A key to learner-centered instruction is knowing your students. We described four kinds of English learners: adequate formal schooling students, limited formal schooling students, long-term English learners, and potential long-term English learners. In your school or classroom, identify an emergent bilingual who fits each of these categories and give reasons for your choice.
3. Choose an emergent bilingual student with whom you have contact in school or outside of school. Interview that student. What type of English learner is he/she? Be specific and list the evidence you used to make your decision. Write a description of the student similar to the examples provided in the chapter.

4. Specific activities that were learner centered were described in this chapter. Choose two and implement them with English learners. Report back.

5. Choose one unit of study you have taught or observed that was learner centered. Be prepared to describe the unit and explain what made it learner centered.

3

Teaching Should Go from Whole to Part

A HIGH SCHOOL WHOLE-TO-PART UNIT

Claude teaches in a middle and high school newcomer center located in a large city in Texas. The principal and the teachers in this school are dedicated to student success and have worked together on principles of academic rigor, high expectations and high support, quality interactions, language focus, and quality curriculum. These principles come from Quality Teaching for English Learners (QTEL), a secondary professional development program. All faculty and administrators participated in the program and are committed to it. QTEL will be discussed further in Chapter 4.

Some of Claude's students are from Asia or Africa, but the majority of them come from Mexico and Central America. Many of the students in Claude's newcomer class are limited formal schooling students who do not read or write at grade level in their first languages. Claude believes that his students need to be involved in authentic, meaningful reading and writing to become competent readers and writers of English. In this class, students read whole texts on topics that are important to them and then write about their reading. There are no isolated vocabulary lists or grammar lessons, and students seldom read the stories in the district adopted basal. A description of a unit on newspapers gives an idea of how Claude supports his students.

The newspaper unit "What can newspapers teach us?" began with a general discussion of the purpose and value of newspapers. Claude invited a speaker from the local paper to talk to his class. The speaker's presentation included an explanation of the various parts of a paper. She showed the class headlines and the different sections, discussing the purpose of each part. During this talk, students were able to examine the various sections of the newspaper from personal copies provided for them. In the following week, Claude arranged a field trip so the students could tour the local newspaper office.

After the guest lecture and field trip, Claude posted on the bulletin board a recent article in *Education Week* about the 55,000 unaccompanied Central American immigrant students, children and youth, who had arrived in the U.S. last year (Maxwell 2014). A large number of these teenage students had arrived in the district where Claude taught, having traveled without adults and having endured many hardships. They, like others, came in the hope of being reunited with family members living in the U.S. Several of Claude's students were these unaccompanied minors. The article included the story of one boy from Honduras and his experiences.

Working in small groups, Claude's students read the article with interest, helping one another understand the text. As the class discussed the article, students related their own experiences or those of others they knew. When Claude invited students to write about the article, the response was enthusiastic. Even students who struggled with writing and had been reluctant to write anything in English made an attempt to respond. All of these newcomers had stories to tell about how they came to the U.S.

Claude's students helped one another edit their writing, and Claude worked with several students individually. With the permission of the students, he posted their responses on the bulletin board around the newspaper article. This activity generated a great deal of interest. Emergent bilinguals from across the campus, especially those who were unaccompanied minors themselves, came to the room to read the news article and the student responses, and then they added their own reactions on sticky notes that Claude had ready for them. The bulletin board became a popular site for reading and writing.

Claude created an activity in which learning could move from whole to part. In the newspaper unit, students learned about the sections of a newspaper. They learned new vocabulary as they read articles and columns that interested them. During the *Education Week* lesson, students responded to a whole article written for a real audience, not part of an article or an adapted, simplified version of an article. Students discussed the article and made personal connections to it. They then wrote their own responses, read each other's papers, and experienced a real audience for their writing from their peers.

A SECONDARY PART-TO-WHOLE LESSON

Betty teaches English language development (ELD) in a large, inner-city high school in California. Her students are mostly Hispanics and Southeast Asians with varied educational backgrounds. One of her classes is for level 2, early intermediate, ELD students. Although the students are grouped by language proficiency, there is still some variation in the language ability of the students in this class. Betty's program is a fairly traditional one in which she uses several part-to-whole activities to build vocabulary and improve grammatical accuracy. Betty is convinced that emergent bilinguals need to build vocabulary and work on grammar.

In a typical period, students come into the classroom and find a list of words drawn from their ESL basal textbook written on the whiteboard. Betty tells the students to look up the words in the dictionary, list the part of speech of each word, and write one sentence for each word. She reminds them that they can work together to look up the words. Most students choose to work on their own. There seem to be two types of students in her classroom: the quiet students who try hard to do their work and to understand the assignment, and the disengaged students who generally pretend to work but spend more time talking than working. Betty frequently reminds those students to get to work.

After most students have finished finding the words, defining them, and writing a sentence for each word, the class reads together from their basal reader. The text is usually a short excerpt from a longer narrative. Students read aloud, taking turns to read sections. Betty occasionally asks students the meanings of words in the story or literal questions from the story. As they answer, Betty is careful to correct their grammar if their answer is not given in standard English. After reading the story, students write answers to the comprehension questions suggested in the text. If students do not finish, the questions are their homework. The following day students exchange papers to correct each other's homework as Betty reads the correct answers.

LEARNING GOES FROM WHOLE TO PART

Claude's unit helped students learn from the whole to the parts while Betty's teaching started with the parts in the hope that students would understand the whole. In this chapter, we look more closely at the commonsense view that when we break a subject down into parts, we make learning easier. In fact, it seems to make sense that smaller units would be easier to understand and learn. This is logical, but it turns out it is not psychological. It is not how our minds work.

We argue that students, especially English learners, first need a sense of the whole to understand the parts. The whole provides an important context in which the parts are naturally embedded. Claude's students worked with the newspaper to get an overview of its parts. They read an article that related to their own experiences and were able to use English to respond to the article meaningfully.

In addition to showing the importance of teaching whole to part in this chapter, we explain that the whole is more than the sum of the parts. For example, the isolated vocabulary lists, the writing of unrelated sentences, and the answering of written questions did not give Betty's students the ability to read and understand whole texts or write meaningful compositions. Studying grammar rules and practicing grammar exercises does not help students write whole, grammatically correct essays or reports. Phonics lessons teaching sounds and letters do not ultimately lead to the reading and understanding of complete texts. The parts do not add up to the whole, as we will illustrate.

When teachers understand both the idea of whole to part and the idea that the whole is more than the sum of its parts, they can better plan lessons for their emergent bilingual students. In this chapter we propose that teachers organize curriculum based on big question themes using the questioning lesson plan. In this way, they support both language and content learning for emergent bilinguals.

THE WHOLE IS NOT EQUAL TO THE SUM OF ITS PARTS

Picture a fictitious classroom filled with thirty inquisitive second graders, many of them emergent bilinguals. The teacher is conducting a lesson centered around a food theme. She tells them she will pass around some food items. They are to look at them, feel them, but not taste them. First she passes out some oregano leaves. She asks the children what they can tell her about it. As they respond, the teacher records the children's answers on the whiteboard. They look at the oregano, they smell it, they feel it. "It's green and it smells funny," says Manuel. "I think I know what it is, it's *perejil* (parsley)!" pipes up María.

The teacher collects the oregano and passes around some mozzarella cheese. The children know that this is cheese, that it's white, and it feels soft, that it doesn't have much flavor. Francisca declares that it is definitely not *queso Oaxaca* that her mother uses to make enchiladas. Again the teacher records the children's responses. Garlic and a package of tube-shaped Italian sausage follow the mozzarella, and then comes a can of tomato sauce. The children are interested, but they aren't sure where all this is going. The teacher next passes out uncooked, wide noodles with scalloped edges. The noodles are brittle and dry. They look and feel nothing like the noodles the Laotian students in the class eat daily.

"Now," the teacher announces, "we are going to taste a special dish using all these things you have looked at. How do you think it will taste?"

"Yucky!" shout several students. "I'm not going to eat it," claims Mo. "Nothing you passed out smelled good or looked like it tastes good."

"It might be good," countered Alicia. "Noodles and tomato usually means Italian food, and I like spaghetti."

"You always bring things we like," added Mai. "I'll try it."

The students in this class are intrigued by the food the teacher has passed around. They try to use their own past experiences with food to predict what the finished dish will be like. However, despite the fact they may have smelled and touched the ingredients, they can't mentally put the odors and tastes together into a final product. The individual tastes of oregano, garlic, sausage, uncooked noodles and tomato sauce simply don't add up to the taste of lasagna.

The fictitious lesson described here at first glance might look like the units we would encourage teachers to use. In many ways the lesson is consistent with our list of principles for effective practice. It appears to be learner centered, and children are engaged. There is lots of interaction. The children have real experiences and are using language.

Although this has many characteristics of a good lesson, it also suggests why some educational practices make learning hard for students. The teacher presented all the ingredients that make up lasagna. Even though the students experienced all the parts of the recipe in isolation, they couldn't predict what the whole, the lasagna, would be like. The taste of lasagna is different from the tastes of its constituent parts. Knowing about the parts doesn't ensure an understanding of the whole.

Phonics Lesson: Whole Does Not Equal the Sum of the Parts

Sally, an elementary itinerant ESL teacher in a rural area in the northwest part of the U.S., was concerned because she was charged with being sure that her ESL students would learn to read. She pulled out small groups of English learners from grades K–3 during reading/language arts time. The students' mainstream teachers told her they did not know what to do with children who could not speak English.

Sally wasn't sure what to do either. She consulted the school reading specialist, even though she knew that he did not have a background in second language teaching. She reasoned that he did know about reading. Talking together, they decided Sally should begin by working on the sounds of English. This seemed to make sense to both of them as the students did not speak English or know the sounds of English.

Sally took some beginning phonics lessons from the specialist to try with her students. She began with the short *a* sound. Giving the students a worksheet with drawings of an alligator, ant, apple, and astronaut and patterns for a capital letter *A* and lowercase *a* at the bottom, Sally began the first phonics lesson: "Look at the paper. Point to the alligator." Sally helped students find the alligator. "Say *alligator*. Listen to the first sound and repeat, *a, a, a*." Sally continued with the same pattern for the other drawings on the worksheet and then had students trace the capital and lowercase letters on the page.

Next, Sally gave the students a worksheet with patterns of the words *alligator*, *ant*, *apple*, and *astronaut* and had them trace the words and say them out loud. She gave the next worksheet to students to do individually. On this sheet students were to draw a line from the letter *a* to the picture of the words that began with an *a*. She found that many students did not know the words in English for *ring* or *mushroom*, both pictured on the page, so she helped them. The final worksheet for the class was one with pictures of a bat, a banana, a cat, and a fan. Students were to say the word, listen for the short *a* sound, and color the picture.

For the next few weeks, Sally did exercises like these with her elementary ESL students working with the sounds *b, c, d,* and *e*. However, she noticed that at first students tried to follow along with the lessons, but they soon became bored or disengaged. They did not seem to understand what they were supposed to be doing at times. Some of the students already knew the words in English they were practicing, while others did not and were often lost. In addition, Sally didn't feel her students were learning enough. She couldn't see how working on these sounds would help her students read the texts the mainstream teachers were already using. For Sally, learning all these separate sounds and words in isolation did not add up to reading whole texts.

While it is often a temptation with emergent bilinguals learning English to simplify tasks and break them into smaller, more manageable parts, doing this actually makes it harder for students to learn. Emergent bilinguals need the whole picture in order to understand the parts. Since the part-to-whole commonsense process is not effective, it is important to understand just how to effectively organize learning. We next look at three ways curriculum has typically been organized in schools.

WAYS TO ORGANIZE CURRICULUM

Schools organize curriculum in different ways. In some schools or classes, there is no discernable connection between and among subjects. In other settings, subjects are linked through a common topic, such as apples or spiders. A third way to organize curriculum is by themes or units of inquiry centered around big questions and then use resources from each subject area to investigate the theme. It is this third, inquiry-based approach that we advocate. In the following sections, we examine each of these ways of organizing curriculum.

The Cha-Cha-Cha Curriculum

The cha-cha-cha curriculum can be found at all levels of schooling. In the elementary grades teachers cover a different topic in each subject. So a second-grade teacher may be working on character and plot in language arts, fractions in math, the water cycle in science, and the contributions of important people in social studies. As the teacher shifts content areas, students have to start thinking about totally different topics. Donald Graves has termed this way of organizing "the cha cha cha curriculum" (Graves 1994). This is difficult for emergent bilinguals who must follow the changes in topics as well as understand the content. The teacher seems to be cha-cha-cha-ing through the day with students trying to follow along but missing the steps most of the time. When teachers have an overarching theme that connects the content learning, students, especially emergent bilinguals, have a much better chance of following the instruction.

At the upper elementary and middle school, each subject is usually treated separately. Within a particular subject, there may sometimes be thematic organization. For example, in language arts, students might be engaged in a unit on exploration. The reading selections and writing activities all relate to this theme. However, the theme of exploration is not carried through into science, social studies, or math.

Students who are studying exploration in language arts might be learning about cell structures in science, solving problems with one variable in algebra, and reading about state history in social studies. Students might begin the day by reading a story about arctic exploration, and then—cha-cha-cha—they switch to cell structures in science. When science study ends—cha-cha-cha—it's time to think about algebra problems. From algebra, students cha-cha-cha to state history. Each subject may have internal consistency, but many ELLs get lost in the transition from one content area to the next. Just when they fully understand that the language arts lesson is about exploration, the teacher moves on to cell structures in science. It takes second language students a few minutes to understand that this is a lesson about cell structures. Each time the teacher changes to a new content area, ELLs lose time figuring out what topic is being studied. They cannot afford to lose this valuable time.

The cha-cha-cha curriculum is more prevalent in middle and high schools because there is more departmentalization. When different teachers teach each subject, it is more difficult to coordinate curriculum. Even when teachers are willing to take the time to work together, there are scheduling difficulties. Very few junior or senior high schools have successfully implemented thematic curriculum despite research showing that thematic instruction is effective (E. García 2002; Freeman and Freeman 1994).

The cha-cha-cha curriculum offers the least support for emergent bilinguals and, in fact, it is not effective for any student. Because there are no links among content areas, students do not revisit ideas. In addition, the vocabulary they are developing as they study in one content area does not naturally recur in any of the other subjects, so there is less chance of students' acquiring the academic vocabulary they need to succeed. A good approach to curriculum should, at the least, link the content areas and help students come to view school as an integrated whole rather than as a series of discrete topics to be studied for a short time each day and then shelved until the next day.

The Gummy Bear Curriculum

A step toward more connected thematic organization is the attempt to unite different subject areas around a common topic. Kucer and Silva (2006) describe this way of curriculum organization as the gummy bear curriculum. They give the example of a theme organized around bears. The teacher has decided to use *Ira Sleeps Over* (Waber 1972) as a central text during the unit of study. This is a story of a young boy who is invited to stay at a friend's house overnight. Despite his sister's teasing, he takes his teddy bear with him for security. The story is about how children use some object for comfort and security. The author could have chosen to have Ira take a favorite blanket or some other toy. He just happened to choose the teddy bear.

However, a teacher moving toward thematic teaching might focus on the bear as a way to unify the curriculum. After all, there is a bear in the language arts story. During science, the class would study about how bears hibernate. In social studies, they could read about how Teddy Roosevelt spared a bear cub, thus creating the teddy bear. In music, students could sing a song about bears, and in art they could draw pictures of bears. Finally, during math the students might engage in a hands-on project that involves counting and manipulating gummy bear candies.

Although attempting to unify the curriculum in this way is a step in the right direction, there are several problems with this approach. In the first place, some of the bear connections are tenuous at best. A creative teacher might find a way to include bears in every subject, but the result is only a superficial unity. *Ira Sleeps Over* is not a story about bears. English learners might recognize the bear element in each subject, but when the teacher moves from language arts to science or any of the other content areas, ELLs would still be lost. In social studies they would be learning about a particular politician and a period of U.S. history, and in math the lesson would be on counting, adding, or subtracting. There is no fundamental connection between a story about a boy who needs some object to feel secure in a new situation and a science reading about how and why bears hibernate.

The problem with the gummy bear approach to curriculum design is that bears, spiders, or apples are only surface-level objects. The real point of each lesson has little to do with these objects. Students should learn about hibernation, and it happens that bears, along with other animals, hibernate. An English learner might think she comprehends the lesson because she knows it is about bears, but unless she understands hibernation she has missed the point. If the teacher is basing lessons on state and federal standards, those standards ask for an understanding of important concepts. Knowing what a teddy bear is would not be listed in the standards. Perhaps the biggest problem with the gummy bear curriculum, though, is that a teacher really has to stretch to connect some subjects to an object like a bear, as in the example of counting gummy bear candies in math.

Curriculum Organized Around Big Questions for Inquiry

A better way to organize curriculum is to explore big questions such as "How does food get from the field to the table?" "How does what we grow help us grow?" or "How does the weather affect our lives?" Wiggins and McTighe (2005) argue that curriculum must deal with big ideas or questions worth investigating. These are questions that do not have a simple answer. During a theme such as "How does food get from the field to the table?" students would use literature and information from the various content areas to build their understanding of plants and plant growth and transportation of products from the farm to the store. The theme might also include smart shopping and healthful eating. Students could use information from language arts, social studies, science, and math as they explore these related topics. Organizing around big questions leads to an inquiry approach to education (Short, Harste, and Burke 1996; Miles 2014).

Teachers can connect curriculum to state and federal standards by basing the big questions on these standards. For example, a grade 1 science standard is to recognize ways that the appearance of animals changes as they mature. Often, grade 1 teachers include a unit on growth and change. Turning the topic of growth into a question such as "How do people and animals change as they grow?" helps focus the curriculum and connects it directly to the standard. This is a big question because it is complex and multifaceted. Students can investigate different aspects of growth and change. The theme also naturally leads into a study of life cycles.

To take another example, a fourth-grade social studies standard requires that students understand the impact of environment on culture. This standard can also be turned into a big question, "How does where we live influence how we live?" Students can begin by studying the local community and then look at other communities that are different from theirs because of differences in the physical environment. A similar standard for secondary students studying world geography is to understand how geographic contexts and processes of spatial exchange influenced events in the past and helped to shape the present. Many standards, like this one, are recycled at higher grade levels so that students can build a deeper understanding of key concepts. At both fourth grade and tenth grade, though, students can approach the ideas through a focused big question.

Teachers can often include the literacy, literature, and math standards within questions based on social studies and science standards. It is important to spend time focusing on literacy and math skills, but they are best learned in the context of literature, social studies, and science. For example, students could read a novel or an informational text about weather and climate change during a unit titled, "How does where we live influence how we live?" They could record the high and low temperatures daily and then graph the results. Both literacy and math skills could be developed as students read and write about this big question. In a study on immigration, students could work to answer the big question, "Who belongs here?" They could discuss reasons immigrants came to the U.S. in social studies, look at immigration patterns and graph them in math, look at where immigrants have come from during different time periods as they study geography, and read biographies and autobiographies about immigrants in language arts.

Basing big questions on standards makes good sense in a time when accountability is being stressed in schools. This approach also is logical because textbooks and supplementary materials available at each grade level reflect the standards. Third-grade students in most states will study the solar system and how the earth orbits the sun and the moon orbits the earth; fourth graders will study how all organisms need energy to grow and that producers and consumers are related to food chains. Teachers at each grade level can meet to plan curriculum together, deciding on the big questions and the materials and methods they will use to engage students in units of inquiry. This sort of horizontal planning is also useful because different teachers at a grade level could teach the theme at different times during the year. This would avoid the problem of two or three teachers attempting to use the same resources at the same time. There might be only one or two good solar system charts available, so it is often more convenient if each third-grade class studies the themes at a different time.

BENEFITS OF ORGANIZING CURRICULUM AROUND BIG QUESTION THEMES

Organizing curriculum around themes is beneficial for all students. However, this approach is particularly important for emergent bilinguals for several reasons. Figure 3–1 lists six reasons for organizing curriculum around big question themes.

1. Because students see the big picture, the English instruction is more comprehensible.

2. Content areas (math, science, social studies, literature) are interrelated.

3. Vocabulary is repeated naturally as it appears in different content area studies.

4. Because the curriculum makes sense, second language students are more fully engaged and experience more success.

5. Teachers can differentiate instruction to accommodate differences in students' language proficiency.

6. Through themes, teachers can connect curriculum to students' lives and backgrounds.

FIGURE 3–1 *Reasons for Organizing Curriculum Around Big Question Themes*

The Big Picture Focus Makes the Input Comprehensible

First of all, a thematic focus provides a context within which students can better understand instruction in a second language. In the same way that it's easier to assemble a jigsaw puzzle if we can look at the picture on the cover of the box, it's easier to make sense of individual lessons when we know they all focus on the same big question. Students engaged in the study of a question such as "How do animals and people change as they grow?" know that each lesson will relate to this topic. Since ELLs have the big picture, they can make better sense of a math lesson in which they compare the growth rate of two animals or of a science lesson in which they study the stages of growth from a tadpole to a frog.

Content Areas Can Be Interrelated

A second reason to organize around themes is that teachers can help students make connections across subject areas. Students investigating a big question like "How does where we live affect how we live?" might do a tornado-in-a-bottle activity and learn about the conditions that cause tornadoes during science, locate areas where tornadoes have struck in the last year during geography, and read a story about a family whose home has been hit by a tornado in language arts. In math, students could study charts showing where tornadoes most often form. They could study how meteorologists use data to predict the formation of tornadoes. They could use weather data to predict the likelihood of a tornado touching down in their area. In classes and schools that organize around themes, knowledge that students gain in one subject area can be used in studying other areas.

When subject areas are interrelated through the focus on a central theme, students keep thinking and learning about the big question as they move from subject to subject or class to class. What they learn in math may apply in social studies or science. They don't put what they learned in math out of their minds when the math lesson is over. The more subjects are interrelated, the greater the chance that emergent bilinguals will understand the instruction. What the students don't fully comprehend during science might become clear when the topic is revisited during social studies or language arts.

Vocabulary Is Repeated Naturally

Maintaining the same topic by focusing on a big question also ensures that key vocabulary will be repeated naturally in the various subject areas. In the past, ESL teachers used repetition to help students learn vocabulary. A teacher might have the class or a student repeat a word or phrase as a way of improving pronunciation and memorizing the words. However, second language acquisition research has shown that we do not learn a new language through imitation and repetition. The problem with repetition is that it can become mindless, much like writing out each spelling word ten times. To acquire some aspect of language, like a word or phrase, students need to encounter it several times in meaningful contexts. By organizing around themes, teachers provide the repeated exposure to meaningful language that students need. Rather than only hearing a word such as *temperature* in science class, an English learner might hear or see it again during language arts, social studies, and math. Since the subjects are interrelated, some of the same vocabulary comes up in each subject area, and this increases a student's chance of acquiring important academic vocabulary.

Because the Curriculum Makes Sense, Students Are More Engaged

Listening to someone speak a language we do not understand well is mentally tiring. Our brains naturally attend to things that make sense, so if a reading passage or a lecture is hard to understand, our attention turns to something else, something we can understand. For this reason, it is critical that teachers do everything possible to make instruction comprehensible for emergent bilinguals. One way to do this is to organize around themes. Even when students don't fully understand the language of a new lesson, they know it is connected to the theme, so they stay engaged for a longer period of time. It is this engagement that leads to both language development and increased subject matter knowledge. If emergent bilinguals can stay focused on the lesson being delivered in English, there is a greater chance that they will learn the concepts and acquire more of the new language. The result is more success in writing papers, presenting reports, or taking a quiz on the subject. When English learners are successful, this success leads to increased motivation to make that mental effort needed to comprehend new subjects in a new language. Thematic organization makes curriculum more comprehensible, making learning more engaging and leading to greater academic success.

Thematic Instruction Allows Teachers to Differentiate Instruction

A fifth benefit of organizing around themes is that teachers can more easily differentiate instruction to meet the needs of emergent bilinguals at different levels of English proficiency. Even when teachers have only three or four English learners in a class, these students may be at quite different proficiency levels. One might be a beginner, while another is at the intermediate level and two more are advanced. As long as all the students are studying the same theme, teachers can adjust assignments to suit the varied proficiency levels of the students. For example, during the theme based on the question, "How does food get from the field to the table?" the beginning student might read a picture book that shows how the fruit, juice, milk, cereal, and toast some Americans eat for breakfast gets from the farm to the store. This student could represent his understanding by drawing and labeling pictures of each step. Intermediate and advanced students could read more challenging books on the topic and demonstrate their understanding by making a complex flowchart, or writing a list or a paragraph to explain how food gets from the field to the table.

Big Question Themes Allow Teachers to Connect the Curriculum to Students' Lives

A final reason for organizing around themes based on big questions is that this approach makes it possible to connect subject matter content with students' lives. Themes based on big questions are universal. Animals and people everywhere change and grow. The weather affects our lives no matter where we live. Since the curriculum focuses on such big questions, teachers can connect subject area studies with students' lives. In fact, emergent bilinguals can often make important contributions to a class by giving examples from countries where they or their parents have lived or experiences they have had.

Discussions that occur during the "How does what we grow help us grow?" theme provides a good example. Some students in the U.S. might eat cereal, toast, and juice for breakfast while a student from Vietnam might have rice and fish. Both students can draw on their own background experience as they learn how food gets from the field to the table. At the same time, the variety of examples coming from a class with students from different backgrounds expands the curriculum and enriches the learning experience for all the students in a class.

Organizing curriculum around big questions provides these six benefits for emergent bilinguals: (1) instruction is more comprehensible, (2) the subject areas are interrelated, (3) vocabulary is repeated naturally, (4) students stay more engaged, (5) teachers can differentiate instruction, and (6) teachers can connect curriculum to students' lives.

THE "QUESTIONING LESSON PLAN"

Teachers at all levels are required to do long-term and day-to-day planning. Too often the day-to-day planning becomes routine, a rote exercise completed because administrators require it. In our work with teacher education candidates, for example, we have found that student teachers are tempted to fulfill the requirement of preparing lesson plans by making lists—lists of page numbers students will read, lists of exercises students will complete, lists of activities students will be doing, and lists of materials that will be needed.

Although we try to get away from this mechanical type of lesson planning, we also realize that it is critical for all teachers to have some plan for the general direction in which the curriculum is headed. Teachers must be able to show administrators, parents, and other teachers that their curriculum does fulfill district and state guidelines. At the same time, teachers should organize their curriculum around big question themes that engage their students in activities that develop language and concepts. A method for planning that we used with student teachers and recommended for experienced teachers is the Questioning Lesson Plan (see Figure 3–2).

The Questioning Lesson Plan

1. What is the question worth talking about?

2. How does the question fit into your overall plan or your bigger question?

3. What content standards does the lesson address?

4. What language standards does the lesson address?

5. How will you find out what the students already know about the question?

6. What strategies will you use to explore the question?

7. What materials will you and the students use to explore the question?

8. What steps will you and the students take to explore the question?

9. How will you observe and evaluate students' learning?

FIGURE 3–2 *The Questioning Lesson Plan*

This lesson plan format is designed to help teachers reconceptualize curriculum as a series of questions generated by the students and the teacher as they explore topics together. The Questioning Lesson Plan encourages teachers to remain focused on the major concepts they want students to understand and on the language students need to access the content they are studying. It asks teachers to consider how each lesson might connect to broader themes. Planning lessons with this format is one way that teachers can put the principles for effective teaching into practice.

Critical to any lesson plan is the development of key concepts. When lessons begin with big questions that relate to students' interests and experiences, students are naturally more motivated to engage in learning. Rather than giving students isolated words or exercises, teachers need to involve students in inquiry that explores topics of interest to them.

Kelly's Questioning Plan

Kelly provides an example of a questioning lesson plan drawn from an engaging big question. Kelly is a fourth-grade teacher in a small farming community in south Texas. Her class has both native English speakers and several Spanish-speaking emergent bilinguals. Since her students' facility with English varies greatly, Kelly wants to be sure to involve all her students in her lessons regardless of their English proficiency.

Kelly and her students had been studying the general theme of health, responding to the big question "How can we maintain a healthy mind and body?" Obesity and smoking are major health issues in south Texas, so the theme was especially relevant. Students had read about and studied both nutrition and exercise. During the "Say 'No' to Drugs" week, school officials expressed alarm at the number of middle school students who had started smoking. Kelly knew that state health standards for fourth grade included understanding the long-term effects of drugs, including nicotine and inhalants, and exploring how external influences affect the use of drugs. The standard also asked students to explore advertising strategies used to encourage drug use. She decided that further exploration of drug use, especially the popular use of tobacco and other inhalants, fit into their big question "How can we maintain a healthy mind and body?" During the unit, Kelly also planned activities to help students meet some of the speaking and listening English language development standards related to presenting information on a topic and understanding information other students present.

Kelly and her students first read and discussed three articles from *Student Science: A Resource of the Society of Science and the Public*. One article discussed how many tweens believed that only occasional smoking would not harm them (Bridges and Raloff 2015). The second article showed how students who smoked also turned to electronic cigarettes or smoking hookahs (Raloff 2013). The third article discussed the dangers of electronic cigarettes (Mascareli 2014).

After reading and discussing the articles and looking at the surgeon general's warning against smoking and the effects of tobacco on health, the students wondered why people would still buy cigarettes and smoke despite the medical evidence. Kelly thought that if she and her students looked at reasons tweens and teens smoke or inhale, they might understand how to avoid smoking and also be able to campaign against it. Following the Questioning Lesson Plan, Kelly's unit on smoking looked like this:

QUESTIONING LESSON PLAN

1. **What is the question worth talking about?**

   Why do young people smoke or inhale? Who or what encourages smoking?

2. **How does the question fit into your overall plan?**

   The students realize that tobacco and inhalants are harmful to one's health, and they need to be aware of the reasons that tweens and teens smoke. This connects with the broad question, "How can we maintain a healthy mind and body" and brings up a subquestion: "How do drugs affect our lives?"

3. **What content standards does the lesson address?**

   115.6 Health Education Grade 4

   4. Health behaviors. The student understands and engages in behaviors that reduce health risks throughout the life span. The student is expected to:

      (C) describe the short-term and long-term harmful effects of tobacco, alcohol, and other substances such as physical, mental, social, and legal consequences;

      (D) identify ways to avoid drugs and list alternatives for the use of drugs and other substances;

5. Influencing factors. The student comprehends ways in which the media and technology can influence individual and community health. The student is expected to:

(A) explain how the media can influence health behaviors; and

(B) describe ways technology can influence health. (TEA 2013, 10, 12)

4. **What language standards does the lesson address?**

§74.4. English Language Proficiency Standards

(2) Cross curricular—listening

(F) listen to and derive meaning from a variety of media such as audio tape, video, DVD, and CD ROM to build and reinforce concept and language attainment;

(G) understand the general meaning, main points, and important details of spoken language ranging from situations in which topics, language, and contexts are familiar to unfamiliar;

(3) Cross curricular speaking

(E) share information in cooperative learning interactions;

(G) express opinions, ideas, and feelings ranging from communicating single words and short phrases to participating in extended discussions on a variety of social and grade-appropriate academic topics

5. **How will you find out what the students already know about the question?**

We will discuss people the students know who are smokers. Are they adults? Are they others their age? Where do they see people smoking? Do people smoke in movies? Do ads promote smoking? Why or why not?

6. **What strategies will you use working together to explore the question?**

We will brainstorm where we see people smoking and who is smoking. Students will interview people they know who smoke. Students will search the Internet for more information. We will use cooperative groups as we discuss our findings.

7. **What materials will you and the students use to explore the question?**

    We will use interview results and any examples of promotion of smoking students find.

    We will search the Internet looking for reasons that tweens and teens smoke.

8. **What steps will you and the students take to explore the question?**

    » Do a quickwrite (write for one minute anything that comes to your mind on the topic or question) on why young people smoke or use electronic cigarettes.

    » Brainstorm places people smoke.

    » Interview smokers.

    » Search the Internet for reasons tweens and teens smoke.

    » Create PowerPoint presentations in groups that show why people smoke and why they should not smoke. Present to other classes in the school.

    » Write and act out role plays showing why tweens and teens smoke and why they should not smoke.

9. **How will you observe and evaluate the students' learning?**

    » Keep anecdotal records of students' contributions to the small and large group discussion. Evaluate PowerPoints.

    » Role plays and PowerPoints will show that the students have answered the question for this lesson.

Kelly's unit on smoking within her health theme engaged her students. By using a big question theme and organizing using the questioning lesson plan, Kelly engaged her students to explore a topic of importance to them. In the process, they learned important health content, and they developed their academic language proficiency by researching topics on the Internet, writing role plays, and preparing and delivering PowerPoint presentations.

A SHIFT TOWARD WHOLE-TO-PART LANGUAGE TEACHING

The recognition that all learning, including language learning, involves a gradual process of differentiating the parts out of the whole has led to a change in second language teaching. Instead of beginning with discrete bits of language, teachers attempt to expose students to a wide range of the target language. They use specific techniques to make the new language understandable. In Krashen's (1992) terms, such teachers make the input comprehensible.

Whole-to-part teaching is critical because emergent bilinguals are not able to learn all the small parts and then assemble them into meaningful wholes. Instead, teachers give students the big picture and, even if they do not understand all the English language instruction involved, they are able to understand key points and vocabulary as they construct meaning. Little by little they are able to pick out the parts, but only because they have the whole to help them understand where the parts fit in. This whole-to-part learning is both more effective and more efficient.

As we mentioned earlier in the chapter, learning whole to part is psychological, it's how our brains learn. Our brains want to make sense of our world. Parts do not make sense, but wholes do. Rob illustrates how teachers can use whole-to-part teaching to help struggling secondary students make sense of U.S. history.

Teaching Whole to Part—U.S. History

Rob was working during a summer session with high school students who had not been successful in previous classes. They were mostly long-term English learners or emergent bilinguals who came to the U.S. as older learners. All had scored low on standardized tests. He wanted to help his students meet the history standard that called for understanding the causes of the American Revolution and the ideas and interests involved in shaping the revolutionary movement.

Rob began a unit on the American Revolution by asking students to investigate the big question "Why do groups of people engage in a revolution?" He wanted his students to talk, read, and write about what revolution meant, why countries had revolutions, where there were revolutions right now, and, finally, what they knew about the American Revolution. He began by bringing to class current newspaper articles and articles he found on the Internet about present-day revolutions. He showed them websites and played video news clips about revolutions happening currently.

Groups of students chose a country where a revolution was occurring. They researched the events that led up to the revolution and the current state of the conflict using the Internet, newspapers, magazines, and other sources. They made a poster with pictures and text answering where the revolution was taking place, who or what groups were involved, and what some of the causes of the revolution were. The students presented their posters to the class. Students from Nigeria, the Ukraine, and Syria talked about rebel groups in their countries.

After students had developed an understanding of what revolutions are and some of the reasons that revolutions occur, Rob focused in on the American Revolution. He read the students a short story about the American Revolution to help make the characters and setting of the period come alive. He projected pictures of the revolution he found on the Internet on the Smart Board and talked through the pictures (retrieved from www.archives.gov/research/military/american-revolution /pictures/). He also showed a film about the American Revolution.

Then Rob and the students read the social studies text information about the American Revolution together. Rob read some sections aloud and had students work in small groups to read other sections. The class compared what they read with the information about revolutions they had already gathered. Groups worked together to decide what the major causes of the American Revolution were, what events and people were important to the outcome, and how the American Revolution could be compared to other revolutions discussed in class.

Students did well in Rob's U.S. history class. Part of their success can be attributed to the rich context Rob provided. Rather than teaching isolated facts, he built a strong background for the concept of *revolution* long before the students encountered that term in their social studies text. By itself, the textbook would not have engaged the students. However, because the students had already studied a current revolution and reported on it, they were better prepared to comprehend the textbook. In addition, Rob scaffolded the reading and supplemented it with pictures and a film. All of these activities resulted in his students' learning academic content and developing academic language.

We have provided in this chapter several examples of whole-to-part teaching in classes with older students. We conclude with the story of one kindergarten teacher and describe how she organized her unit around the questions "How are bugs the same and how are they different?" and "How can I find out?" These questions fall under the kindergarten standards for science that call for students to understand how scientists observe, record, and report information.

Teaching Whole to Part—Observe Like Scientists

"Itsy Bitsy Spider went up the water spout. Down came the rain and washed the spider out. . . . " (Trapani 1996). These are the beginning lines of the well-known song about spiders that many native English-speaking preschoolers and kindergartners sing inside and outside school across the country. However, the children enthusiastically singing this song in Isabel's kindergarten class are not all native English speakers. In fact, only about half of her students came to school this fall speaking English fluently. Her students have several different first languages including Spanish, Vietnamese, Khmer, Arabic, and several languages of India, including Urdu and Punjabi.

Isabel has been teaching in her urban district for five years, and she has found that each year more students enter her classroom as English learners. Because of this, her district has provided professional development to help Isabel and other teachers better meet the needs of their emergent bilinguals. She learned how to help her students to acquire English and learn the kindergarten curriculum by organizing her curriculum around big question themes based on the standards.

As she planned units of study, Isabel was sure to meet the state content-area standards. In science kindergarten students are expected to ask questions, gather information, and communicate their findings. In addition, they should be able to identify the properties of organisms. During this unit Isabel planned to teach her students about the differences between spiders and insects by having them notice that spiders have eight legs while insects have only six. She wanted her students to become little scientists, so one of her questions was "How do scientists observe, record, and report information?" Two smaller questions within her theme were "How are bugs the same and how are they different?" and "How can I find out?"

In addition to science standards, Isabel wanted to support her students as beginning readers. In language arts, kindergarten students are expected to develop their oral language vocabulary. They also should learn to identify letters of the alphabet and match letters and sounds in words. Isabel planned different activities to help her students develop important beginning reading skills through her science unit.

Songs are especially effective for teaching language and introducing content. Isabel and her students sang together a counting song about elephants balancing on a spider web, "One Elephant, Two Elephants" (Wainman 1982). She wrote the words on large song sheets and clipped the songs to her standing song chart. The children sang the songs together as a student volunteer tracked the words. Isabel also asked the Spanish speakers if they knew the song in Spanish, *"Los elefantes"* (Ada 1991), which is similar to the elephant song in English but has a different tune. Since some students were familiar with the song in Spanish, Isabel put those words up on the song sheet, too, and the whole class sang it in Spanish led by the Spanish speakers and a tape recording of the song.

Isabel then asked the students what the songs had in common. The children immediately called out, "Elephants and spider webs." Next, Isabel asked the students what they knew about spiders and wrote down student responses: "They are bugs." "They can bite you." "I don't like spiders." "They eat flies." "They make webs." "Baby spiders come from eggs." After the class had discussed spiders, Isabel read them *The Very Busy Spider* (Carle 2006). All the students wanted to feel the raised spider web on each page, so Isabel allowed one student to come up each time she turned a page. The children talked about the spider web catching the fly at the end of the story. When they talked about spiders and flies, Isabel asked them what the two had in common. "They are bugs!" several children replied.

Isabel then read *I Spy a Bug* (Latour and Latour 2014) to the students. It is about a girl who explores all around her yard for bugs and describes her investigation in rhyme. The teacher then took her students on an exploration of the schoolyard to see what bugs they could find. She brought some jars and told the students not to touch the bugs but to tell her when they saw one by saying, "I spy a bug!!" She then collected the bugs and put them into jars.

The class found a caterpillar, a ladybug, a cricket, a beetle, and some ants. During the next several days, the teacher and students spied and caught a fly, a butterfly, a moth, and a bumblebee, and one mother brought in some fireflies that she and her son had caught the night before. Each bug was put in a separate jar on a table, and Isabel wrote the name of the bug on a large strip of paper.

Because her students speak several different languages, Isabel teaches mainly in English. Although she has few resources in Vietnamese, Khmer, Arabic, or the several Indian languages of her other bilingual students, whenever possible she encourages students who speak those languages to talk in their home language about what they see and understand and to bring in resources they have at home. When working in small groups, Isabel previews or reviews lessons in Spanish with her Spanish-speaking students before teaching the lesson in English. She uses resources she has in Spanish. For example, Isabel read her Spanish speakers two bilingual limited text books: *Where Do Insects Live? ¿Dónde viven los insectos?* (Canizares and Reid 2003) and *What Do Insects Do? ¿Qué hacen los insectos?* (Canizares and Chanko 2003). The children were fascinated by the pictures and commented on the bugs they recognized. Since the text is limited and predictable and the pictures helpful, Isabel encouraged her students to read the texts along with her and then read them in pairs in both Spanish and English.

Next, Isabel read the whole class a limited text book in English, *Bugs, Bugs, Bugs* (Reid and Chessen 1998). After identifying bugs they knew, Isabel asked the students to choose a bug to draw and write about. Isabel told the children they could look at the bugs in the jars, use the books she had read, or use other books in the room about insects to get ideas for their drawing and writing including *Have You Seen Bugs?* (Oppenheim 1986) and *The Big Bug Search* (Young 2010). With Isabel's guidance, the children began to make some important observations as they looked at the insects in the jars and the books, talked together, drew, and wrote. Some students noticed that spiders have eight legs, but that beetles, ants, bees, and butterflies have only six. Isabel put up large posters of an insect and a spider and discussed the difference in number of legs with all the children.

As the students learned the concepts of science, Isabel also worked with the children on sounds and letters. Isabel began by inviting children to share their picture and what they had written on their drawing. Students hung their pictures around the room under letters of the alphabet; so *ants* were under the letter *A*, *beetles* and *bees* were placed under the *B*, and *crickets* were hung under the *C*. Then Isabel took out some word strips and asked students to pin up the large printed words under the letter of the alphabet that the word started with. When they were finished, the student pictures and the large printed insect words covered the wall under the alphabet.

To work on ending sounds, Isabel reread some of the bug books and asked the children to look for rhyming sounds. The children were delighted with the description of the firefly on page one of *I Spy a Bug*: "I spy a bug with its belly so bright. It flies and it flies and lights up at night" (Latour and Latour 2014, 1). They called out the rhyming words *bright* and *light*.

Isabel worked on other concepts and language as the students continued the unit. For example, they observed and read about camouflage (Heller 1992), and they learned the language of comparison and contrast as they talked about how insects and spiders are the same and how they are different. Isabel organizes her teaching so that all her students can see the whole before they learn the parts. Figure 3–3 is a short bibliography of some of the insect books and songs Isabel used during the unit.

CONCLUSION

Throughout this chapter we have discussed the importance of teaching emergent bilinguals by organizing curriculum around big question themes. Rather than teaching students who are learning English by cha-cha-cha-ing through the day, changing topics and using different vocabulary each time the subject changes, teachers are encouraged to organize their teaching around big question themes. This gives the students the big picture, and then teachers can connect the details to that big picture idea.

A useful way of getting at the big picture is to consider asking students big questions that really matter. Simply picking a topic like "the farm" does not get at key concepts students need to know. Instead, asking "Why is agriculture important to our lives?" encourages students to investigate different important concepts instead of simply learning the names of farm animals and crops. Students can study how animals are cared for on a farm, what products come from animals, plant growth

Ada, Alma Flor. 1991. *Días y días de poesía*. Carmel, CA: Hampton-Brown.

Canizares, Susan, and Pamela Chanko. 2003. *What Do Insects Do? ¿Qué hacen los insectos?* New York: Scholastic.

Canizares, Susan, and Mary Reid. 2003. *Where Do Insects Live? ¿Dónde viven los insectos?* New York: Scholastic.

Carle, Eric. 2006. *The Very Busy Spider*. New York: Scholastic.

Heller, Ruth. 1992. *How to Hide a Butterfly and Other Insects*. New York: Grosset and Dunlap.

Jackson, Ian. 1998. *The Big Bug Search*. New York: Scholastic.

Latour, David, and Melissa Latour. 2014. *I Spy a Bug*. Self-published.

Oppenheim, Joanne. 1996. *Have You Seen Bugs?* New York: Scholastic.

Reid, Mary, and Betsy Chessen. 1998. *Bugs, Bugs, Bugs*. New York: Scholastic.

Trapani, Iza. 1996. *The Itsy Bitsy Spider*. Boston: Houghton Mifflin.

Wainman, Margaret. 1982. *One Elephant, Two Elephants*. Port Coquitlam, BC: Class Size Books.

Young, Caroline. 2010. *The Big Bug Search*. Glasgow, UK: Usborne.

FIGURE 3–3 *Insect and Spider Bibliography*

and organic farming, and how products get from the farm to the table. Teachers can bring in the various content areas as students graph plant growth or animal production, study climate effects on plants and animals, consider technology and how it has changed farming, and compare farming methods across countries. This kind of in-depth whole-to-part study meets the new standards that are required, allows for creative teaching that engages students, and supports the language development that emergent bilingual students need.

As we have discussed teaching through whole-to-part learning through big question themes in this chapter, our examples have included themes that teach both language and content. In reality, one cannot separate the principles of "Learning goes whole to part" and "Lessons should teach academic language and content." Claude taught students about newspapers and how to access relevant information from them, and he encouraged his students to write responses to newspaper articles of interest to them. Rob helped his students learn key concepts in U.S. history. Isabel helped her students understand how to compare and contrast spiders and insects and how to recognize rhyming words. She also taught them how scientists investigate. These teachers taught whole to part to help their emergent bilinguals develop both academic language and subject matter content.

APPLICATIONS

1. Observe a teacher at any grade level who has emergent bilinguals in his or her class-room for at least two hours. Is the teacher cha-cha-cha-ing through the curriculum or do you notice an overall big idea being explored? In other words, do the lessons hold together and do lessons move from whole to part? How? If you observe at the secondary level, ask the teacher if he or she coordinates with other teachers around a theme. Also ask if the teacher teaches extended units of study.

2. Write a lesson for a grade level of your choice using the Questioning Lesson Plan. Share with your classmates or a colleague.

3. Teach a lesson following the Questioning Lesson Plan. Be prepared to share back how the lesson went.

4. Forming a big question is not always easy. Look at the topics that follow. Choose five of them. Write one or two big questions for each topic. Be prepared to share your questions.

Our community workers	Civil rights	The Holocaust
The water cycle	Exports and imports	The Civil War
City and country life	Women's rights	Immigration
Oceans	Government regulations	Supply and demand
Deserts	The rain forest	Distribution and consumption of goods
Protecting our environment	Monopolies	
	The solar system	Poverty in the U.S.
Global warming	The Great Depression	Dictatorships
The three branches of the U.S. government		

4

Teaching Should Develop Academic Language and Content

Natascha is a sixth-grade language arts teacher in a rural school near the Texas border with Mexico. Some of her students are native English speakers and others are recent arrivals with adequate schooling. However, most of her students are long-term English learners who started school speaking Spanish and have developed conversational Spanish and English but not grade-level academic proficiency in either language. Natascha knows that all of her students must meet the language arts standards for her grade. She doesn't have time to teach language first and then teach content, so she teaches academic language and academic content in every lesson.

One unit Natascha taught illustrates how she teaches both academic language and content to help her students meet standards. A grade 6 standard for language arts requires students to analyze in detail how a key individual, event, or idea is introduced, illustrated, and elaborated in a text. Natascha chose *Esperanza Rising* (Ryan 2000) as the text to teach this standard. This is a culturally relevant text for her Hispanic students (Ebe 2015). Although this book is sometimes used at lower grade levels, Natascha knew she could use it to teach the concepts and skills her students needed to meet the standard. She also knew that many of her students had difficulty reading, so she decided to use a text that was accessible and could help them build reading proficiency.

Natascha wanted to be sure all her students could understand the literal meaning of a text with the main idea and details, so the first activities she planned focused on writing a summary. She began by having them make a summary glove of different chapters. After the students had read the first chapter, *"Las uvas"* ("The Grapes"), for example, she passed out blank sheets of paper and asked her students to put their left hand palm down on the paper and trace their hand. She demonstrated how to do this. Next, she had them write the word *summary* on the palm. She explained that a good summary includes answers to the questions, "who?" "when?" "where?" "what?" and "why?" Finally, she had students label the thumb and fingers of the hand using these key question words, starting with *who* over the thumb.

Once all her students had finished making the summary glove, Natascha worked with them to decide what to put on the thumb and each finger. The students, with Natascha's help, decided that *who* should be Esperanza, Papá, Tío Luís, and Miguel, and they wrote this on the thumb of their glove. They continued with the answers to the other questions. After they had answered the five *wh-* questions, each student used the information to write a brief summary on the palm of their glove. Natascha used the first chapter to model the process of completing the summary glove. For subsequent chapters, students worked individually or in pairs to complete a glove. Natascha was able to give extra help to her beginner-level students as the other students wrote their answers. After the students finished their summary gloves for each chapter, Natascha posted them on the bulletin board. Students read each other's summaries and, in the process, solidified their understanding of each chapter.

The summary glove provides emergent bilinguals with a visual scaffold for writing a summary. All her students benefited from this approach. She scaffolded summarizing by helping them organize the task with a series of concrete steps. Writing a summary is an important language arts content objective. At the same time that Natascha taught content, she also taught language. During this activity, her students were given practice in forming and using *wh-* questions during the class discussions. They learned that for questions starting with *who*, the verb follows, as in "Who was in the chapter?" Following the other *wh-* words, students must insert "did" to ask questions like "Where did the chapter take place?" By teaching *wh-* questions and summarizing, Natascha taught both academic language and content.

After all her students had completed the summary glove project, Natascha had them write a more complete summary that included information to answer each of the five *wh-* questions. Students at different levels of English proficiency responded in different ways. Her beginners completed a graphic organizer with a labeled picture for each section. Her low intermediate students drew pictures and wrote simple sentences in their summaries. More advanced students and native English speakers wrote paragraphs. Students also worked in groups at different proficiency levels. Each group created a graphic representation for one of the chapters in *Esperanza*

Rising and presented their poster to the class. Natascha put these on the bulletin board, and students used them to review key events and characters in the book.

As an additional activity to teach summary writing, Natascha assigned students to create what she called a CASPAR chart as they read each chapter. The letters in CASPAR stand for *characters*, *adjectives*, *setting*, *problem*, *action taken*, and *resolution*. The chart was constructed using a large piece of colored paper and gluing six narrow strips of paper across the top. These were labeled with the letters *C A S P A R*, and they could be lifted up to read the words the letters represented, such as *character* and *setting*. Below each strip, students listed key words. For example, under *character* one student put *Esperanza*, *Papá*, *Miguel*, and the other characters in the chapter. Under *adjectives*, she listed words like *happy*, *rich*, *excited*, *sympathetic*, and *nervous*. Through this activity students learned about key language arts concepts, such as character, setting, problem, and resolution. At the same time, they began to focus on the descriptive adjectives the author used to make her writing more vivid. Throughout the unit, Natascha worked with her students to include descriptive adjectives as they wrote about the characters in the novel.

The students used their summaries and CASPAR charts to complete the next two activities. The first was to complete a Story Hill, a graphic often used in language arts classes. The key elements of the plot are represented as a hill with the setting, characters, and problem on one side, the climax on the top, and the problem/resolution, conclusion, and theme/moral at the bottom of the other side. Students filled in details on the Story Hill charts and posted them around the room.

As a follow-up activity to the Story Hill, Natascha asked students to complete a Story Trail. For this project, students created a poster for each chapter. The poster included a short written summary and pictures of the setting and characters. Students drew a line in the center of the poster showing the mood during the different parts of the chapter. For example, the *"Las uvas"* chapter begins with Esperanza very happy because it is her birthday. She is waiting for her father to come for the celebration. Then she gets the news that her father is missing. At the end, her father's murdered body is brought to her. The line students drew in the center of the poster went downward, showing how the mood changed from high to low as the chapter progressed.

As students developed a good understanding of the story elements, the plot, and the mood, Natascha introduced activities to help them make text-to-self and text-to-text connections. To begin, she gave students a chart to teach them to make the text-to-self connections. The chart is divided into two columns. In the first column are "What the text says," "What do you already know?" "What have you experienced?" and "Text-to-self connection." Students write their answers in the boxes of the second column. For example, one student wrote that the text told about how

Esperanza dealt with sadness over her situation and that her friend comforted her. Then he wrote that he knew good friends are important because they can help in times of trouble. The student recalled an experience he had when he was sad and a friend helped him feel better. Finally, he connected his experience with Esperanza's experience in the chapter.

This series of questions scaffolded the instruction for Natascha's emergent bilinguals. They recorded the big ideas from the text, wrote what they knew and had experienced on the topic, and then made the connection between their experience and the experience described in the text. Natascha worked with her students to fill out the chart for the first chapter, and then students worked individually or in pairs to complete the information for the other chapters.

Natascha extended this activity to include connections between *Esperanza Rising* and another novel her students had read, *The House on Mango Street* (Cisneros 1984). She worked with the class to complete a chart with three columns, titled "Esperanza Rising," "My Own Experience," and "House on Mango Street." The students brainstormed different important ideas from the books and made connections to their own experiences. For instance, both *Esperanza Rising* and *The House on Mango Street* had as themes the importance of family and the need to grow up fast. Students shared how their family worked together and how they had needed to grow up quickly when they immigrated.

As a further extension, Natascha researched topics and informational texts related to each chapter. She created a chart with a column that had a brief chapter summary and another column with topics and books related to events in the chapter. For example, for the chapter in which Esperanza and her family leave Mexico by train, Natascha listed the geography of Mexico and California, transportation, railroads, and jobs, and included informational texts for each topic. Students then worked in groups to read these resources and report back. This activity helped students build background and also led to discussions about the differences in the structure and language of novels and informational texts.

As a project to help students summarize what they had learned so far, they were given a template for a cube on colored paper. On the six sides they listed the protagonist, antagonist, conflicts, resolution, adjectives, and climax. They assembled the cubes, which were hung on strings from the ceiling.

After students had studied part of the standard relating to the development of events in a text, Natascha focused on how an individual is introduced, illustrated, and elaborated. The language arts standard Natascha was working on requires students to analyze in detail how a key individual, event, or idea is introduced, illustrated, and elaborated in a text. The summary activities focused on events. Now, Natascha had students look at character development.

Each student chose one of the main characters. Then Natascha gave them colored index cards. On the front of one card they wrote the name of the character; the other cards were labeled with the words *feelings*, *relationships*, *changes*, *conflict*, and *point of view*. With Natascha's help, students found specific information from the novel that they wrote on the back of each card. For example, one student wrote that Esperanza was mean and spoiled on the back of the first card, and for Esperanza's feelings that she felt sad. The series of cards were strung together and hung up in the room. As a follow-up students cut out a doll figure of their character from a template and listed the character's attributes on the doll. The dolls were also posted up in the classroom. As they wrote the attributes, they added new descriptive adjectives to their vocabulary.

Language arts standards include finding textual evidence to support a claim, so Natascha had students work together in small groups to choose one character and list that character's physical description, personality, and relationship to other characters. They put this information on three strips of paper. Then, for each characteristic, students found a supporting quote from the novel and put the quote and the page number on the back of each strip under the heading "textual evidence." One group chose Miguel. They listed characteristics such as "he works hard and is respectful" for personality; "he is young, tall, and has black hair" for physical description; and "he has a close relationship with his family" for relationships. They found a quote for each characteristic. For example, for the physical characteristic "tall," they found the supporting quote "At sixteen Miguel was already taller than his parents" (16).

As a final activity, students were assigned one of the characters. They divided a poster into three parts to represent the character's past, present, and future. Then they drew a picture and wrote a paragraph for each time period. Depending on their level of English proficiency, students wrote longer and shorter paragraphs, but all the students could participate because Natascha had carefully scaffolded this activity by engaging her students in the previous projects on character. By completing this project students met the standard to analyze how an individual is introduced, illustrated, and elaborated in a text.

Natascha spent several weeks teaching *Esperanza Rising*. Her students learned literary concepts such as character, plot, and theme. They were able to summarize chapters and analyze character. They also found textual evidence for claims they made. At the same time, they learned about the structure of a novel and differences between this genre and informational texts. Further, they learned how to use descriptive adjectives and to ask and answer *wh-* questions, among other language skills. In the process of teaching this novel, Natascha provided sheltered instruction to teach both academic language and academic content.

CONTENT-BASED ESL

Natascha scaffolded instruction for her emergent bilinguals to ensure that they could learn the language arts content as they increased their English proficiency. However, schools have not always differentiated instruction to meet the needs of English learners. In many districts instruction given in English excluded some students from access to a meaningful education. This began to change in 1974 when Chinese parents in San Francisco sued the school district for violation of the civil rights of their children. The school district claimed that the Chinese students were given an equal education because they were provided the same materials and taught the same content as native English speakers. The Chinese parents argued that by teaching non-English speakers in English, a language they did not understand, the district was denying them an equal opportunity to learn and discriminating against them under Title VI of the Civil Rights Act of 1964. The Supreme Court sided with the parents in the Lau *v*. Nichols case. Although it did not require a specific program for English learners, the Supreme Court did issue guidelines for districts to follow. These guidelines called for schools to identify English learners and to provide special services that would give them access to the core curriculum.

According to the Lau decision schools could meet these requirements in different ways, including bilingual instruction and ESL (Crawford 1999). Students could be given some instruction in their home language or be placed in ESL classes. ESL teachers could pull out groups of students or work with mainstream teachers by providing extra support in the classes. In many classes the Natural Approach was used, although some teachers used ALM or Grammar-Translation. However, administrators and teachers soon recognized that if they tried to teach emergent bilinguals English first and then content, they would fall far behind their classmates. For that reason, they began teaching both language and content simultaneously in content-based ESL classes or in bilingual classes where content was taught through the primary language while students learned English (Brinton, Snow, and Wesche 1989; Snow and Brinton 1997).

In these classes, teachers often organized the curriculum around themes based on science or social studies. For example, a content-based ESL class for younger students might study community members and their roles, while a class for older students might focus on life cycles. They used different strategies to make the academic content comprehensible. While the primary focus in content-based ESL classes was on language development, teachers used subject matter content to teach English so that students learned both language and content (Schifini 1985).

In traditional ESL classes, teachers taught conversational language around topics such as food, clothes, and weather. However, for emergent bilinguals to develop the language they needed to discuss, read, and write in the content areas, conversational English was not sufficient, and teachers began to teach academic language. Cummins (1981) conducted research on immigrant students in Canada. He found that students developed two types of language proficiency: conversational language and academic language. His studies showed that it takes about two years to gain proficiency in conversational language, but that it takes five to seven years for students to reach grade-level proficiency in academic language. Cummins defined academic language as being context reduced and cognitively demanding. Other researchers found similar results for the length of time it takes to develop academic language (Collier 1989; Thomas and Collier 1995).

Academic language includes the different registers of language used in schools. It is more like written language than spoken language. The goal of schools is to teach academic content and also to teach the academic language needed to comprehend and produce the academic language of each discipline. Students with academic language proficiency can talk, read, and write like scientists in science class, like social scientists in social studies and history classes, like mathematicians in math class, and like literary scholars in language arts and English classes (Freeman and Freeman 2009).

LANGUAGE OBJECTIVES

To teach academic language effectively, teachers should develop language objectives. Lesson planning begins by identifying content objectives. The technical vocabulary of the content area should be considered part of the content objectives. For example, in teaching the structure of an atom, a teacher will explain that an atom has *protons* and *neutrons* in the *nucleus* and *electrons* in the *orbital*. The italicized words are technical terms that a teacher would need to use in teaching the concept of atomic structure. These terms are labels for key concepts in science, so they should be listed under the content objectives.

Once a teacher decides on the content objectives, he asks, "What language forms and functions will my students need to discuss, read, and write about this content?" The teacher may choose one or two aspects of language to teach. Language forms can refer to different things, such as verb endings, comparative forms, possessives, types of questions, punctuation, or descriptive adjectives and adverbs. Students use language forms to carry out functions, such as summarizing, describing, explaining, or comparing and contrasting.

If the content objective in a language arts class is to write about a recent experience with an identifiable beginning, middle, and end, a language objective could be to use signal words to show time sequence such as *first*, *then*, *next*, and *finally*.

Another language objective could be to use the correct form of regular past tense verbs. A third possible language objective would be to use descriptive adverbs to modify actions.

In a science class, a content objective might be to make a pocket garden and observe changes in seeds grown under different conditions. The teacher might begin by asking students to write the procedure they will follow for making the pocket garden, observing the seeds, and recording the results. A language objective would be for students to use the imperative form of verbs, such as *choose, moisten,* and *place.* A different language objective would be for students to use prepositional phrases to show location, such as *in the plastic bag* and *under the table.* The teacher could use sentence frames to scaffold this structure: "Place the seeds in _____."

In a math class, the content objective could be for students to order objects by length and to compare the lengths of two objects indirectly by using a third object. A related language objective could be to add the comparative and superlative suffixes *-er* and *-est* to one- or two-syllable adjectives, as in *longer* and *longest.* Another possible language objective could be to write sentences showing comparison, using the frame "_____ is shorter than _____." More advanced students could write compound sentences with a coordinate conjunction, following the pattern "A is shorter than B, but it is longer than C."

As a final example, the content objective for students in a social studies class could be to compare and contrast geographic features of an area. One language objective could be to write complex sentences with signal words showing contrast, such as "The western part of the state is flat; however, the eastern part is mountainous." A second language objective could be to use the correct form of present tense verbs to agree with the subject, as in "The river *runs* south," and "The rivers *run* south."

As these examples show, teachers should base language objectives on the content objectives. They should consider the function of the language, such as describing, comparing, explaining, or analyzing, and then write language objectives by considering the language forms students would need for these functions. Language objectives should be developed keeping students' current proficiency levels in mind. Developing both content and language objectives is an important first step in teaching academic language and subject matter content.

REASONS TO TEACH ACADEMIC LANGUAGE AND ACADEMIC CONTENT

There are four reasons to teach both academic language and academic content. See Figure 4–1.

1. Students learn language and content at the same time.

2. Teaching language and content keeps language in its natural context.

3. Students have a real purpose for using academic language.

4. Students learn the academic vocabulary of the different content areas.

FIGURE 4–1 *Reasons to Teach Language and Content*

Students Learn Language and Content at the Same Time

In the first place, when teachers teach both language and content, students learn language and content at the same time. There is no need, and indeed there is no time, to teach language first and content later. In the same way that children growing up in a bilingual environment can develop two languages simultaneously, English learners in classes where teachers focus on language structures and forms as they teach literature, science, social studies, and math learn academic English as they learn the academic content. In the earlier stages of language development, teachers need to use more techniques to make the English instruction comprehensible, so the amount of content that can be taught must necessarily be reduced. As students gain increased English proficiency, they can learn more content in English. Nevertheless, at every stage of language development, emergent bilinguals should also be learning academic content. Developing high levels of academic English and grade-level academic content knowledge and skills takes time, so it is important that emergent bilinguals learn academic English and subject matter from the start.

Teaching Language and Content Keeps Language in Its Natural Context

A second reason for teaching language and content is that this approach keeps language in its natural context. It is natural to talk about the hypotenuse of a triangle if you are studying geometry. Math is the natural context for this word. As they learn this word, students understand how it is related to other words in the semantic field, such as *triangle*. It is easier to learn words in context than in isolation or as part of a list of unrelated words. Key words for different subject areas are best understood as part of a network of related terms needed to understand some aspect of a subject. In the area of literature, for example, it is easier to learn a term like *rising action* in the process of talking about the development of plot. The student comes to understand *rising action* as one phase of plot development that is related to other words, such as *climax* or *resolution*. Content-based language teaching naturally lends itself to presenting vocabulary in context.

When teachers in different content areas include a focus on language, English learners develop proficiency in the different genres of the subject. For example, in science students learn how to write procedures, procedural recounts, and reports. In writing a procedure, students put items in a numbered list and use the imperative verb form for each step. For example, the first three steps of a procedure for a pocket garden would look like this:

1. Choose three kinds of seeds.
2. Moisten a paper towel.
3. Place the seeds in the wet towel.

On the other hand, when writing a procedural recount, students use paragraphs and past-tense verbs to describe what they did, as in "First, we chose three kinds of seeds. Then, we moistened a paper towel and placed the seeds in the towel." For a report, they gather information and present it in paragraphs with a main idea and supporting details. Learning to write these different genres of science as students study science keeps the language in its natural context.

Students Have a Real Purpose for Using Language

A third reason for teaching language and content together is that students have reasons to use the language they are learning. They are not simply memorizing words for a test, words they will forget very soon. Instead, they need to use different language structures as they listen to lectures, talk with classmates, read textbooks, and write reports. Use of the language forms and functions of a content area leads to deeper learning and greater retention. An English learner studying geometry will develop a better understanding of *hypotenuse* as she listens to the teacher explain the parts of a triangle, reads proofs in her textbook, and then engages in problem-solving activities. An emergent bilingual studying literature will come to understand the structure of a story plot and the terms for the different phases of the plot as he writes a summary of a short story. In each case, the students are motivated to learn the academic English they need to talk, read, and write about academic content.

Students Learn the Academic Vocabulary of the Different Content Areas

A final reason for teaching language and content is that students learn the academic vocabulary of the different content areas. As the previous examples show, students learn key words such as *hypotenuse* or *rising action* in the process of listening, reading, talking, and writing about academic subjects. Students also come to understand that in different contexts the same word takes on different meanings: In math, students learn their multiplication *tables*. In chemistry, they might study the periodic *table*. In geology, they encounter the water *table*. And as they study different subject areas, they consult a *table* of contents. They also learn to gather information from charts and *tables*. Studying a word like *table* as part of a list would never prepare a student to learn the different meanings of the term as it is used in various content areas.

FROM CONTENT-BASED ESL TO SHELTERED INSTRUCTION

For many ESL teachers, the transition to teaching content-based ESL posed problems. In the first place, especially in middle school and high school, ESL teachers felt they lacked knowledge of the content. Most ESL teachers had background in language arts, but they were less confident when asked to teach science and math concepts. A second difficulty was in finding time for the ESL teacher to meet with the mainstream teacher or teachers whose content they were expected to teach. This was particularly difficult when the ESL teacher had to travel to more than one school and to work with several different teachers.

In some schools the ESL teacher and the content teacher taught as a team. This worked well if the two teachers had time to plan together and if they maintained an equal status in the classroom. Team teaching was not successful in classes where the ESL teacher played a subordinate role. This was also an expensive model for schools to implement since there were two teachers for each content-based ESL class.

Content-based ESL classes were designed to help emergent bilinguals develop academic knowledge and proficiency in English. However, students exiting these classes seldom achieved levels of English proficiency that enabled them to succeed in mainstream classes. Often students were exited as soon as they had developed conversational proficiency. As the research shows, academic language proficiency takes longer to develop.

Content-based ESL generally focused on language and used academic subject matter as the content of lessons. A second approach, sheltered instruction, involved teaching emergent bilinguals with a focus on academic content. Sheltered instruction classes took many different forms, but, in general, in these classes teachers presented grade-level content and sheltered the instruction for emergent bilinguals by using a number of techniques common to ESL classes along with other techniques, such as cooperative learning, designed to make the academic content comprehensible. Generally, sheltered classes were for students at the intermediate or advanced level of English proficiency, and the classes were taught by mainstream teachers (Echevarria and Short 2010; Zwiers 2007).

A program model for older students proposed by Krashen (1985) included a component called sheltered content. In this model, students were taught some subjects in their primary language, some in sheltered classes, and some in mainstream classes. As students became more proficient, they were transitioned from primary language instruction to sheltered instruction, and then they were mainstreamed. For example, students might take social studies classes at first in their primary language. Later they would have a sheltered social studies class, and when they became more proficient in English they would be mainstreamed in social studies.

Content-area teachers needed professional development in how to shelter the content by using ESL techniques. Not surprisingly, most mainstream teachers found that they could not cover the same amount of material in a sheltered class as in a class with native speakers. In addition, they lacked materials adapted for ESL students. Further, most mainstream teachers had not had classes in ESL methods, second language acquisition, linguistics, or cross-cultural communication as part of their teacher education. And, while they could learn a few techniques for sheltering instruction, most districts did not provide the long-term professional development teachers of sheltered instruction classes needed. Figure 4–2 lists ways teachers can make academic content comprehensible.

Cognitive Academic Language Learning Approach (CALLA)

One method developed for sheltered classes is the Cognitive Academic Language Learning Approach (CALLA). It is an "instructional system designed to develop academic language skills in English for students in upper elementary and secondary schools" (Chamot and O'Malley 1989, 111). CALLA is primarily designed for students at the intermediate to advanced stages of English proficiency. The authors state, "learning a language has more in common with learning complex cognitive skills than it does with learning facts, isolated pieces of information, or even meaningful texts" (112). The idea, then, is that second language students will learn English through an organized approach to the content area materials they need to study in the regular classroom.

Three components comprise CALLA: (1) grade-appropriate content, (2) academic language development, and (3) instruction in learning strategies. In CALLA classes, students first study content materials in science and mathematics because these subjects are less language dependent than social studies and language arts. In science, students receive comprehensible input through hands-on activities. Mathematics has an international sign system and somewhat restricted vocabulary.

If at all possible, preview the content in the students' first language. You may use a student to do this.

1. Use visuals and realia. Always try to move from the concrete to the abstract.

2. Use gestures and body language.

3. Speak clearly and pause often, but don't slow speech down unnaturally.

4. Say the same thing in different ways (paraphrase).

5. Write key words and ideas down. (This slows down the language.)

6. Use graphic organizers such as Venn diagrams, semantic webs, and charts.

7. Use PowerPoints, Smart Boards, and media including video clips and other visuals.

8. Make frequent comprehension checks.

9. Have students explain main concepts to one another working in pairs or small groups. They can do this in their first languages.

10. Above all, keep oral presentations or reading assignments short. Collaborative activities are more effective than long lectures or assigned readings.

FIGURE 4–2 *Making Academic Content Comprehensible*

Later, students begin to work in social studies and literature, which involve more language. Teachers learn a number of ways to provide context for the content.

As students explore various content areas, they also develop the academic language they need, the second component. Since much of the academic language used in the content areas is abstract, particularly the language of textbooks and lectures, the input is made comprehensible through the use of maps, models, manipulatives, demonstrations, written responses, and discussions. As students become actively involved in the content, they learn the academic language they need.

The third component of CALLA, learning strategy instruction, helps students consciously develop techniques for working with content area materials. In the CALLA model, teachers first find out what learning strategies students already use by interviewing them and having them "think aloud" as they do a task. After strategies are identified, teachers provide students opportunities to practice them. Chamot and O'Malley (1994) identified three major types of strategies and developed activities for each type: metacognitive, cognitive, and social-affective. Metacognitive strategies include advanced organization, selective attention, and self-evaluation. These strategies help students plan, monitor, and evaluate their own learning. Cognitive strategies, such as grouping, note-taking, imagery, and inferencing, encourage students to manipulate content material in different ways. Social-affective strategies, such as cooperative learning, give students a chance to interact in order to ask questions and clarify the content.

CALLA teachers develop five-phase lesson plans that include (1) preparation, (2) presentation, (3) practice, (4) evaluation, and (5) expansion. For example, in a social studies lesson on the branches of the U.S. government, during the preparation stage the teacher might have students describe the form of government in their home countries. He might ask questions like "Do you have a president? a king?" "Who makes the laws?" "Do you have senators, a supreme court, a congress?" After students have discussed government in their own countries, the teacher might move into the presentation stage by listing the three branches of the U.S. government on the board and explaining the roles and responsibilities of members of each branch. Then, the teacher shows a video describing each of the branches and showing pictures of members of the executive, judicial, and legislative branches. For the practice stage, students, working in groups, would read a short article with illustrations that explains the roles and responsibilities of people in each of the three branches. Then they write a summary of the article. For evaluation, the students could work in three groups. Each group would create a PowerPoint presentation explaining one of the branches. These presentations would include images and information gathered from the Internet. For expansion, students could choose a current controversial law being considered at the state level and describe how the law was introduced and what different branches of state government will be involved in getting the law passed or keeping it from becoming law.

Chamot and O'Malley wrote *The CALLA Handbook* (1994) to explain their model and to provide sample lessons. After O'Malley's death, Chamot published a learning strategies book with colleagues (Chamot et al. 1999). She also updated CALLA in a book chapter, showing that it could be applied to younger students (Chamot 2005). In 2009 she published a second edition of the *CALLA Handbook*. Many teachers have found both the model and the materials extremely helpful as they work to teach content to emergent bilinguals.

Distinguishing English Language Development from Sheltered Instruction

California and some other states make a clear distinction between content-based ESL classes focused on language development and classes that shelter grade-level academic content. The classes that teach language using academic subject matter as the content are referred to as English Language Development (ELD) while those that shelter grade-level content are designated Specially Designed Academic Instruction in English (SDAIE). This is a helpful distinction because it clarifies the goals of each program and resolves the problems that result from trying to shelter grade-level academic content when English learners are at the early stages of English language development (Freeman and Freeman 1998).

Los Angeles Unified School District (LAUSD) is the second largest school district in the U.S. and has the most ELs. The district provides professional development for their teachers on the differences between ELD and SDAIE as well as appropriate instruction in each type of class. The English Learner Master Plan (2012) provides details of how students are assessed, placed in classes, and instructed. Additional materials on the district's website, including PDFs and PowerPoints, were developed to provide teachers with professional development (retrieved from http://notebook .lausd.net/portal/page?_pageid=33,1170728,33_1181823&_dad=ptl). In the following sections, we explain how the district distinguishes between ELD and SDAIE and the instructional strategies teachers should use in each type of class.

Figure 4–3 lists some key differences between ELD and SDAIE. As the figure shows, the goal of ELD is language development, and the goal of SDAIE is to teach grade-level content. In ELD classes, students learn some academic content, but teachers emphasize teaching academic language. In SDAIE classes, on the other hand, students increase their language proficiency, but teachers stay focused on teaching academic content. In the LAUSD model, ELD instruction is delivered in English while SDAIE makes strategic use of the students' home languages. ELD classes use content texts at a grade appropriate for the students' proficiency levels. For students at a beginning ELD level, for example, the texts might be those designed for students in a lower grade. SDAIE classes use grade-level texts that native English speakers use. In ELD classes, instruction is suited to students' ELD level while in SDAIE classes, core content is taught using careful scaffolds. Finally,

ELD	SDAIE
Goal is English language development.	Goal is to teach grade-level content.
Content learning is a by-product of learning English.	Learning the English language is a by-product of learning content.
Instruction is in English.	Instruction is in English but can include primary language support.
Uses rich content through grade-appropriate texts.	Uses grade-level texts.
Teacher delivery is differentiated according to ELD levels.	Access to core is through intentionally planned scaffolds according to ELD levels.
Teachers assess students' language development.	Teachers assess students' academic content knowledge and skills.

FIGURE 4–3 *ELD and SDAIE (adapted from LAUSD handout)*

in ELD classes, language development is assessed, and in SDAIE classes, academic content is assessed.

Like other districts, LAUSD classifies English learners into one of five English language development levels: beginning, early intermediate, intermediate, early advanced, and advanced. Other states and organizations, such as TESOL (Teachers of English to Speakers of Other Languages) and WIDA (Word Class Instructional Design and Instruction), use different labels for these levels, but the language proficiency descriptors of students at each level are quite similar. Figure 4–4 lists an adaptation of the levels and descriptors found in the LAUSD Instructional Programs for English Learners parent brochure.

The LAUSD master plan for elementary students in the mainstream English program shows that English learners at levels 1 through 3 receive ELD instruction in language arts, math, science, social science, and health. Students at levels 4 and 5 receive SDAIE instruction in these subjects. All English learners receive SDAIE instruction in art, music, and physical education. At the secondary level, the plan is similar but the academic core content is taught in ELD classes for levels 1 and 2, and SDAIE is used for levels 3 to 5.

ELD teachers use a variety of techniques common to ESL classes, such as those listed in Figure 4–2, to help students move through the early levels of language development. These classes focus on specific language forms and functions. The emphasis is on oral language development, but reading and writing are also included.

SDAIE classes are designed to give emergent bilinguals access to core content through scaffolded instruction. There are four critical components of SDAIE lessons (retrieved from http://notebook.lausd.net/portal/page? _pageid=33,1170752,33_1181827&_dad=ptl, February 13, 2015). These are (1) content, (2) connections, (3) comprehensibility, and (4) interaction. Teaching the *content*

ELD Levels	Descriptors
1. Beginning	Limited receptive or productive skills. May use words or short phrases. May remain silent.
2. Early intermediate	Oral and written production limited to words or short phrases or questions they have memorized. Receptive language ability is still limited but continues to increase.
3. Intermediate	Oral and written production expands to sentences and paragraphs or more elaborated discourse. Students understand most of what is said.
4. Early advanced	Students can write paragraphs and short compositions. They can communicate more complex ideas orally. They understand almost all of what they hear.
5. Advanced	Students use more extensive vocabulary, including some technical vocabulary, and can read and write grade-level academic texts with sufficient scaffolding.

FIGURE 4–4 *ELD Levels (adapted from LAUSD parent brochure)*

involves determining the key concepts and skills from state standards, designing lesson objectives that focus on specific concepts and language, and using state-adopted curriculum materials. Teachers should build *connections* between what is to be learned and what students already know, including knowledge gained from their previous content learning, the processes or routines and skills they have learned, and their personal experiences.

Comprehensibility is the third critical element. Teachers should use visual clues such as pictures and diagrams. They should control the range of their vocabulary, repeat new key words in different contexts, and check often for comprehension. The final essential element for SDAIE instruction is *interaction*. Teachers are encouraged to use a variety of groupings, use modeling and sentence frames to scaffold instruction, have students use targeted academic language, and ask different types of questions. Teachers in LAUSD are given a lesson plan template that includes spaces for them to show how they will include these elements along with a plan for instruction that includes several steps: activating prior knowledge, introducing main concepts and objectives, providing input and modeling, engaging students in guided and independent practice, evaluating, and reviewing the lesson.

Los Angeles Unified has a well-developed professional development program for teachers. The district continues to refine their program and to train their teachers in delivering ELD and SDAIE instruction. Many other districts have also established programs to teach emergent bilinguals academic language and academic content.

ENGLISH LANGUAGE PROFICIENCY STANDARDS AND ASSESSMENTS

As the number of emergent bilinguals has continued to increase, even in states that previously had few English learners, most states now require prospective teachers to take classes to prepare for teaching second language students. They also require current teachers to take classes or attend professional development to equip them to teach emergent bilinguals. At the same time, methods and materials for teaching sheltered English have been developed and adopted by school districts.

Federal mandates and initiatives have increased the need for states to attend to the academic progress of English learners. In particular, the reauthorization of the elementary and secondary education act, titled the No Child Left Behind Act of 2001 (NCLB 2002), follows an accountability model that requires schools to test students on a regular basis and report the results. The results include scores of each subgroup, one of which is Limited English Proficient students. Schools that do not show Adequate Yearly Progress (AYP) that meets the standards set in NCLB for each group are subject to various penalties.

Title III of the No Child Left Behind Act, which focuses on English learners and is titled the English Language Acquisition, Language Enhancement, and Academic Achievement Act, lists several purposes, one of which is:

> to hold State educational agencies, local educational agencies, and schools accountable for increases in English proficiency and core academic content knowledge of limited English proficient children by requiring—
>
> (A) demonstrated improvements in the English proficiency of limited English proficient children each fiscal year; and
>
> (B) adequate yearly progress for limited English proficient children, including immigrant children and youth. (Retrieved from www2.ed.gov/policy/elsec/leg/esea02/index.html February 14, 2015.)

In addition, each state must report the number of English learners reclassified as fully English proficient. A positive aspect of NCLB is that it forced schools to allocate more resources and training for teaching English learners. To comply with NCLB, states developed English language proficiency standards and assessments to determine how well emergent bilinguals were progressing toward a high level of language proficiency. The WIDA (World Class Instructional Design and Assessment) organization works with many states to help them develop both their English language proficiency standards and their assessments, aligning them with the state's academic content standards (retrieved from www.wida.us February 14, 2015).

In addition the TESOL organization (2006) developed and published new *PK–12 English Language Proficiency Standards*. There are five standards. Standard 1 is: "English language learners communicate for social, intercultural, and instructional purposes within the school setting" (2). Standard 2 is: "English language learners communicate information, ideas and concepts necessary for success in the area of language arts" (2). The remaining three standards use identical wording for mathematics, science, and social studies. The previous TESOL standards had focused on conversational language, and the new standards signal the shift to the focus on academic language.

The TESOL publication includes a series of model performance indicators to guide the development of English language proficiency assessments. These indicators state what students in different grade-level clusters and at different levels of English proficiency can do in each mode (listening, speaking, reading, and writing) for topics in each content area. Each indicator includes the language function, such as *describe* or *explain*; the content they should communicate; and the support or strategy the teacher provides.

For example, in science on the topic of weather and natural disasters for the writing mode, a level 1 student should be able to "Draw and label charts of features, conditions, or occurrences using information from newspapers or the Internet"; a level 3 student should be able to "Compare features, conditions, or occurrences between two areas (e.g., native country and the U.S.) using information from multiple sources"; and a level 5 student should be able to "Interpret the global impact of varying features, conditions, or occurrences from modified grade-level source material" (85). Students could do this by comparing the temperature or rainfall of two countries.

As this example shows, students at different levels of English proficiency can all produce writing on the same topic. However, students at different proficiency levels can be asked to write in different ways with different kinds of support. In this example, a level 1 (beginner) student would "draw and label" using information from a newspaper or the Internet. A level 3 (intermediate) student would "compare" using multiple sources. Comparing requires students to write paragraphs or short essays. A level 5 (advanced) student would "interpret" using grade-level source material. At each level, students need to do more complex writing, and they receive less support. A newspaper or the Internet is easier to read for information than grade-level source material.

Additional pressure for schools to prepare emergent bilinguals academically comes from the Common Core State Standards (CCSS). This initiative developed by the Council of Chief State School Officers and the National Governors Associate for Best Practices includes rigorous college and career readiness standards for English language arts and mathematics, with additional standards for literacy in history/social studies, science, and technical subjects that were released in 2010 (www.core standards.com). In addition, the National Research Council, the National Science Teachers Association, the American Association for the Advancement of Science, and Achieve, a nonprofit education reform organization, have partnered to produce Next Generation Science Standards (retrieved from www.nextgenscience.org /next-generation-science-standards; February 14, 2015).

These new standards focus on conceptual understanding and literacy development. Students must solve problems, develop arguments based on evidence, and write reports, arguments, and narratives. The standards for English language arts shift the emphasis of instruction from fiction to informational text. The standards for literacy in the content areas require science and history/social studies teachers to teach students how to read and write academic texts in those subject areas. The math standards, as well, require students to develop the conceptual understanding needed to read and interpret word problems and to write explanations of the steps they take to solve problems. The science standards also require students to develop concepts they can discuss, read, and write about.

Several professional books have been written to prepare teachers of English learners to meet the Common Core State Standards. For example, in his book *Building Academic Language: Meeting Common Core Standards Across the Disciplines, Grades 5–12*, Zwiers (2014) describes a number of activities designed to build academic language for emergent bilinguals with an emphasis on oral language. The author connects the different activities to specific standards. Another useful book is Boyd-Batstone's *Helping English Language Learners Meet the Common Core: Assessment and Instructional Strategies K–12* (2013). This book includes both instructional strategies and ways to assess English learners.

The California Together organization has analyzed the impact of the new standards on emergent bilinguals, and they published "Raise Your Voice on Behalf of English Learners: The English Learners and Common Core Advocacy Toolkit" (retrieved from www.californianstogether.org/reports/; February 8, 2015). The organization points out that the new standards focus on the language students need to choose appropriate registers in different academic contexts. Students need to understand how to write a history report, describe the steps in a science experiment, or explain their reasoning for solving a problem in math. Students can only do this if every teacher is both a content teacher and a language teacher.

California Together notes that many of the aspects of the new standards align with research-based best practices for English learners. Teaching to the standards requires teachers to actively engage students in interactive, inquiry-based activities and to teach the academic language of each subject area. This call for a shift from teacher-centered to student-centered pedagogy is promising; however, the organization also notes that instruction for English learners in many schools does not employ the practices that are recommended. Emergent bilinguals are not being prepared to meet the new standards, in part because many have been enrolled in reading and math interventions and have not developed adequate background knowledge in science and social studies or high levels of literacy and math. For many emergent bilinguals, instruction has been at a low level, and it will take time to implement practices to meet the new standards.

Federal mandates such as the No Child Left Behind Act, which requires extensive testing of all students and imposes sanctions on schools that do not show progress, have focused attention on education for English learners. The Common Core State Standards and the Next Generation Science Standards are more rigorous than previous standards, and the assessments for these standards will be difficult for English learners to pass. Meanwhile, states have developed English language proficiency standards and aligned them with their content standards. The TESOL and WIDA organizations have also developed assessments to measure English learners' growth in language proficiency.

State departments of education and individual school districts have responded to these mandates and initiatives by hiring new teachers who are trained to teach emergent bilinguals and by providing professional development for current teachers. Some districts, such as Los Angeles Unified, have the resources to provide professional development for their teachers. Many other districts lack the expertise to provide this sort of professional development, so they adopt programs and training that have been developed by different researchers or organizations. In the following sections we describe some of the most widely used programs that have been designed to equip teachers to teach both academic language and subject matter content.

Guided Language Acquisition Design (GLAD)

Project GLAD is a model of professional development that has been used for over thirty years to train teachers to use sheltered instruction. The training focuses on strategies to develop both language acquisition and literacy. According to the Project GLAD website, "The strategies and model promote English language acquisition, academic achievement, and cross-cultural skills" (retrieved from www.project glad.com). This model, supported by government grants, was developed at a school district in Southern California. Currently Project GLAD trainers conduct training sessions throughout California and in Texas, the two states with the greatest number of emergent bilinguals.

GLAD describes its program by listing the *what* and the *how*. The *what* is the organizational structure. GLAD uses an integrated, balanced approach to literacy. Reading, writing, speaking, and listening are integrated across the various content areas, and students are also taught metacognitive strategies. The *how* consists of the steps in the training. These include two days of research and theory plus a series of strategies teachers can use. This is followed by four or five days of demonstration lessons. There is also follow-up coaching and an opportunity for some faculty to become GLAD trainers.

GLAD is a well-established model of professional development that has been implemented in a number of school districts. It is research based and uses strategies for both language and literacy acquisition. Districts with long-term GLAD professional development have been recognized as exemplary. GLAD has been used in more than 1,000 school sites and has certified over 1,200 trainers. It has been used in a variety of ESL and bilingual programs.

Quality Teaching for English Learners (QTEL)

Quality Teaching for English Learners (QTEL) was developed by Walqui and her colleagues at WestEd, a nonprofit research and development agency in California. The model is based on Walqui's work with school districts across the country. QTEL has been researched and implemented primarily at the middle and high school levels.

It is extremely challenging to work with secondary-level emergent bilinguals because they are so diverse and have only a limited time to reach grade-level norms in the academic subject areas. As Short and Fitzsimmons (2007) point out, these students face double the work of native speakers because they have to learn English and learn academic subjects in English. The QTEL model is designed to accelerate learning for older emergent bilinguals and equip them with the academic language they need to succeed in school.

The model has five principles and, for each principle, associated goals.

1. Sustain academic rigor.
2. Hold high expectations.
3. Engage students in quality interactions.
4. Sustain a focus on language.
5. Develop quality curriculum.

The first principle's goal is to promote deep disciplinary knowledge and engage students in disciplinary concepts and cognitive skills. The second principle is to *hold high expectations*. Teachers may interpret a students' lack of English proficiency as an inability to do academic work. However, QTEL encourages teachers to hold high expectations for all students from the beginning. The goals that follow are to engage students in high-challenge, high-support tasks and to engage students in developing their own expertise. The third principle for the QTEL model is to *engage students in quality interactions*. Language and content knowledge are developed during interactions with peers, so the goal is to engage students in sustained inter-actions with teachers and peers as they construct knowledge together. The fourth principle is to *sustain a focus on language*. The goal is to promote language learning and disciplinary language use through meaningful interactions. Teachers should not simplify communication or academic content. Instead, they should focus on the academic language students need. The final principle is to *develop quality curricu-lum*. The goal is to scaffold learning (Ward 2010). As Ward concludes:

> Whether anchored in textbook or teacher-designed lessons and units, quality cur-riculum must incorporate the learners' lives and experiences, the context in which they live, and the multilinguistic and multicultural composition of the classroom, school and community. (28)

Teachers who have gone through QTEL professional development engage all their students, even those at beginning levels, in rigorous academic content. They use manipulatives and models to help students think about difficult concepts.

Students are seated in clusters of three or four and interact as they complete assignments. They are given language scaffolds, such as sentence frames, to carry out different tasks. For example, in a geography class studying landforms, students were assigned different parts of the United States and asked to identify landforms in that section of the country. Looking at two-dimensional relief maps of their assigned areas, students discussed the landforms using the sentence frame "In the _____ region of the United States, there are _____ [number] kinds of landforms. There are _____, _____, and _____." Students completed the sentences identifying the parts of the country using terms like "In the *Southwestern* region of the United States, there are *three* kinds of landforms, *mountains*, *deserts*, and *canyons*."

Students make charts, graphs, and other visuals to represent their ideas. In schools using the QTEL model, graphic displays line the halls. Teachers encourage students to use all their language resources as they learn academic content in English; so, students who speak the same first language may be grouped together and use their first language and English as they solve problems and carry out projects. Teachers serve as facilitators and guides. Rather than lecturing, they spend most of their time moving around the class from group to group answering questions and offering suggestions.

QTEL has been successfully implemented in a number of schools. It targets secondary emergent bilinguals at different proficiency levels. In addition to the teacher professional development, WestEd has helped to design materials and curriculum for teaching older learners key concepts from each of the content areas and the language needed to communicate that content.

Sheltered Instruction Observation Protocol (SIOP)

The most widely used model for professional development in the U.S. is Sheltered Instruction Observation Protocol (SIOP). This model has been used with both ESL and mainstream teachers. Researchers at the National Center for Research on Education, Diversity, and Excellence (CREDE) developed SIOP in the early 1990s. The researchers reviewed techniques that had been shown to be effective for teaching emergent bilinguals as well as approaches to professional development that had been effective.

The result of the early research was the development of an observation tool that could be used to assess how well teachers implemented key practices for English learners. CREDE received funding for a large research study that had three goals. These were to

1. develop an explicit model of sheltered instruction,
2. use that model to train teachers in effective sheltered strategies, and

3. conduct field experiments and collect data to evaluate teacher change and the effects of sheltered instruction on LEP [limited English proficient] students. (Echevarria, Vogt, and Short 2012, 15)

The research was carried out at the middle school level in four large districts, two on the west coast and two on the east coast. Teachers were trained to use a set of techniques and strategies and they were observed and assessed using the observation tool. SIOP was first used with a small group of teachers and refined, and then it was implemented with a much larger group of teachers during a three-year period.

The observation instrument continued to be refined as teachers and researchers considered how best to implement the strategies. During this time, the researchers realized that the observation tool could also be used as a guide for planning lessons (Short 1999). Since the early study, additional research has been carried out in schools implementing SIOP. In addition, a number of books have been produced to explain the model and show how it can be applied in different subject areas and at different grade levels. There are separate books on using SIOP for teaching science (Short, Vogt, and Echevarria 2011), mathematics (Echevarria, Vogt, and Short 2010), language arts (Vogt, Echavarría, and Short 2010), and history-social studies (Short, Vogt, and Echevarria 2011). These books include model lessons and units at different grade levels for teaching the subject.

There is a lesson plan checklist for teachers to use as they plan lessons following the SIOP model. Lessons are assessed using the SIOP protocol, which includes the same items with a five-point rating scale used to evaluate the lessons. There are thirty items on the checklist. These are divided into three sections: (1) preparation, (2) instruction, and (3) review/evaluation.

Preparation for a SIOP lesson includes writing content and language objectives; choosing and listing the content concepts to be taught; identifying supplementary material to be used, such as graphs or models; listing ways to adapt the content as necessary to accommodate different proficiency levels; planning meaningful activities that integrate content concepts; and language practice. While all of these are important for planning effective lessons, they take time to write, so teachers often choose one or two of these components to focus on and then gradually add more.

The second section of the checklist, instruction, has several parts: building background, making input comprehensible, implementing specific strategies, planning for interaction, providing time for students to practice and apply what they have learned, and using appropriate techniques for lesson delivery. Each of these parts, in turn, is further broken down; for example, building background includes explicitly linking concepts to students' backgrounds and explicitly linking past learning to new concepts. The practice/application section lists providing hand-on materials and/or manipulatives, providing activities for students to apply content and language knowledge, and providing activities that integrate reading, writing, listening, and speaking.

The last section is review/evaluation. This section includes giving a comprehensive review of key vocabulary, giving a comprehensive review of key content concepts, providing feedback to students regularly, and conducting assessments of student comprehension and learning throughout the lesson on all lesson objectives (Short 1999). As can be seen, the checklist for lesson planning and the evaluation tool are comprehensive and explicit. This has made the SIOP attractive for school district personnel.

Although many districts have adopted SIOP, it takes long-term professional development for teachers to implement all aspects of this model. In some cases, districts or individual schools have only offered limited training for teachers. All the components are grounded in research and best practices, but the planning that is involved is very time-consuming, especially for a teacher who teaches several different classes or subjects each day. In addition, personnel who assess the implementation of the model need to be knowledgeable about all the components. As a result, in some schools teachers use a few strategies from SIOP without fully implementing the model.

A Critique of SIOP

Crawford and Reyes (2015) have written a book critiquing SIOP. They point out that while sheltered instruction, as conceived by Krashen (1985), was, in effect, a late-exit bilingual program, SIOP is frequently used as a stand-alone ESL program. In addition, while sheltered classes in Krashen's model were reserved for students at the intermediate and advanced stages of English language development, SIOP is often applied with students at beginning stages.

SIOP includes a number of techniques for making the input comprehensible; however, there is also a strong emphasis on direct teaching of language. This raises the question of whether the developers of SIOP take what Krashen would call an *acquisition approach* in which language is picked up naturally when students receive comprehensible input in the target language, or a *learning approach* in which learners develop language as the result of direct teaching. As a result, Crawford and Reyes question whether SIOP has a consistent theoretical base.

In addition to questioning the theoretical basis for SIOP, Crawford and Reyes examine the research base. The claim that SIOP is a valid and reliable measure of sheltered instruction is based on a study conducted by the authors of SIOP. In their study, the SIOP researchers asked four teachers who were experienced in sheltered instruction to view six 45-minute videos of lessons. In three of the lessons, teachers used sheltering techniques consistent with the SIOP features, and in the other three, the teachers did not use the SIOP features. The four teachers all agreed that the three videos that showed teachers using sheltering techniques scored higher on the SIOP rubric. This was a small study involving only four teachers. In addition, the basis for judging whether the lessons were sheltered was the SIOP rubric. There was no attempt to show that SIOP equals sheltered instruction.

However, SIOP is widely used, and follow-up studies have focused on whether or not ELs in SIOP classes achieve at higher rates than ELs in classes that do not provide instruction with the SIOP features. A review of the published studies by the federal Institute of Education Sciences concluded that no evaluation study of the model meets its evidence standards and so the Institute cannot draw any conclusions as to the effectiveness of SIOP. Krashen (2013) reviewed five studies that provided comparative evidence regarding the model's effectiveness. Four of the studies were conducted by SIOP researchers and one by independent researchers. Three of the studies showed no significant difference between classes with teachers trained in SIOP and teachers with no training. In the other two studies, there was a small positive effect size for students in classes with SIOP trained teachers. If more evidence for the effectiveness of SIOP can be shown in future research, the claims the publisher of the SIOP materials now makes would be strengthened.

Despite the lack of a consistent theoretical base or strong research evidence, SIOP continues to be widely used as a model of sheltered instruction. Like many other program models we have discussed, SIOP reflects expert opinion of best practices for teaching emergent bilinguals.

CALLA, GLAD, QTEL, and SIOP are four of the most widely used methods for teaching both academic content and academic language. They share a number of features and use the research-based strategies that Saunders and his colleagues (Saunders, Goldenberg, and Marcelletti 2013) recommend. As the number of emergent bilingual students continues to increase, more teachers will be educated to use instructional approaches such as these.

PLANTS AND SEEDS

We began this chapter with the description of an extended unit that Natascha developed around the novel *Esperanza Rising* to teach academic language and language arts content to her emergent bilinguals. We conclude with another unit—a science unit about plants and seeds that Rosa, a first-grade bilingual teacher, developed. Like Natascha, Rosa organized around units of study and taught both academic language and content to her students.

Rosa is a first-grade teacher in a small farming town in Iowa. Many of her students began school in pre-kindergarten as non-English speakers. About half of her students are native English speakers. In the past fifteen years the number of Spanish-speaking emergent bilinguals has more than doubled in Iowa (Batalova and McHugh 2010). Families have come to the area because there is work in the meat packing industry and in agriculture. Rosa came to the area with her family as a migrant child. Now, she has finished college and has a job in her district as one of the few bilingual teachers. The district has set up a dual language strand within the school. Teachers in the strand teach content in Spanish and English to both native English and native Spanish speakers. In this way, all the children who are in the dual language strand become bilingual and biliterate by the end of elementary school. Rosa is the dual language teacher in the first grade.

Rosa organizes her curriculum around themes, and she teaches language and content. She also draws on her students' home languages and cultures. She knows that her students need academic language and content knowledge to succeed in school. Science content fascinates her first graders and can be made comprehensible through visuals and hands-on activities. The science standards for her grade level include carrying out field investigations, asking questions, and drawing conclusions. In addition, students should be able to observe nature and to identify and label living things in nature.

To meet these standards, Rosa and the other first-grade teachers plan a unit on plant growth answering the big question "How do seeds grow into plants?" In the process of answering this question, they investigate sub-questions, such as "What makes a seed grow into a plant?" "What are the stages of plant growth?" and "How long do seeds take to grow into plants?" The teachers share activity ideas and put together a text set that supports a range of readers around this theme. During the unit, Rosa, as the dual language teacher, introduces concepts in both languages and reads books in both English and Spanish. Figure 4–5 lists the books Rosa used during this unit.

Rosa starts her unit by bringing in a large jar filled with many different kinds of seeds. She shows the jar to the class, walking around the room so that everyone can see what is in the jar. Then she asks, "What are these things in this jar?" Her students answer enthusiastically, "Seeds!" Then Rosa asks them if they can identify any of the seeds. Some children recognize corn; others recognize the beans, the pumpkin, and the watermelon seeds. Some children even recognize lettuce seeds and pepper seeds, explaining that they help their mothers plant those seeds in their family garden. Some of her emergent bilinguals know the names of the seeds in Spanish and, as the English words are used, they begin to pick up the new vocabulary.

Ada, Alma Flor. 1990a. *Just One Seed*. Carmel, CA: Hampton-Brown.

————. 1990b. *Una semilla nada más*. Carmel, CA. Hampton-Brown.

Blackaby, Susan. 2003. *Plant Packages: A Book about Seeds*. North Mankato, MN: Capstone.

Bunting, Eve. 1996. *Sunflower House*. New York: Trumpet.

Carle, Eric. 2009. *The Tiny Seed*. New York: Little Simon.

Gibbons, Gail. 1991. *From Seeds to Plants*. Carmel, CA: Hampton-Brown Books.

Heller, Ruth. 1999. *The Reason for a Flower: A Book About Flowers, Pollen, and Seeds*. New York: Penguin Putnam Books for Young Readers.

————. 1983. *La razón de ser una flor*. New York: Scholastic.

Hutts Aston, Dianna, and Sylvia Long. 2014. *A Seed Is Sleepy*. San Francisco, CA: Chronicle Books.

Jordan, Helene. 2000. *How a Seed Grows*. New York: HarperCollins.

————. 1996. *Cómo crece una semilla*. New York: HarperCollins.

Krauss, Ruth. 1945. *The Carrot Seed*. New York: Harper Trophy.

————. 1978. *La semilla de zanahoria*. Translated by A. Palacios. New York: Scholastic.

Lucca, Mario. 2001. *Plants Grow from Seeds*. Washington, DC: National Geographic Society.

————. 2003. *De las semillas nacen las plantas*. Washington, DC: National Geographic Society.

Marzollo, Jean. 1996. *I'm a Seed*. Carmel, CA: Hampton-Brown.

McMillan, Bruce. 1994. *Growing Colors*. New York: William Morrow & Co.

Nelson, Kadir. 2015. *If You Plant a Seed*. New York: HarperCollins.

Rattini, Kristin Baird. 2014. *Seed to Plant*. Washington, DC: National Geographic.

Rajczak, Kristen. 2011. *Watch Corn Grow*. New York: Gareth Stevens Publishing.

Robbins, Ken. 2005. *Seeds*. New York: Atheneum.

FIGURE 4–5 *Plants and Seeds Bibliography*

Seed Growth

Rosa plans several activities focused on answering the question, "How does a seed grow into a plant?" She begins by reading two limited text books, *Seeds to Plant* (Rattini 2014) and *If You Plant a Seed* (Nelson 2015). She follows this with another book, *How a Seed Grows* (Jordan 2000). Later she reads the Spanish version of this book, *¿Cómo crece una semilla?* (Jordan 1996). The next day she reads *Plants Grow from Seeds* and *De las semillas nacen las plantas* (Lucca 2001, 2003). These limited text books show different kinds of seeds and the plants that grow from the seeds, provide key content information, and are accessible for all the students in her dual language classroom even when she is reading in their second language.

After reading and discussing the books, Rosa has the students form groups of four with two native English speakers and two native Spanish speakers in each group. The students push their desks together, and she gives each group a plastic bag with a variety of seeds. She tells them to put the seeds that are the same together. The children group similar seeds and talk about the seeds in both Spanish and English as they work. When they are finished, Rosa puts a large piece of butcher paper on the wall. She draws a circle in the center and writes the words *seed* and *semillas* in it. Then she asks the students if they can identify some of the seeds in their bag. She begins with one group. They know which are the bean seeds. Spanish speakers tell her it is the seed of the *frijol*. Rosa draws a line from *seed/semillas* and makes a small circle. In this circle she writes *bean* and *frijol*. She continues this activity until each group has identified one type of seed. The most difficult is the tiny carrot seed. As each group responds, Rosa adds to the web she has drawn.

Rosa then reads additional books about plant growth. The first book is *Growing Colors* (McMillan 1994), a book of colorful photos showing various fruits and vegetables. The students and the teacher identify the fruit from the plants and talk about the colors, shapes, and the textures. They decide, for example, that an orange is round, orange, and smooth; an ear of corn is long, oval, yellow, and bumpy; and raspberries and blackberries are red, black, oval or round, and rough. Rosa writes some of these descriptive words on the board, and the students use comparative forms as they talk about how the fruits and vegetables are the same and different. For example, they might say, "The ear of corn is bigger than the orange" or "The raspberries are rougher than the orange." Rosa also writes a sentence frame on the board, "The ____ is ____-er than the ____," and students use this scaffold as they discuss the fruits and vegetables.

Next, she hands out a blank chart with the word *seed* written at the top of the first column and the words *color*, *texture*, and *shape* heading the other columns. Working in their groups, the children examine their seeds again. They write the name of each type of seed on the chart and then fill in a description for each kind of seed. Students then share their descriptive words and Rosa adds the words to the web that she made earlier. Through this activity Rosa teaches the vocabulary terms for the fruits and vegetables. This builds her students' content knowledge. She also teaches academic language, including descriptive adjectives and comparative endings and structures.

Now that the students have started to develop vocabulary and concepts related to seeds, Rosa moves on to the topic of seed growth. Rosa reminds her class about a story they read in kindergarten, *The Carrot Seed* (Krauss 1945), and takes out the big book version of the story. To help the children remember the story, Rosa shows the pictures and has the children tell her what is happening in the story. Then the class reads the story together, chiming in at familiar places. This is the story of a boy who patiently waits for his carrot seed to grow. Rosa points out that it takes a long time for carrot seeds to grow. The next day during language arts, Rosa and the students read *Just One Seed* (Ada 1990a) in English and then *Una semilla nada más* (Ada 1990b) in Spanish the following day. These pop-up big books have a story that has many similarities to *The Carrot Seed* because the mother, father, brother, and sister tell the boy in the story that the seed he has planted will not grow. He takes care of the seed and, in the end, it is a huge sunflower that is not only beautiful but produces seeds for people and animals to eat. *The Carrot Seed* and *Just One Seed* provide the perfect opportunity for Rosa to reinforce concepts related to plant growth and to help students develop academic language as they use language forms and structures. The class works with Rosa to complete a Venn diagram comparing and contrasting the two stories.

Another story that Rosa reads to the children from her text set of books on plants and seeds is *I'm a Seed* (Marzollo 1996), a story told from the point of view of two different seeds as they grow, one into a flower and the other into a pumpkin. The students discuss the steps of plant growth for each plant, and they also discuss the differences between fiction and informative text. The part of the story telling about how the plants grow contains facts, but the students recognize that since the seeds talk to each other, this is fiction. Drawing on the information in all the books, Rosa and the students list the steps involved in a seed growing into a plant. Then she guides students as they convert this information into a paragraph. She models how to use the cardinal numbers *first*, *second*, *third* in English and *primero*, *segundo*, *tercero* in Spanish to show the sequence.

To continue to develop content knowledge and language, the class reads several other books about plants, plant growth, and seeds, including *The Reason for a Flower: A Book about Flowers, Pollen, and Seeds* (Heller 1999) and the Spanish version, *La razón de ser una flor* (Heller 1983); *Plant Packages: A Book About Seeds* (Blackaby 2003); *Sunflower House* (Bunting 1996); *The Tiny Seed* (Carle 2009); and a relevant book for children living in Iowa, the corn state, *Watch Corn Grow* (Rajczak 2011).

After the various activities, Rosa asks the students what they think their next project will be. "We're going to plant seeds and grow plants!" they answer excitedly. The next day, Rosa has the children make their own plant journals with construction paper. She explains that they will draw and write about how their plants grow. They will record information and report what they find, like scientists do.

They will also refer to the many books they have read in class and look at books such as *Seeds* (Robbins 2005) and *A Seed Is Sleepy* (Hutts Aston and Long 2014) that tell them more about different kinds of seeds and how they grow.

During science time, the students choose their seeds, wet paper towels, wrap their seeds, and put them in plastic bags. Rosa has some groups put their seeds on a windowsill where they will get sun and has other groups put their seeds inside a cabinet where it is dark. Still others are placed in the refrigerator in the classroom. She explains that the students will conduct an experiment to find out how these different conditions influence plant growth.

During the next several days, students record in their plant journals the date and the number of days since the seed was put into the wet paper towel. They also draw a picture of the plant and label it to record how the seeds are sprouting. In addition, they write one or two sentences based on their observations of the plant growth. As the plants sprout and grow, they measure and graph them, comparing the growth in different environments: sun, dark, and cold.

Rosa's students eventually transplant the healthy sprouts in dirt to watch them grow over the coming month. Rosa's unit on plant growth helped her students develop both language and content. Rosa's students answered the questions, "What makes a seed grow into a plant?" "What are the stages of plant growth?" and "How long do seeds take to grow into plants?" They read and talked about texts of differing levels of difficulty that were connected by a common theme. They compared and contrasted the seeds and how they grew. The students read fiction and informational texts. They also read graphs and charts and kept their own plant journals. Throughout their theme study the students were learning academic content and, at the same time, academic language needed to meet the science standards, becoming more proficient language users.

CONCLUSION

The fourth principle is that teachers should teach both academic language and academic content. Emergent bilinguals face double the work of native English speakers because they need to learn academic English, and they need to learn academic content taught in English (Short and Fitzsimmons 2007). Teachers have responded by developing methods for teaching language and content.

Content-based ESL involves teaching ESL using academic subject matter as the content. In these classes, teachers focus on teaching English through social studies, language arts, science, and math. This is a shift from earlier communicative methods that taught the language needed for everyday activities outside of school, such as clothes, food, shopping, and the weather.

Over time, a distinction has developed between content-based ESL and sheltered classes. Teachers in sheltered classes teach grade-level content and use techniques to make the academic content comprehensible. In sheltered classes the focus is on teaching content while the purpose of content-based ESL classes is to teach English. Content-based ESL came to be called English language development, and in California the sheltered classes designed for intermediate and advanced students were called SDAIE.

As these changes were taking place, federal mandates and initiatives required states to assess students and report their results. There was a move toward accountability and new, more rigorous standards were developed. In addition, states were required to develop English language proficiency standards and ways to assess growth in English. The TESOL organization and WIDA helped develop performance indicators that could be used to assess English learners.

Teacher education programs in many areas include classes in how to teach emergent bilinguals, so new teachers are better prepared to teach all their students. In addition, school districts and different organizations have implemented professional development programs aimed at equipping teachers to work effectively with English learners. Some of the most widely used methods or programs include CALLA, GLAD, QTEL, and SIOP. As the number of emergent bilinguals continues to increase, new methods will be developed to provide all students with academic content knowledge and the academic knowledge needed to communicate that content.

APPLICATIONS

1. Both Natascha and Rosa taught their English learners academic content and academic language by scaffolding instruction. List some of the ways that these teachers scaffolded their instruction to make the content comprehensible.

2. In Figure 4–2 we list several ways to make content comprehensible. Try one of these that you have not used before. Describe what you did and evaluate the effectiveness of this technique.

3. We discussed and gave examples of language objectives. Review the content standards for your grade level in one subject area. Choose one standard and write a content objective to meet the standard. Then write one or more language objectives that are based on the language demands of this content objective.

4. Write a performance indicator that you could use to assess one of your language objectives. Tell what beginning, intermediate, and advanced students would need to do to meet the objective.

5. Draw a Venn diagram and use it to show similarities and differences between ELD and SDAIE classes. Be prepared to share this with classmates.

6. List some of the classes or professional development you have had to better prepare you to teach emergent bilinguals. What has been most useful? What specifically made the class or training useful? Prepare to share this with classmates.

5

Teaching Should Be Meaningful and Purposeful

MEANING AND PURPOSE FOR FUTURE TEACHERS

This chapter opens with a cultural graffiti board that was created in a teacher education course by future teachers of emergent bilingual students (see Figure 5–1). Groups of students in this course, called "Establishing a Supportive Learning Environment in the Bilingual Classroom," produced the graffiti board after completing several other activities to help them consider their own cultures. Every activity built on the previous ones as students answered the question, "What is culture?"

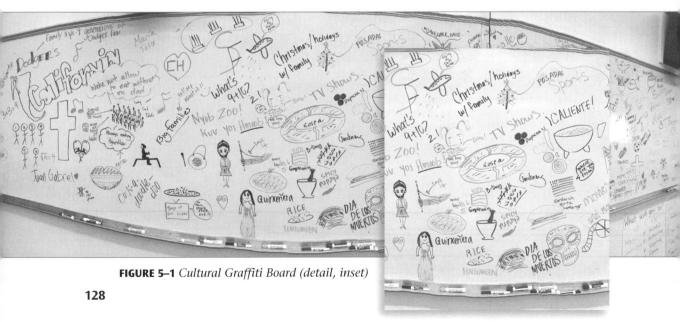

FIGURE 5–1 *Cultural Graffiti Board (detail, inset)*

128

Mary and Elizabeth, the professors for the course, first organized students into groups. Each group represented as great a variety of cultures as possible so that different voices could be heard during group discussions. Some of the students were Anglos with a variety of backgrounds, others were Hmong, and the majority were Latinos. The groups were first asked to define the term *culture*. They were told not to look up a definition, but to consider their own experiences and ideas. Some of the groups defined culture as their home language and ways they did things at holidays. Others mentioned typical cultural dishes and strict rules. Still others mentioned expectations like going to college or being married in the church. The groups shared their definitions with their classmates.

After considering the various definitions of culture, each group made a mandala. The groups were given a template to complete, and each student in the group chose one aspect of his/her culture and represented it on the outside circle of the group mandala. After sharing the drawings, the group decided what all the members of the group had in common and wrote that in the middle. For example, a group with two students of Mexican background and one of Hmong background found they had a lot in common, including food, religion, sports, family, language, and celebrations (see Figures 5–2 and 5–3). Another group representing Hmong and Mexican cultures chose just one commonality, family (see Figure 5–3).

After completing the mandalas the students in each group wrote one stanza for a group "I Am from" poem. Figure 5–4 lists some possible choices students were given to complete their lines of the poem. The students were also given examples, including "I am from Texas and Mexican parents," "I am from always respect your

FIGURE 5–2 *Cultural Mandala 1*

FIGURE 5–3 *Cultural Mandala 2*

"I Am from" Poem

I am from _____ (place of birth) and _____

(nationality, family ancestry, place).

I am from _____ (things you were told as a child) and

_____ (a song or saying from your childhood).

I am from _____ (specific item from your childhood) and _____

(objects from your home).

I am from _____ (a religious memory) and _____

(family foods).

FIGURE 5–4 *Samples for "I Am from" Poem*

elders and ranchero music," and "I am from baking Christmas cookies and freckles, from Joyce, my mom, and Fred, my dad." They then wrote their individual stanzas. Once finished, each group put the stanzas together and shared their group poem with the whole class.

Since all of the students were studying to be teachers, they were asked to draw a classroom organizational plan and decide how they could display their culture in that classroom. Students chose things like the Mexican flag, posters of soccer teams, piñatas, or photos of people dressed in traditional clothing at celebrations. This led to the class creation of the cultural graffiti wall pictured in Figure 5–1. Previous activities had given students multiple ideas about what they could contribute to the wall, and, as the photo shows, students included words in their home languages (English, Hmong, and Spanish), customs (*Día de los Muertos*, Day of the Dead), costumes (Hmong New Year), traditional dishes (*pozole*, Mexican soup and rice), family celebrations (birthday, *Posadas*), music (*Los Tigres del Norte*, a Mexican musical group), sports (soccer ball, Dodgers), and religion (cross).

The culture graffiti wall pulled together students' reflections of their own cultures and those of their classmates. One final activity to make the students think even more deeply on the topic of culture was the Culture Venn diagram. Students were given the following directions:

- Partner up with someone in your group.
- Each of you pick a shape that represents your culture.
- Draw your shapes overlapping (like a traditional Venn diagram).

- On the outside sections, write characteristics of your culture.
- On the overlap, write about how your cultures are similar.

Each pair of students used a different piece of poster paper and worked to think of something that represented their culture. Figure 5–5 shows Jessica's representation of the Hmong drum so often used in both festivals and funerals in traditional Hmong culture, and Gregoria's drawing of the nopal cactus that is symbolic of both arid landscapes in Mexico and the fruit that is often eaten and used for different purposes. Within each symbol the students wrote reflections of their own culture. Then they wrote what they had in common in the overlap section.

After these activities, the students in this teacher education class looked again at their original definitions of culture, added to them, and then read articles to see how others had defined culture. The approach Mary and Elizabeth took in using these different activities represents the principle for this chapter, "Teaching should be meaningful and purposeful." The activities were not only meaningful for the students because of the connections to their own cultures but purposeful as well. These future teachers considered how to include culture into their own teaching

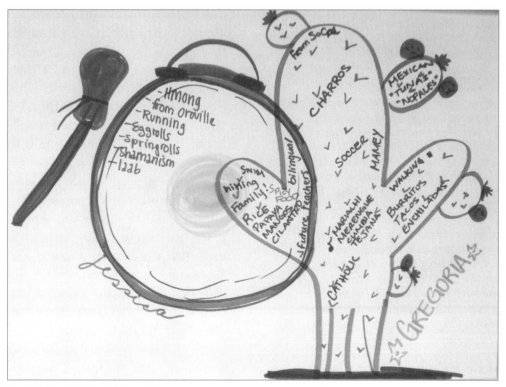

FIGURE 5–5 *Cultural Venn Diagram*

in the future. They could see the extensive scaffolding that could and should take place for students to understand concepts like culture more deeply. They also could see that the activities were purposeful because they could adapt these activities with their own future students.

ENGAGEMENT THROUGH PUBLISHING

Teachers we have worked with have found different ways to make teaching meaningful. Mike, an extremely creative fourth-grade teacher who engaged the multilingual, multicultural students in his classroom in activities that had meaning and purpose for them, provides an example. One project Mike used was a class newspaper that the students named *28 Times*. Their classroom number was 28, so the students named their paper after the location, like the *New York Times*.

Mike's students read several issues of the local newspaper. They noticed the editorials often discussed things that needed improvement in their city, so they decided to write their own editorials that focused on how to improve their school. Giving students the opportunity to write and publish in the newspaper engaged Mike's students. They had a choice of what to write about. "Are the Bathrooms Your Playground?" is a good example of one student's editorial on how to improve the school (see Figure 5–6).

The author had a clear message: cleaning up the bathrooms would improve his school. In the process of writing their editorials, Mike's students learned to write a new genre. Since the piece was published and distributed around the school, the students were motivated to use conventional English forms in their writing. This newspaper project was meaningful for Mike's students because they wrote about something

Editorials
Roeding Talks Back

ARE THE BATHROOMS YOUR PLAYGROUND?

Messy, messy, messy. The bathrooms are so messy. They are dirty and paper towels are laying almost everywhere. I would like the bathrooms to be cleaner and for people to treat the bathrooms like their own bathroom. Is this what your bathroom at home looks like? I mean, why would our Roeding School students play around in the bathrooms? I think the students should know better than to mess up the bathrooms. You don't want your bathroom to be dirty, or paper towels lying everywhere do you? I think we all want our school bathrooms to be clean.

FIGURE 5–6 *Student Editorial: "Are the Bathrooms Your Playground?"*

that was important to them, improving their school. There was also a definite purpose for the editorial. The author was eliciting support from other students in keeping the bathrooms clean.

The newspaper production was of particular significance to the emergent bilingual students in Mike's classroom because it gave them a voice. Cummins (2011), in discussing English learners (ELs), explains:

> EL students are often implicitly or explicitly defined by what they lack (i.e., their limited English proficiency). This is why creative writing (in English and/or their home language) that is shared with multiple audiences (e.g., through school, community, or international websites) is particularly significant for students from EL and/or marginalized communities. (145)

The *28 Times* project was creative writing that was shared throughout the school and supported students' language growth, membership in the school community, and understanding of one genre of writing.

Mike organized his class so that all students, including his English learners, could show what they learned. He did this by involving them in various projects, including art, drama, construction, and video as well as through their writing. Besides the publication of the newspaper, *28 Times*, Mike's students were immersed in varied and exciting learning experiences over the years that he taught in this inner city school. Projects included the following:

- *"Eureka*—A History of California" was the title of a student-created museum that featured a range of exhibits about their state, including life-sized dioramas with student actors depicting important historical events and students as docents leading tours for parents and other students through the exhibits in the classroom museum.
- "Under the Sea" was a student-created, oversized portable scene that filled the classroom with animated sea creatures created by the students. The exhibit began with a California coastal tide pool and moved out under the waves into a kelp forest and finally into the murky depths of the Pacific Ocean.
- "28 Roeding Mall" was a December activity that derived its name from the name of the school, Roeding. Student entrepreneurs raised money by making and selling a variety of items, including holiday cookies and candies, Hmong New Year treats and ornaments, holiday cards, and stickers. The students created business names, logos, and newspaper advertisements that they included in *28 Times*. They also produced a shopping guide with full-page advertisements. Besides distributing their guide throughout the school,

students scripted and produced a radio commercial aired over the school intercom and a video commercial shown to the student body during lunch hour a day before the mall opened. Two days before the winter break, students opened their mall and sold their "products."

ENGAGEMENT

All these projects engaged Mike's students in learning. A great deal has been written about the importance of engagement for student learning. Strong, Silver, and Robinson (1995) asked students and teachers about the kind of work they found engaging and the work they hated to do. Respondents said that "work that was repetitive, that required little or no thought, and that was forced on them by others" (1) was work they hated. On the other hand, "work that stimulated their curiosity, permitted them to express their creativity, and fostered positive relationships with others" (1) was engaging. The activities that Mike, Mary, and Elizabeth involved their students in were all engaging because they stimulated curiosity, allowed students to be creative, and encouraged positive social interaction.

Strong and his colleagues suggest the acronym SCORE to represent the goals of people who are engaged. SCORE stands for *success, curiosity, originality, relationships,* and *energy.* They point out that students who are engaged want to succeed, they are curious, they are encouraged to express themselves in original ways, they are involved with others as they work, and they do all this with energy. As we reflect on the mandala project, the cultural graffiti wall, the *28 Times* publication, the "Under the Sea" classroom project and others, it is clear that all of these goals for engagement were met.

Success

What, then, exactly must teachers do to help students meet the goals for engagement? First of all, it is important to convince students that they can succeed. Too often students are given a project but they don't know what successfully completing the project involves. For that reason, teachers must clearly articulate the criteria for successful completion and give feedback as students work on a project. Some teachers show students a rubric that lists expectations and that will be used to evaluate their work so that students know the expectations for success.

In addition to understanding the expectations, students must also be taught the skills they need to complete the project. This requires careful scaffolding. Mike's students needed to understand newspapers and the function of editorials. They read several issues of the local newspaper and discussed different aspects of writing editorials, such as writing good leads and supporting points with specific examples.

Mary and Elizabeth's students built their understanding of culture through the activities they were involved in and their interaction with their classmates. When students do succeed, that success must be celebrated, and students must be given credit for having achieved their goals.

Curiosity

Teachers should understand that students are naturally curious. However boring, repetitious school tasks do not arouse curiosity in learners. The job of teachers is to pique students' curiosity about different aspects of the curriculum. They should help students see big questions as interesting problems to investigate. When given a topic, students should be allowed to generate questions they want to answer, questions like "How do animals become extinct?" "What causes a light bulb to light up?" "Why does the earth move when there is an earthquake?" Teachers help students take a scientific approach to the questions they investigate as they follow the steps a scientist takes. Teachers also organize their lessons so that students can work in groups as they answer their questions and come up with new ones.

Students are more curious when they make personal connections with the topics they are investigating. Mary and Elizabeth helped their students connect with their own cultures as a way to get them to think more deeply about the question, "What is culture?" Mike had his students write about how to improve their own school. Any topic in the curriculum can be made personally relevant. For example, when we lived in South Texas, several teachers had students explore weather extremes after a hurricane. Children were interested in what caused the hurricane, and this led to interest in other kinds of extreme weather, including tornadoes and blizzards.

Originality

With the demands of state and federal standards, teachers often do not see how they can allow their students' originality. They worry that students must have command of the content they will be tested on rather than thinking about what students learn when really engaged. Allowing students to explore questions in different ways—doing web searches, carrying out interviews, taking field trips, or conducting hands-on experiments—are important ways to move students beyond finding answers in a textbook.

It is also important that students be encouraged to show what they have learned in ways other than filling in bubbles on a test or writing an essay exam. Fortunately, new standards, especially English language proficiency standards, generally assess using performance indicators. When teachers value student art responses, dramatic interpretations, group debates, and constructions, they foster creativity and enable students to demonstrate their knowledge in original ways. These kinds of student responses engage students because they have an audience for their work. As a result, they become more creative. In addition, when students see the work of others, new ideas come to them for future projects.

Peer Relations

When teachers foster the development of a classroom community, there are opportunities for all the students to work together and contribute. But positive peer relations do not occur simply by having students work together on a project. We work in a sixth-grade classroom weekly where the teacher has fostered an atmosphere of collaboration among the students. She sets clear expectations for students. They sit in groups of four and work on interesting projects. The teacher changes groups weekly, and students don't complain and ask to work with their friends. No matter what group they are placed in, students respect one another, value each other's contributions, and help each other. In this classroom, peers work together to complete different kinds of projects, including planting and caring for a biome, doing an experiment to understand sedimentation, and creating a poster to show continental drift.

Energy

Energy is created when students are engaged. In Mary and Elizabeth's classroom, one could feel the energy as students worked on their mandalas, created their "I Am from" poems, designed plans for their own classrooms, and completed the class cultural graffiti wall. The energy was positive. Students were creative, and they felt successful because they could use their originality and share it with others. Nou Lor, a Hmong student teacher, texted Mary after the class, telling her:

> Thursday's class activity was very fun, interactive, and allowed each student to learn more about one another's cultural background values. It allowed us to find similarities among cultures (building a sense of community within the classroom). I felt a sense of belonging and connection with all my classmates.

Nou Lor's comments show that students respond positively to teaching that is meaningful and purposeful.

Pedagogies of Engagement

Meaningful and purposeful teaching is engaging. Educators at all levels have identified the importance of engagement for learning. Smith and his colleagues (2005) discuss pedagogies of engagement for college students. Based on a review of the literature on effective classroom practices, they suggest that classrooms that engage students use problem-based learning where students work together in groups to solve key problems in their fields. This type of learning has several features: learning is student-centered, it occurs in small groups, teachers are facilitators or guides, problems are focused and stimulating, and new information is acquired through student-led learning. As Smith and his colleagues state: "to maximize students' achievement, especially of complex and content-dense materials, instructors should not allow students to remain passive" (100). When teaching is meaningful and purposeful, students are never passive. They are actively involved in the subjects they are studying.

LITERACY ENGAGEMENT

Engagement in literacy is often seen as the key to student success. However, students seldom find meaning and purpose in the texts they are expected to read in school. Daniels and Zemelman (2014) list several problems with content-area textbooks. Although the texts are often very long, frequently more than one thousand pages, they are superficial; they cover a great number of topics but do not go into detail on any topic. They are hard to read. Rather than presenting a coherent narrative, they are a kind of storage bin of discrete facts. They are poorly designed. There is often so much on a page, including visuals and sidebars, that students aren't sure what to attend to. Even though they are authoritarian, many textbooks are inaccurate and leave out important information. They are written to meet standards, but they are not user friendly for students. All of these factors make it hard for teachers to make reading textbooks meaningful or purposeful.

Teachers need to supplement textbooks to make learning meaningful and purposeful. Daniels and Zemelman (2014) suggest giving students a balanced diet of reading. This requires using both textbooks and other genres; assigning some readings and letting students choose other assignments; mixing fiction and informational texts, including classics and contemporary works; finding some books that are hard and others that are easy, some that are long and others that are short; and using multiple texts rather than relying on one textbook. Teachers also need to teach specific strategies to give all their students, including their ELs, access to the texts they are expected to read. Unless teachers do these things, many students will not be engaged in literacy.

Cummins (2011) argues that literacy engagement is "a primary determinant of literacy achievement both for English learners (ELs) and underachieving students generally" (242). He points out that the case for literacy engagement as a primary determinant for achievement is logical, because emergent bilinguals need to develop academic language and academic language is found primarily in printed texts. For this reason, it is crucial for emergent bilinguals to be engaged in reading academic texts.

Cummins goes on to say that the claim for the importance of literacy engagement is also empirical; that is, it is supported by research. Krashen (2004) has conducted a review of the research showing the benefits of free voluntary reading. In addition, a report by the Program for International Students Assessment (PISA) (Brozo, Shiel, and Topping 2007/2008) provides evidence of the importance of literacy engagement. This report is especially important because it shows that literacy engagement is more important than socioeconomic status as a predictor of high reading achievement. Since many emergent bilinguals are from low socioeconomic backgrounds, the PISA findings are encouraging.

Brozo and his colleagues explain that the PISA exam measures how well students are prepared for the challenges of today's knowledge societies. To be prepared, students must perform different kinds of reading tasks designed to measure "the capacity of students to apply knowledge and skills and to analyze, reason, and communicate effectively as they pose, solve, and interpret problems in a variety of situations" (305).

The exam requires students to find one or more pieces of information in a text and make a broad generalization; it asks students to develop an interpretation by drawing inferences and using information from one or more parts of the text; it requires students to reflect on the content of the text and relate the text to their own experiences; and it asks students to critically evaluate ideas presented in a text. All of these requirements can only be met if students have high levels of academic language proficiency.

Brozo and his colleagues explain that engagement in literacy was measured by a questionnaire asking students a series of questions about their literacy. Students who read more, read a variety of materials, read for enjoyment, and used strategies as they read were defined as highly engaged readers. A key finding of the 2010 report was that students who were highly engaged in literacy had higher reading achievement than students with moderate or low levels of engagement. This held true even when comparing students of lower socioeconomic status with those with higher status. Highly engaged readers with low socioeconomic status had greater achievement than moderate or low engaged readers with higher status. Engagement was the key, and students become engaged when they see a meaning and purpose in reading.

Guthrie and Davis (2003) also conducted research on the importance of engaging students in literacy. They were especially concerned about middle and high school students. In their research, Guthrie and Davis found that beyond elementary school, students found reading boring, few students enjoyed spending time reading interesting content area texts, and teachers seldom helped students appreciate reading or involved students in meaningful projects with reading. Based on their research, Guthrie and Davis list classroom practices that encourage students to read. These include organizing teaching around thematic units that have big ideas and answer student questions, facilitating hands-on activities and real-world interactions, using interesting texts, providing opportunities for student choice and input, and scaffolding reading by using different reading strategies.

An important finding from Guthrie and Davis' research on engagement in reading is that students who have knowledge and learning goals are more motivated than students with performance goals. Students who read to gain knowledge and learn new information are much more engaged than students who read simply to do well on a test or to achieve a high score on a report. Engaged students have an intrinsic motivation to read and do not need extrinsic motivation in the form of high grades or praise from others. They read because they find that reading is meaningful and serves a purpose.

Culturally Relevant Books

Krashen (2004) points out that the more people read, the more their reading comprehension will improve and the more capable they will be of reading from a variety of genres, including academic content texts. Research shows that students read better and read more when they read culturally relevant books (Freeman, Freeman, and Freeman 2003; Rodriguez 2009; Feger 2006; Goodman 1982; R. Jiménez 1997; Ebe 2010, 2015). Developing a collection of culturally relevant texts takes a concentrated effort. Not all books about Spanish speakers, for example, are relevant to all Latino students (Rosario and Cao 2015). Some books merely perpetuate stereotypes. Others, especially those published in Spain, contain settings and events that are unfamiliar to most Latino students in the United States. Still other books contain fairy tales or legends, and students have trouble connecting personally to such books. However, an increasing number of culturally relevant books are being published.

Just what makes a book culturally relevant? Figure 5–7 provides a rubric that teachers and students can use to determine whether or not a book is culturally relevant.

Teachers we have worked with have used the rubric in various ways. Many have used the rubric to evaluate and choose books to use with their students. Some have read a book that they thought might be culturally relevant to a single English learner and then asked the student the questions on the rubric. They have been

Cultural Relevance Rubric

1. Are the characters in the story like you and your family?

Just like us . . . . Not at all

| 4 | 3 | 2 | 1 |

2. Have you ever had an experience like one described in this story?

Yes . . . . No

| 4 | 3 | 2 | 1 |

3. Have you lived in or visited places like those in the story?

Yes . . . . No

| 4 | 3 | 2 | 1 |

4. Could this story take place this year?

Yes . . . . No

| 4 | 3 | 2 | 1 |

5. How close do you think the main characters are to you in age?

Very close . . . . Not close at all

| 4 | 3 | 2 | 1 |

6. Are there main characters in the story who are: boys (for boys) or girls (for girls)?

Yes . . . . No

| 4 | 3 | 2 | 1 |

7. Do the characters talk like you and your family talk?

Yes . . . . No

| 4 | 3 | 2 | 1 |

8. How often do you read stories like these?

Often . . . . Never

| 4 | 3 | 2 | 1 |

Adapted from Ebe 2010

FIGURE 5–7 *Cultural Relevance Rubric*

excited about how the children connect to the events and can extend the reading by comparing characters and events to their own families and experiences. Other teachers have had older students read a book they believed fit the questions on the rubric and then had students individually fill out the rubric. Still others have used the rubric as a basis for class discussion of a text they read aloud to the class or that the class read for a literature study. In the following sections, we give examples of books that fit each question from the rubric.

Question 1: Are the characters in the story like you and your family?

Francisco is a Spanish/English bilingual teacher working with Latino children in the Bay Area near San Francisco. He received Ada's book (2002) *I Love Saturdays and Domingos* as a gift because he and his Anglo wife have two children with English-speaking and Spanish-speaking grandparents. The characters in this book mirror Francisco's own family. The book is about a girl who spends Saturdays with her English-speaking Anglo grandparents and Sundays (*domingos*) with her Spanish-speaking Hispanic grandparents.

Francisco read the story to his class and then explained that his children have English-speaking and Spanish-speaking grandparents like the characters in the story. This led to a discussion of what the children in the class did with their grandparents and whether they spoke English or Spanish with them.

Jenna, a third-grade teacher, teaches in the Lower East Side of New York City. Eighteen of her twenty-four students are emergent bilinguals, most of Asian backgrounds. For her graduate class in reading, she was asked to choose a culturally relevant book and read it with one of her students. Jenna chose Jane, an excellent student whose parents were immigrants from China. Jane and her family often speak Mandarin at home and maintain many traditional Chinese customs in their new country.

The book Jenna chose was *The Year of the Book* (Cheng 2013), a chapter book about Anna, a fourth-grade American-born Chinese girl who reads as a kind of escape. She is frustrated by her inability to understand how to be friends with classmates at school and by the fact that her Chinese-born mother does not speak English perfectly. Anna does not speak Mandarin and resents having to go to Chinese school on Saturdays.

Jenna's paper for her graduate class describing her experience with using *The Year of the Book* shows how students connect to books when they can relate to the characters. After reading several chapters with Jane, Jenna reflected on many interesting remarks Jane made as they discussed the Cultural Relevance Rubric questions. Jane noted that the main character did not speak Mandarin, but Jane told her teacher that "even if you are Chinese you don't have to speak your cultures' language." When asked if she often read books like these about her culture, Jane's response was "I don't read Chinese books, but I like books like this because books like this is about my culture. If I read about my culture, I can read and learn more about what my culture's custom is." Clearly, Jane responded to the characters and the situations in *The Year of the Book*. Even though the main character did not speak Mandarin like Jane does, the main character was her age dealing with friendships and was from Jane's culture. These connections helped Jane relate to the book.

Question 2: Have you ever had an experience like one described in this story?

When Myra read the bilingual book *My Tata's Remedios/Los remedies de mi tata* (Rivera-Ashford 2015) to her Latino students who were recent immigrants from Mexico, she discovered how culturally relevant texts engage students and encourage discussion. This book describes how Aaron's grandfather (*tata*) teaches his grandson how he uses herbs, dried flowers, and teas to help heal family members and neighborhood friends. As one person after another comes to grandfather's house with bee stings, itchy feet, diaper rash, burns, infected eyes, toothaches, and colds, Aaron's *tata* prepares a *remedio* (remedy) for each of them using the plants he has collected from his garden and the surrounding area.

Myra's second graders attend school along the Mexico/U.S. border. Many are newcomers, and all come from homes where Spanish is spoken. From the very beginning of Myra's reading of the book in Spanish, her students began making comments about their experiences with remedies. "*Mi mamá me hace té de manzanillo cuando me duele el estómago.*" (My mother makes me chamomile tea when I have a stomach ache.) "*Mi tata puede sobar a la gente cuando les duele algo.*" (My grandfather gives massages to people when they hurt.) "*Mi abuelito tiene la sábila en su jardín.*" (My grandfather has an aloe vera plant in his garden.) "*Mi abuela también me dió clavos cuando me dolía un diete.*" (My grandmother also gave me cloves when I had a toothache.)

Because of the students' engagement with the book, Myra asked the students if they wanted to interview their family members and collect recipes that different family members use for remedies. All the students were excited about this project. That night for homework the students asked their family members about different remedies they knew. They wrote down how the remedies were prepared. The next day the students shared what their parents, their aunts and uncles, and their grandparents told them. With these results the class made a bilingual book in both Spanish and English of remedies, describing how the remedies were prepared. They decorated the covers of their books and took them home to give to a family member. All of Myra's students were engaged, and they developed both oral and written literacy skills through the activities she developed around this book.

Another book that relates to the idea of natural healing and to many ELLs' experiences is *Friends from the Other Side: Amigos del otro lado* (Anzaldúa 1993). This book, like *My Tata's Remedies/Los remedies de mi tata*, is especially appropriate for students who live along the border of the United States and Mexico. Natascha, a middle school teacher, chose this book to read to her students for a graduate project on exploratory talk (Gramigna 2005). As Natascha learned in her *literatura infantil* (children's literature) class, exploratory talk encourages students to explore their own feelings, ideas, and beliefs and draw on their backgrounds to connect the books they read with their own experiences (Barnes 2008, 1990). As students participate in discussions about culturally relevant texts, teachers encourage them to respond with different meanings and interpretations. Key to exploratory talk is that the teacher stimulates conversation but does not lead it. Typical exploratory talk questions include "What do you think about . . . ?" "What part or character in the story did you like most?" "What do you remember?" "What else would you like to know?" "What does the story remind you of?"

Natascha chose the book *Friends from the Other Side: Amigos del otro lado* in part because her students were doing an inquiry unit on immigration. This powerful story tells of Prietita, a girl who befriends Joaquín, an undocumented boy who is taunted by his friends and classmates. Prietita stands up for Joaquín and provides food and moral support for the boy and his mother. The story brings out the fear that undocumented families suffer when the *migra* (border patrol) comes to the neighborhood. The *curandera* (healer) is a key character in the story as she gives the mother and son shelter and helps them cure sores they got when crossing the contaminated river.

The four middle school students Natascha read with for her project were labeled as struggling readers and had the characteristics of long-term English learners (LTELs) since they had been in this country attending school six or more years, appeared unengaged with school, and struggled with reading, writing, and understanding English. These LTELs showed, however, that when their teacher used exploratory talk, encouraging them to connect the story to their experiences, they were capable of much more than they appeared to be. As Natascha explained in her project paper for this class:

> *A pesar del bajo nivel académico y motivacional que los niños presentan en la clase regular de lectura y escritura, . . . al exponer a los niños a estrategias del habla explorativa planteado por Gramigna, éstos lograran demostrar que son capaces de comprender, interpretar y desarrollar el pensamiento crítico al realizar conexiones personales e intertextuales con el cuento narrado.*

In spite of the low academic and motivational level that these students showed in their regular reading and writing class, . . . upon exposure to the exploratory talk strategies suggested by Gramigna, these students were able to show that they were capable of understanding, interpreting, and thinking critically as they made personal and intertextual connections with the narrative.

Because the book talks openly about undocumented characters, Natascha encouraged students to discuss their own experiences,

Se abrió la puerta a la discusión y a las múltiples interpretaciones sobre la denominación "mojado." Los niños estuvieron de acuerdo con haber escuchado la denominación antes y algunos compartieron historias de parientes y familiares que también cruzaron el río y a los que los han llamado "mojados." Reflexionaron además sobre la importancia de venir a vivir y a trabajar a los Estados Unidos como causas nobles y que valen la pena, aún cuando la gente se burla de ellos.

The door was opened for discussion [on the topic of undocumented people] and for discussion of the many interpretations of the label "wetback." The students all agreed they had heard the label before and some shared stories of relatives and close friends who also crossed the river and those people who had called them "wetbacks." They also reflected on the importance of coming to live and work in the United States as a noble goal and worth the effort even when people ridiculed them.

The exploratory talk that took place allowed Natascha's students to discuss themes in the book *The Friends from the Other Side*, including friendship and conflicts with friends, inequality, economic hardships, and legal issues. Exploratory talk and a culturally relevant book allowed Natascha's students to move beyond *"la mera recuperación de datos que se hayan a un nivel superficial"* (the mere regurgitation of facts that are found at a superficial level) and instead encouraged her students to share *"múltiples inferencias e interpretaciones"* (multiple inferences and interpretations).

Khadijah Goes to School—A Story About You (Hussain 2015), written by a first-generation Pakistani Canadian, is another culturally relevant book that many immigrant students in North America can connect with because it relates to their own experiences. The book opens right to left and is read as Arabic language books are read. It is the story of a young Muslim girl who is new to a public school in Canada. She is uncomfortable there and feels unaccepted. She continually asks her Baba (father) why she should go to school and is told that she goes to school "because you learn so much." However, Khadijah is not convinced and wishes she didn't have to go to school.

The book, illustrated by children, is both whimsical and deep. Reviewers believe the book dispels myths and misinformation about Islam, and that it challenges stereotypes, racism, and bigotry. But the book does more than that—it explores human potential. Khadijah eventually sees that learning is a part of life and understands that she must start by asking questions. Ultimately, she is told that the secret of learning is to read. Two pages from the book show how the phrase "to read" is represented in many different languages and images.

Question 3: Have you lived in or visited places like those in the story?

Teachers should consider the setting as well as the characters and experiences described in a story. Nikki teaches fifth grade in an inner-city community in Harlem in New York City. She chose the short story "The Streak" from a book of short stories entitled *145th Street* (Myers 2015). Walter Dean Myers, the book's author, is himself from Harlem, and he writes about life in Harlem. Nikki reasoned that the story would be particularly good because it is situated in places that she knew her students visited frequently, such as bodegas, corner delis, and park basketball courts. In addition, the dialect used by characters in the story was familiar to students. Finally, the book is called *145th Street* and the students attend school on 122nd Street, so the proximity added an important connection for her students.

Another story that takes place in New York City is *Abuela* (Dorros 1997), a fanciful, beautifully illustrated tale of a young immigrant girl, Rosalba, who, while walking in the park with her grandmother, imagines what it would be like if she could fly. In the story she and her grandmother then fly over New York City exploring the city from above. Ebe (2011) explained how Amanda, a second-grade teacher working in New York City, used *Abuela* with Jessica, one of the quietest English learners in class. Amanda reported that as she read the story, Jessica's eyes lit up, and she began telling her teacher how she goes to the park with her *abuela* and drinks lemonade. Amanda explained how Jessica responded to the book.

> Her voice was even louder than usual (she constantly whispered in class when she spoke in English) as she explained that the pictures of the neighborhood in the book looked like the apartment building where she lived. She even told Amanda that her cousin unloaded fruit just like Rosalba's cousin does in the story. (37–38)

Many of the connections Jessica made to the story were because of the setting. She related to the places Rosalba and her grandmother went. After their reading and discussion of the story in English, Amanda encouraged Jessica to take the Spanish version of the story home to share with her family.

Mary, the high school reading and language arts teacher we wrote about earlier who taught along the Texas/Mexico border, chose the young adult version of *Enrique's Journey* (Nazario 2014) to read with her students. She chose the book because of frequent news of unaccompanied minors arriving in large numbers from Central America in her border city in Texas. *Enrique's Journey* is the true story of a Honduran teenager in his eighth attempt to come to the U.S. to escape intolerable conditions in his home country and to find his mother, who had left him with relatives eleven years earlier in search of a better life. The book tells of Enrique's traumatic journey, one that thousands of others have also taken—his ride on *el tren de muerte* (the death train), his encounters with gangs, the support from others he meets on the journey, and the struggles he faces when he finally reunites with his mother after he crosses the Texas border.

While all of Mary's English learners were from Mexico, and many had come from nearby Mexican cities, they could relate to Enrique's experiences because they had heard the stories of children like him. They knew that the difficult part of the journey was in Mexico where gangs were a serious problem and starvation and overexposure were common. Several of Mary's students had family members who had direct experiences with these refugees in Mexico, and the stories about them were similar to what they read about in this book. In addition, there was a refugee detention center for these undocumented minors located just outside their city, and students had heard stories of the children in this center waiting to be reunited with their families. Local newspaper articles also featured the plight of the refugees and the traumas they had lived through. This book directly connected to the area where Mary's students lived, and that made it more relevant for them.

Question 4: Could this story take place this year?

When Yvonne read *Going Home* (Bunting 1998) to her graduate class, she realized quickly that this book was especially relevant to educators. In this story two children raised in the United States reluctantly travel back to rural Mexico with their parents to spend Christmas with relatives there. On the trip they begin to understand the sacrifices their parents have made for them. After reading the story, one teary-eyed teacher raised her hand and said, "That story taught me how important it is that my students go back to Mexico for the holidays. I've always complained and wondered why parents take their children out of school. I understand a bit better now."

The following week, a high school teacher reported that she had read the book to her students. That reading had led to a discussion in which several of her students talked about how their views of living in the United States were different from their parents' views and how hard it was for them and their parents to understand and appreciate each other. The book is especially valuable because it reflects the current reality of many Mexican American students and their connections to their parents' experiences in Mexico.

Books about Chinese New Year are certainly current for students now living in North America and especially so for those in New York City where many Chinese New Year celebrations are shared not only with Asians but with the entire New York City community. Some books teachers have used include a board book for young learners, *Bringing in the New Year* (Lin 2013), and two other books for younger children, *Chelsea's Chinese New Year* (Bullard 2012) and *My First Chinese New Year* (Katz 2012).

Ebe (2015) reports on how one of her graduate students, Laura, used *My First Chinese New Year*. Laura read the book to one of her Chinese-American students who "usually does not engage in a lot of conversation" but responded enthusiastically to *My First Chinese New Year*. Laura explained that for the first time the student eagerly retold the story and talked about the characters. She was able to retell the parts she liked best and share her background knowledge and experiences about the topic. She explained in detail her knowledge about receiving the money in the red envelope and the meaning of the dragon dance discussed in the story.

Question 5: How close do you think the main characters are to you in age?

Barbara, a bilingual teacher, finds that her native Spanish-speaking first graders love to hear stories that relate to their own cultural and social experiences and that are also about children their own age. Barbara teaches in a rural school where many of the students are from migrant families. Her students enjoyed the story *La mariposa* (Jiménez 2000, 1998). This book was originally a chapter of Jimenez' *The Circuit* (1997) and has now been converted into a children's book beautifully illustrated by Simon Silva. Barbara read the Spanish version of the book first, and the students discussed it. Her students told her, *"Es triste porque Francisco no tiene amigos"* (It's sad because Francisco doesn't have friends), and they connected to his brother Roberto helping him. *"Mi hermano me lleva a la escuela también, maestra."* (My brother brings me to school too, teacher).

Later in the year, while the students were engaged in an insect unit, she reminds them of the story she had read earlier in Spanish. That reading served as a preview as she read them the English version (Jiménez 1998). In the story, the young boy sits in the back of the class and observes a caterpillar that turns into a butterfly. The metamorphosis parallels the change the young boy is going through. Barbara's students related this part of the story to the cocoon they had been watching in their own classroom as part of their insect unit.

Cecilia's Year (Abraham and Abraham 2004) is a chapter book about a fourteen-year-old girl living on a farm in New Mexico in the 1930s just after the Depression. Cecilia has dreams of going to high school and getting an education so that she can work in an office or become a teacher. However, her parents don't see these dreams as realistic and want her to revise her dreams and become a homemaker and mother.

Each chapter is organized around the months of the year and the routines of farm life. Natascha, the middle school teacher who used *Friends from the Other Side*, read this book with her middle school students who, like Cecilia, were soon to go into high school. Her students lived in a rural border community in Texas, so they could relate to much of what was described in the book. Natascha wanted her students to connect to the book and also see that they could expand their dreams for the future. As one of her writing assignments, she asked her students to write about what they planned to do in the future. This led to a unit on different professions, and Natascha invited a local business owner, a policeman, a doctor, a nurse, and a college professor to speak to her students about their work and the importance of education to achieve their own goals. *Cecilia's Year* helped Natascha's students, who were the same age as Cecilia, to think more deeply about their own futures.

The book *Waiting for Papá: Esperando a Papá* (Colato Laínez 2004) is relevant for students who are seven or eight years old, and also for immigrant children whose families are separated with some living in the U.S. and some living in the home country. The main character, Beto, has been waiting for his father to come from El Salvador for three years, but his father cannot get official papers to come to the U.S. As he celebrates his eighth birthday, Beto reflects on the violence and loss his family suffered before he and his mother left El Salvador. When he writes a letter to his father for a class assignment, his teacher arranges for him to read it on the radio on a station that supports immigrants. This leads to unexpected support for the family. This story is relevant for many children who have been separated from their parents and relatives and who have suffered the disappointment of delayed reunions.

Question 6: Are there main characters in the story who are: boys (for boys) or girls (for girls)?

Linda teaches English as a second language (ESL) in a large urban high school in Fresno, California. She read aloud *América Is Her Name* (Rodríguez 1998). This book is about a Puerto Rican girl in the big city. Linda's female students found this book especially relevant because the character is a city high school girl who struggles with teachers and school officials who don't understand her. Linda's students see the main character, América, develop pride in her cultural roots. América has a teacher like Linda who encourages her students to write poetry about their lives and experiences in both English and their native languages.

Linda also found books that the boys in her class found relevant. Her high school boys enjoyed Gary Soto's (2006) *Buried Onions*, a story about an older teenager, Eddie, who is trying to escape the violence in the large city where he lives during the heat of summer. Many of the boys in Linda's class can see themselves in the main character of this powerful story, especially since the book actually takes place in Fresno. The violence in Fresno is reflected in Soto's image of a huge onion buried beneath the city streets giving off vapors in the heat, vapors caused by the tears the violence creates. This image is one that Linda's students who live in a city in the hot Central Valley of California understand well.

Xavier Garza has written several books about *lucha libre,* literally meaning "freestyle wrestling." *Lucha libre* is a form of wrestling popular in Mexico and other Spanish-speaking countries. Wrestlers wear colorful masks that have special significance for each wrestler, and their wrestling style is distinctive. Garza's books are popular among Spanish-speaking boys familiar with *lucha libre.* Garza's action-packed bilingual English/Spanish books include *Lucha Libre: The Man in the Silver Mask* (Garza 2005), *Maximillian and the Mystery of the Guardian Angel: A Bilingual Lucha Libre Thriller* (Garza 2011), *Maximillian and the Bingo Rematch: A Lucha Libre Sequel/Maximiliano y la Revancha de lotería: La Continuación de la Lucha Libre* (Garza 2013), and *The Great and Mighty Nikko!: ¡El gran y poderoso Nikko!* (Garza 2015). The last book is a counting book that even young preschoolers and kindergartners can enjoy. In it, Nikko is admonished by his mother for not settling down to go to sleep because he is playing with his action figure *luchadores.* Nikko imagines his bed is a wrestling ring and on each two-page spread, he adds more *luchadores* to the ring until he reaches nine and he, the tenth *luchador,* the "great and mighty Nikko" defeats them all before falling asleep. Our five-year-old grandson, Romero, loves counting the *luchadores* on each page, decides which masked fighters are the "good guys" and which are the "bad guys," and imagines himself to be one of the superheroes.

The Name Jar (Choi 2001) is a book about a young Korean girl who goes to school in the United States for the first time. On the way to school, someone asks her what her name is and all the children laugh at how it sounds. When she gets to her classroom, she refuses to tell anyone her real name. After several days, the teacher devises a way to give her a name by putting out a jar and asking the children to write a name for her and place it in the jar. Her classmates discover her real name and its beautiful meaning, and then everyone puts her real name in the jar. This story has a happy ending, but it reflects an experience that is not at all uncommon for newcomers to this country. Although the story is about a girl, the message of this story is important for boys and girls alike.

Question 7: Do the characters talk like you and your family do?

The students in Charene's eighth-grade English language arts class in New York City speak a variety of home languages including Arabic, Bengali, French, Fulani, Haitian Creole, and Spanish. Charene looks for ways to encourage students to draw on their first languages. Her use of the book *Inside Out and Back Again* (Lai 2013) provided her with the opportunity to not only draw on their first languages but also show them how they could use their first languages in their own writing. *Inside Out and Back Again* tells about Ha, a young Vietnamese girl leaving her country after the fall of Saigon and coming to the United States. The book provides a rich description of Vietnamese traditions and the feel of home and Ha's difficult transition in her move to Alabama. The entire story is written in verse and includes many examples of translanguaging between Vietnamese and English.

The story itself connects to many of the immigrant students in Charene's class, but few noticed the use of language within in the book. After the students read a chapter in which the author describes New Year's Eve celebrations using both English and Vietnamese words, their teacher grouped students at tables into same home language groups. On their tables was a sheet with the following questions, both in English and translated into the students' home languages: "The author uses a lot of vocabulary words in Vietnamese in this book. Can you explain your thinking as to why she didn't use all English words? How are you able to infer the meaning of the Vietnamese words?" Some of the students talked to each other using their home languages about these questions while others discussed the questions in English. They then wrote individual responses to the prompt in their journals.

As a follow-up activity, Charene asked students to share New Year's traditions from their home countries orally and then write about their traditions following the model verses used in the book. Her students were to incorporate their home language (usually names of traditional foods and clothing that is worn) as Lai did in her book. The students' poems were edited at home where parents could help add cultural information and check the home language additions. This book and the follow-up activity validated students' home languages and cultures (Ebe 2016).

Another teacher, Bria, teaches in an elementary school in the Bronx in New York City. Many of the families in the neighborhood struggle economically, and many of her students are English learners. For her master's-level course in teaching reading, she did a case study with Jesus, an emergent bilingual from Mexico who had trouble with reading comprehension. Bria chose Jesus for this assignment because he appeared to be an unengaged reader. Bria reasoned that using a culturally relevant book might motivate Jesus.

The year before Jesus was in Bria's class, he was taught reading using basal materials that were not relevant to immigrant students. The texts used in the program would score a 1 (the lowest level) on the cultural relevance rubric for Jesus. She decided to read an authentic text titled *Waiting for the Biblioburro* (Brown 2011) to Jesus and the other students in her class. The story, based on the experience of a teacher and librarian from Colombia, is about a little girl from Colombia who loves to read and write. However, she lives in a remote village and only owns one book that she reads over and over. One day a *bibliotecario* (librarian) carrying books on his burro comes to town and shares his books with the children in the village. The illustrations depict a rural village in Colombia and reinforce the text by providing a good text-picture match.

Bria thought Jesus would be able to relate to this story because in Jesus writer's notebook he wrote a personal story about being bored in the summer when he visited his grandparents who lived on a remote farm in rural Mexico. In addition, there are Spanish words infused throughout the story, and Bria knew Jesus and his family spoke Spanish at home.

When Bria first started reading *Waiting for Biblioburro* aloud to the class, she asked Jesus to help her whenever she came across a Spanish word. At first he refused to help her, so Bria turned to the whole class and asked for help. She explained what happened next.

> Every time a Spanish word came up the room erupted with noise. Everyone was eager to tell me how to pronounce it. I wasn't aware how many of my other students speak Spanish. Two students in my class who are very low academically raised their hands more during this read-aloud than they have all year. By the end of the read-aloud Jesus was pronouncing the Spanish words for me with the others. I think that he was initially hesitant because he may have been embarrassed. Although I selected this text for Jesus, I was pleasantly surprised how many of my other students connected with the text because of the language used.

As Bria followed up with text-based questions, students were able to answer the questions more readily than they had with any other story they had read that year. As Bria wrote in the conclusion of her paper:

> Even for the students who have never been to Colombia or left the Bronx they were still able to connect to the text because of the Spanish language. This read-aloud was an eye-opener to show me the importance of exposing students to literature they can connect to, and it makes my job easier because students are eager to engage in the lesson.

Question 8: How often do you read stories like these?

As educators, we need to find books that connect to our students' lives and everyday reality. Often, we also need to expose all the students in our classrooms to the realities of their classmates' lives. For example, there are few books for young children about Islam and Muslim traditions and customs. Muslim families are not always understood by children unfamiliar with Islam and Islamic cultural traditions. A beautiful book that validates Muslim children and helps non-Muslim classmates appreciate and understand them is *Golden Domes and Silver Lanterns: A Muslim Book of Colors* (Khan 2012). This creatively illustrated book shares in rhyme such things as the golden dome of the mosque, the blue hijab mother wears to cover her head, and the red rug father kneels on to pray five times a day. Muslims and non-Muslims alike highly recommend this book as one that sensitively and beautifully represents present-day Muslims.

María learned how seldom some of her minority high school students at a Harlem High School had been exposed to texts that really connected to their experiences when she read the story, "What's a Mexican?" to an eleventh-grade Dominican student, M. María chose this excerpt from the blog "Between Worlds: Racebridges for Schools" for M. because although she was Dominican, she did not speak much Spanish and did not have the physical characteristics of most of her Dominican classmates. María also wanted to read the script of this story with M. because she was struggling with reading and seldom showed much engagement in reading.

María reported on her choice and her experience for her master's in reading course. She wrote:

> It is important to realize that although people come from different parts of the world, not everyone looks the same and there is no single way that a person should or should not look. I chose this student because, like many of her classmates, she is only decoding and is not truly understanding what is going on with what she is reading. I think that reading a culturally relevant text will help her work on her reading skills.

"What is a Mexican?" is told by storyteller Olga Loya, and the script and video of this story can be found online at Racebridges for schools (http://racebridgesfor schools.com/wp/?p=1811). This story is part of Loya's "Being Mexican-American: Caught Between Two Worlds—Nepantla" (www.racebridgesforschools.com/olga _tracks/nepantla.html), a series of MP3 soundtracks that include Loya's stories about her search for identity as a woman of Mexican descent who had denied her cultural heritage and language growing up but regained it as an adult. She explains that as a young girl when people said "but you don't look Mexican," she was glad. As a young adult, she tells how she attended a speech given by Caesar Chávez, the

Mexican farm worker, labor leader, and civil rights advocate. He spoke about the pride he had in his Mexican heritage. For the first time, Olga realized that she had not acknowledged her Latino cultural background.

María read over the excerpt with her student, M., and then asked her the questions from the Cultural Relevance Rubric. When asked the first question, "Are the characters in the story like you and your family?" M. showed that she related to the story when she answered, "Me and my family are not Mexican, but I think we're exactly the same. Except I'm Dominican and live in New York." Although M. had not lived in or visited the places Olga Loya mentioned, she did relate to some of the other questions and the theme of Loya's story. She told María, "People always tell me I don't look Dominican. People always think that I'm mixed." Like Loya, who told about being surprised and embarrassed when friends told her she had an accent, M. commented, "I was told I have an accent before, but I still don't believe it." She was inspired by the storyteller's success in life and her pride in herself. She told her teacher, "I feel like if you're Hispanic or black, no one takes you seriously, so no one thinks that you can be successful . . . and I know that I will be successful. I don't care what everyone else thinks. I'll show them just like the girl in the story." Perhaps the most important message for teachers came from M.'s response to the last question, "How often do you read stories like this one?" M. responded honestly:

> I barely read. And when I do it's for school. And they never read these kinda things in school. It's always about Europeans or white people or something. Or a black guy. I don't think I have ever read anything about a Hispanic person. That's so sad.

María's experience with M. is one that made her consider the texts she uses with her students. In the conclusion of her case study for her reading class she wrote:

> Like M. said, this story was completely different from the readings we have read together. The texts we have read were outside of her interests and were pretty irrelevant to her. We have not read a single text that involves a Latino, but rather blacks and whites. The times I have read aloud with M. she has to go back to the reading to answer questions, or asks to reread the text quietly to herself. My one surprise came from the fact that she read the story to me aloud and was able to recall the whole thing.

Unfortunately, there are often too few books that do connect to the cultures and experiences of the diverse students in our classrooms. As an assignment for Yvonne's graduate class in second language acquisition, students were asked to read a culturally relevant book to a student or group of students and administer the rubric. Yvette, a bilingual teacher who teaches in rural Texas along the border, read *Family Pictures: Cuadros de mi familia* (Garza 2005) to one of her students. The book related to the lives of her students by depicting familiar experiences—the family birthday party with a piñata, making tamales with the family, cleaning *nopales* from the cactus, and a cakewalk for scholarship money for Mexican Americans to go to college. After reading and discussing the rubric questions, Yvette was appalled when the student she interviewed answered *"nunca"* (never) to the question "How often do you read stories like these?" *"¿Nunca?"* Yvette asked again. "Never!" her student insisted.

Our concern is that many emergent bilinguals do not have access to culturally relevant books. Classroom libraries do not have enough books. Even when there are enough books in English or in students' native languages, few of those books have the characteristics that the culturally relevant rubric calls for: few books are about the present experiences of the students, few books have characters that look

Abraham, Susan Gonzales, and Denise Gonzales Abraham. 2004. *Cecilia's Year*. El Paso, TX: Cinco Puntos Press.

Anzaldúa, Gloria. 1993. *Friends from the Other Side: Amigos del otro lado*. San Francisco: Children's Book Press.

Brown, Monica. 2011. *Waiting for Biblioburro*. Berkeley, CA: Tricycle Press.

Bullard, Lisa. 2012. *Chelsea's Chinese New Year*. New York: Millbrook Press Trade, Lerner Publishing.

Bunting, Eve. 1998. *Going Home*. New York: HarperTrophy.

Cheng, Andrea. 2013. *The Year of the Book*. Boston: HMH Books for Young Readers.

Choi, Yangsook. 2001. *The Name Jar*. New York: Knopf.

Colato Laínez, René. 2004. *Waiting for Papá: Esperando a papá*. Houston: Arte Público Press.

Dorros, Arthur. 1997. *Abuela*. New York: Penguin Putnam Books.

Garza, Carmen Lomas. 2005. *Family Pictures: Cuadros de familia*. 15th anniversary edition. San Francisco: Children's Book Press.

Garza, Xavier. 2005. *Lucha libre: The Man in the Silver Mask*. El Paso, TX: Cinco Puntos Press.

———. 2011. *Maximillian: The Mystery of the Guardian Angel: A Bilingual Lucha Libre Thriller*. El Paso, TX: Cinco Puntos Press.

———. 2013. *Maximillian and the Bingo Rematch: Maximiliano ¡La revancha de lotería!* El Paso: Cinco Puntos Press.

———. 2015. *The Great and Mighty Nikko!: ¡El gran y poderoso Nikko!* El Paso, TX: Cinco Puntos Press.

FIGURE 5–8 *Cultural Relevance Bibliography*

like and talk like the students, few books have settings the students recognize, and few books use the same languages the students speak.

The student responses in the stories told by Yvette and María illustrate the importance of using at least some culturally relevant texts. There was a time when one might have argued that there were not many culturally relevant texts available. However, now there are many books and other text resources that connect to students' cultural heritage and present lives and realities. Bilingual and ESL conferences at state and national levels display many such books from different cultures. Teachers can also find many culturally relevant readings by searching online. Figure 5–8 is a bibliography of culturally relevant texts used in this section.

Hussain, Asim. 2015. *Khadijah Goes to School—A Story About You*. 2nd edition. Canada: Self-published (LogixPlayer Inc.).

Jiménez, Francisco. 1997. *The Circuit: Stories from the Life of a Migrant Child*. Albuquerque: University of New Mexico Press.

———. 1998. *La mariposa*. Boston: Houghton Mifflin.

———. 2000. *La mariposa*. Spanish edition. Boston: Houghton Mifflin.

Katz, Karen. 2012. *My First Chinese New Year*. New York: Square Fish.

Khan, Hena. 2012. *Golden Domes and Silver Lanterns: A Muslim Book of Colors*. San Francisco: Chronicle Books.

Lai, Thanhha. 2013. *Inside Out and Back Again*. Brisbane, AU: University of Queensland Press.

Lin, Grace. 2013. *Bringing in the New Year*. New York: Knopf Books for Young Readers.

Myers, Walter Dean. 2012. *145th Street: Short Stories*. New York: Random House Children's Books.

Nazario, Sonia. 2014. *Enrique's Journey*. YA version. New York: Delacourt Press.

Rivera-Ashford, Roni Capin. 2015. *My Tata's Remedios/Los remedios de mi tata*. El Paso, TX: Cinco Puntos Press.

Rodríguez, Luis. 1998. *América Is Her Name*. Willimantic, CT: Curbstone Press.

Rosario, Vanessa Pérez, and Vivien Cao. 2015. *The CUNY–NYSIEB Guide to Translanguaging in Latino/a Literature*. New York: CUNY–NYSIEB Graduate Center.

Soto, Gary. 2006. *Buried Onions*. Wilmington, MA: Houghton Mifflin Harcourt.

TEACHING IDIOMS

One of the greatest challenges of learning a new language is mastering the idioms of the language. Because language learners are acquiring a new language and new vocabulary, they often take things literally. Idioms, on the other hand, require emergent bilinguals to understand the figurative meaning of a word or phrase. For example, the idiom "killing two birds with one stone" does not contain difficult words. Most emergent bilinguals learning English would understand the literal meaning of the individual words, but they would not understand the figurative meaning of the expression—accomplishing more than one thing with only one action or solving two problems with one solution. Students of a new language must learn to interpret the intended meanings of the idioms that people around them use every day.

Mary taught high school English to beginning ELs. She knew that they struggled to understand idioms in the stories they read. She wanted to find a meaningful and purposeful way of helping her students begin to understand idioms they encountered in their reading. She began work on idioms by reading a page from a text aloud. Each time she came to an idiom such as "Has the cat got your tongue?" she stopped to think aloud: "This doesn't make much sense. There's no cat in this story. I guess I can't take this literally. It must be an idiom." She went on to show how she could often figure out the meaning of the idiom from the context.

Having introduced the idea that idioms express a figurative meaning, Mary passed out a list of traditional idioms. Students chose one idiom. They drew a picture showing the literal meaning and wrote the figurative meaning. For example, one student chose "Feel blue" and drew a picture of a girl with a blue body. She then wrote at the bottom of the page the figurative meaning as "Feel sad." Other student examples included idioms such as "fat cat," "My ears are burning," "feeding frenzy," "A closed mouth catches no flies," and "Wake up and smell the coffee." Figure 5–9

FIGURE 5–9 *Idiom "Wake up and smell the coffee."*

shows an example. The students shared their drawings in small groups, and then Mary posted them on the bulletin board for everyone to see.

Mary's students took an interest in idioms. They started to bring in idioms they heard other teachers or students use. They wanted to understand the meaning of these idioms, so this unit on idioms was meaningful. Mary kept a list of expressions up on the bulletin board of the idioms students brought in. Some of the examples students found were current slang, like *dawg* and *butter*, so the class discussed the difference between idioms and slang. While both involve the use of figurative language, idioms enter into the language and are used for longer periods of time than slang, which changes rapidly.

To meet language arts standards, Mary worked with small groups of students in the next phase of the unit. She read a short story to them that contained several idioms. Each time they came to an idiom, Mary helped guide the students to use their background knowledge and the context of the story to figure out the meaning. With Mary's support, students began to recognize idioms and to develop strategies for determining their meaning.

The third stage of the unit on idioms involved the students in a collaborative learning activity. Mary divided the students into pairs and gave each pair a different short story that contained idioms. Students worked together to identify the idioms and to determine what they meant. They made a list of the idioms they found. They also tried to think of a similar idiom in their first language, and if they discovered one they wrote it down as well. For example, for the idiom "Actions speak louder than words," one pair explained the idiom as "It means you can be judged better by what you do than by what you say." This native Spanish-speaking pair added a Spanish version, *"Una acción vale más que mil palabras"* ("One act is worth more than one thousand words"). Students enjoyed being "idiom detectives." After they all finished, they took turns sharing several of their idioms and the first-language equivalents.

In the next step, students were given a short play script with idioms underlined. They were directed to apply the strategies they had learned to determine what each idiom meant. For example, Pedro used the context to decide that when one character was described as having a chip on his shoulder, it must mean that something was bothering him. After figuring out the meanings of these idioms, the students tried writing their own short scripts using the same idioms or others they had studied earlier in the lesson. One pair of boys started their script quite creatively:

> **Carlos:** Hey, Juan, Do you know what happened to me? <u>Make a shot in the dark.</u>
> **Juan:** I don't know.
> **Carlos:** I crashed my car. My car is <u>dead as a doornail</u>. It's going to <u>cost me an arm and a leg</u>.

Students performed their short scripts for each other giving them a chance to develop their oral English. As they read their plays, their peers enjoyed identifying idioms in each one.

Mary carefully scaffolded her unit on idioms through several steps. She modeled how to think about idioms and how to determine their meaning. As idiom detectives, students practiced identifying and finding the figurative meaning of idioms. The students enjoyed illustrating the literal meanings. They compared idioms in English with some in their native language. The final play-writing assignment required them to work together to put the skills they had learned into practice and gave them the opportunity to develop their oral English. These activities followed the principle, "Teaching should be meaningful and purposeful to engage students."

THE FUTURE UNIT

To conclude this chapter on the principle that "Teaching should be meaningful and purposeful to engage students," we describe another unit that Mary taught. This was a future unit answering the question, "What might the future tell us about the present?" Mary used the unit with her newcomer and second-year emergent bilinguals as well as her regular English high school students. Mary taught the same content and concepts to all her classes, but provided scaffolding and paced her lessons to meet the needs of her students with varying English proficiency.

The students attended a large high school along the Mexico/Texas border. The school has an almost 100 percent Hispanic student population, most of whom are of Mexican descent. The students in Mary's classes varied: some were native English speakers, some were adequate formal schooling students who had moved across the border to attend high school, and some were long-term English learners who struggled with academic Spanish and English. Mary's students were a mix of freshmen, sophomores, juniors, and seniors, and they all needed to meet the language arts standards if they hoped to graduate from high school and continue on to college.

As Mary looked at different standards in language arts, she identified several she wanted to work on with her students during this unit. They included developing the ability to answer literal and inferential questions about a short story, developing an understanding of figurative language, developing an understanding of story elements, developing the ability to support statements with evidence from a text, and developing the ability to write different genres including journal writing, newspaper articles, poems, and letters.

Future Poster

To begin the unit, Mary gave the students a future poster assignment, asking them to imagine what life would be like in 2053. She asked them to include drawings and labels of what clothing, sports, new laws, schools, and new inventions might look like. Figure 5–10 is a sample future poster showing each element, including a new law that does not allow people to walk in the streets—instead, they must fly. In school, students go to class, and the teacher inserts a computer chip in students.

Literacy Strategies with "The Star"

To engage her students in this unit Mary chose several science fiction short stories she thought the students would enjoy. Students read the stories on their own, read and discussed in pairs, or read with Mary depending on their English proficiency. Mary first gave the students "The Star" (Claes 2015), a short story she found on the

FIGURE 5–10 *Future Poster*

Internet about a famous singer with gold albums and Grammy awards who faces the end of her fame and fortune when nuclear bombs and radiation destroy the modern world.

After reading and discussing the story and with a focus on the big question, "What might the future tell us about the present?" Mary assigned a journal entry answering the questions, "How do you think the world will end?" and "How would you react?" Most students answered that they thought there would be natural or man-made disasters. Students then worked together on a story map where they filled in setting, time, place, characters, problem, plot, events, and resolution—literary concepts that were all part of one of the language arts standards. In the context of this fascinating story, students could easily pick out these elements, although they concluded that this story had no resolution since it ends with the main character thinking she will still be a star tomorrow when it is clear that all the characters are doomed to die.

Finding textual evidence to support conclusions was something else that students needed to be able to do. Mary had students work together to answer literal and inferential questions and then support their answers with textual evidence. For example, for the question, "How did the father react?" the students answered, "The father is a realist. He knows what is happening." They then quoted the part of the story where the father says, "There are diseases and radiation poisoning spreading all over the country."

As part of their study of figurative language, students took lines from the story and rewrote them adding figurative language. So, for example, two students changed, "You roll your eyes and tell them" to "You roll your soccer ball eyes." They rewrote passages to include personification. One pair wrote, "The stars dance in the night."

To encourage students to write longer narratives that would be interesting to them, Mary gave the following assignment: "You are a star. Write about a typical day in your life." Teenagers often fantasize about becoming a famous star, so all the students eagerly embraced this writing assignment. They enjoyed reading one another's assignments posted later on the bulletin board. Mary followed this activity with a paired writing assignment, giving the students these directions: "You are a star and the world is ending. Write a tall tale about your experiences." Her goal here was to encourage students to incorporate figurative language—metaphor, simile, personification, and hyperbole—into their writing and help them to include key story elements. She also wanted them to write in a new genre.

Students chose stars like Britney Spears and Michael Jackson and storybook heroes like Harry Potter to bring into their tall tales. This activity with "The Star" was so engaging that students saw a meaning and purpose for completing it.

Literacy Strategies with "The Pedestrian"

Another story that Mary included in her future unit to help her students develop key language arts concepts and build language proficiency was the short story "The Pedestrian" (Bradbury 2014). It takes place in a world where no one reads anymore. Mr. Mead, a writer, walks through a dark city where no one comes out of their homes because they are all watching television. He has never seen another person on his nightly walks in ten years. On one fateful night an automated police car stops him and makes him get into the car. Because it is inconceivable that anyone would do anything at night but stay inside watching TV, the car takes him to a psychiatric center to be studied.

The students were fascinated by this story and understood Bradbury's message immediately. After they read the short story and discussed it, the students filled out a flowchart of the events from the beginning to the end of the story. Next, they created a small poster. They were asked to choose a quote from the story, paraphrase it in their own words, and write a short paragraph making a text-to-self-connection. One student chose a quote about Mr. Mead walking on deserted streets and commented on how he felt when he walked on the street at night and there were no other people around. Another wrote about the police car stopping Mr. Mead and related an incident when the police stopped him and his friend and interrogated them. These quotes, paraphrases, and personal connections posters were carefully completed on colored paper with colored markers and displayed on the wall. Students then walked around the room, read each other's posters, and wrote short comments on sticky notes to put on the posters.

Two other activities followed that related to the poster activity. As she did with "The Star" Mary gave students a sheet with literal and inferential questions and asked them to find the textual evidence for their answers. Then she asked students to choose four quotes from the story that stood out for them. They were to write the quote and tell how the quote connected to something else in the story, something from another story, something from their life, or something from the life of someone else they knew.

She involved her students in other activities to build their understanding of figurative language. These activities were similar to those she used for "The Star." Mary knew that her students needed several opportunities to develop a good understanding of key concepts, such as figurative language. One interesting addition that she made was for a journal entry. She reminded the students of the part of the story where Mr. Mead was taken to the mental hospital. Then she asked them to "write a journal from Mr. Mead telling what happens to him in the mental hospital. In your journal entry include one metaphor, one simile, and one example of alliteration."

One student wrote about how he wondered why no one had come to ask for him since he had "vanished into thin air." Another wrote that he was "losing his mind" in this "creaky cracked up crazy institution."

Literacy Strategies with *The Hunger Games*

All of the activities students completed with the short stories provided a foundation for their work with the futuristic novel *The Hunger Games* (Collins 2008). Students, even the newcomers, were all familiar with the movie version, which was about to come out in theatres. Many had been reading online about the actors and the filming of the movie. Mary chose this book because she knew that all her students would want to read it, even those who never had read anything that long in English before. They also had some background about the plot and the setting of the book.

Mary realized that it was critical that the students understood what was happening at the beginning of the novel. With the newcomer emergent bilinguals, Mary read to and with them. Sometimes she provided a preview in Spanish of what students were about to read in English. Mary also put students in groups after reading a section and allowed them to use their first language to orally summarize what she had read to them. Her second-year students read in pairs and discussed what they had read in both English and Spanish.

Found Poem

When Mary was sure that most of her students understood the first section of the book, she explained the first activity, creating a *found poem*. A found poem takes prose from any topic and, using the topic and the vocabulary from the source document, creates a poem. Mary structured the assignment carefully with the following instructions:

Pick the most important word from the beginning of this section.

- 2 adjectives from your section
- 3 verbs from your section
- 4 nouns from your section
- 3 adverbs from your section
- 2 different adjectives from your section
- a word that represents something important from the end of your section

Decorate and add a drawing to your poem.

Mary scaffolded the writing of the poems for the newcomers, helping them choose the key important words and working with them to find words that fit the parts of speech. With her second-year emergent bilinguals, Mary also provided individual support and had students work in groups to brainstorm ideas and discuss drawings to illustrate their poems. Figure 5–11 shows one group's work, the found poem "Gamemakers."

FIGURE 5–11 *Found Poem "Gamemakers"*

Sequence, Tone, and Actions

Mary planned assignments that would show that students understood each section of the book and that they were developing the concepts required by the standards. One assignment was for students to create a page that listed the key characters in a section of the book; summarize the beginning, middle, and end of the section and its tone; and include quotes representing talking, thinking, action, and seeing. This was a complex assignment, so Mary first provided the students with an example and discussed it with the class. One group of students used the section where the main character, Katniss, volunteers to fight for her district to replace her younger sister, who was chosen in the lottery. The students listed the characters. Next, they summarized the beginning, middle, and end of the section and identified the tone as tense. Then they found appropriate quotes: For talking—"I volunteer." "I gasp." "I volunteer as tribute." For thinking—"I don't need to shove through the crowd." For action—"I push her behind me." And for seeing—"He's looking at me with a pained expression." This was difficult for the students, but they were able to succeed because Mary had provided background through earlier activities with the short stories, and then she worked closely with individuals and groups as they completed the assignment.

Valentine Assignment and Facebook Page

Students were reading *The Hunger Games* in February. The novel and the characters seemed to lend themselves to having students choose two characters and have one write a valentine to the other. Mary included specific instructions for the valentine. Students had to tell why they were sending the card, what they liked about the

FIGURE 5–12 *Valentine*

person, their favorite memories of the person, and their hopes for a future together. Figure 5–12 shows one student's elaborate valentine to Gale from Katniss, which includes many specific details from the novel.

The valentine project was followed by another project that engaged Mary's students and also required them to show that they understood details about the characters in the novel. Each student created a Facebook page for one of the characters. It was clear that students understood what Facebook pages included, so they eagerly added drawings, friends from the novel, and profile information for the character they chose. For example, a Facebook page of Katniss included a cover photo drawing of the woods with a profile picture of Katniss with her bow and arrow. Below this was her profile information, including the fact she lived in District 12 and attended a District 12 school. When she commented she hated The Capitol, the creator of this Facebook page had characters in the novel respond with likes and comments. Pages also included "Recent Activity" sections and comments from friends about Katniss.

Newspaper Project

As the students were completing the novel, Mary assigned them a newspaper project. They had written in journals, composed a valentine letter, created a Facebook profile, and now Mary had them write in different newspaper genres. She brought in copies of local newspapers and discussed the different sections with the class. She then told them they would work in small groups to create a newspaper for District 12 that included the following pages:

> **Page 1.** A breaking news story from any part of the novel plus an advertisement
>
> **Page 2.** Obituaries of five of the tributes that had died up to this point in the novel

Page 3. Advice column: One character writes asking for advice about something from the story and the advice that the person answers. This was accompanied by a comic strip (minimum five squares) with a scene from the story showing the problem the character is having.

Page 4. Weather for the week

Page 5. Write as a sports report: Write what has happened in *The Hunger Games* so far.

Like the other creative assignments, the students eagerly tackled this one. In one group's advice column Katniss asked about eating wild berries while hunting in the woods, and her sister, Prim, told her to never eat the nightlock berries. These berries are a key detail as the novel unfolds.

Students were creative in their descriptions of the sports pages, showing they had listened to sports broadcasters. One Sports News page began, "There is Katniss running as fast as she can with an arrow and a bow in her hands, jumping some obstacles." The obituary page had little text but also showed that students found details in the text about contestants in the Hunger Games who had died (see Figure 5–13).

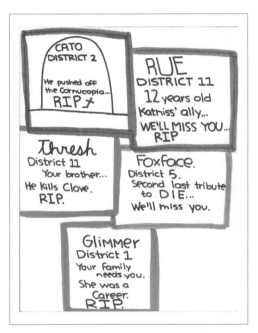

FIGURE 5–13 Hunger Games *Obituaries*

CD Soundtrack Project

The valentine, Facebook, and newspaper projects were followed by a complex group project asking students to create a soundtrack for the movie adaptation of the novel. When Mary taught this unit, the movie was still being filmed. Students were required to choose music that fit the mood/tone of different parts of the story. The instructions for this project were specific and detailed:

> Directions for the Soundtrack Project: Create a cover for a soundtrack CD for *The Hunger Games*. On the back cover list fourteen songs you included in the soundtrack. For each of the fourteen songs, on a separate paper write the name of the song and the artist/group. What part of the book will this song be for? Write the page and sentence before the song comes on. Explain why you put this song here.

Mary's students talked together and shared ideas about the songs they would choose. To complete this project, students needed to thoroughly understand the novel and think about what songs would be appropriate at key points in the novel. Mary's emergent bilinguals were familiar with music in both English and Spanish. They identified songs in English by artists such as Katy Perry, and in Spanish artists such as Motel and Pepe Aguilar. They were engaged in this project. It was meaningful for them because it connected what they were doing in school with their funds of knowledge (Moll 1994), their interest in popular music that was developed outside school.

Future Unit Literary Terms Dictionary

To support the English language development of her emergent bilingual students and to meet the standard for developing content-specific vocabulary, Mary had her students make and keep a Future Unit Literary Terms Dictionary. As the students read the various short stories and the novel, they created individual dictionaries with academic vocabulary. In addition to learning literary terms such as *setting* and *protagonist*, the students studied how writers use action verbs and descriptive adjectives to make their writing memorable. They included these terms in their dictionary.

Each entry included the title of the story, the vocabulary term, a sentence from the story with the term, a synonym of that term, and a drawing if appropriate. For example, one student chose the action verb *slammed* from "Harrison Bergeron." She wrote this sentence from the story: "He slammed them back into their chairs." Then she drew a picture of a person pushing someone into a chair and listed the synonym, "hit hard." Students kept these dictionaries throughout the unit and used them as a reference for their own writing.

Future Unit Review and Student-Created Future Stories

To conclude the unit, Mary involved students in two final activities. First, to review the stories, she had students answer literal and inferential questions about the stories. For each reading she asked them, "What was the author's prediction about the future?" and "What can our society do to keep the prediction from coming true?" Students were also asked to look back at the future poster they had made at the beginning of the unit and describe one of the predictions they had made.

For the final project, students worked in small groups to create a book that takes places in the future. Students used their imagination to write a book as they considered what life would be like in the future. Book titles included *The Flying Shoes*, *Fighting for Love*, and *Johnny of the Future*. The students enjoyed reading each other's finished stories.

CONCLUSION

As teachers consider what kinds of activities will best help their students learn the content they are teaching, they should keep in mind the principle, "Teaching should be meaningful and purposeful to engage students." When students are given repetitive tasks that do not interest them or are required to memorize information that they have no connection with, they are likely to quickly forget what they learn, or they may not learn it at all. Students were engaged in Mary and Elizabeth's Graffiti Wall and other culture-related activities because the future teachers could draw on their own experiences as they developed a definition of culture. The activities were meaningful and purposeful because the teachers knew they could use them in their own future teaching.

Culturally relevant books are meaningful to students because they connect with their life experiences. These books engage them in reading. Emergent bilinguals, in particular, need to be able to draw on their background knowledge as they read in another language. When they see themselves or their languages in the books they read they are motivated to read.

The idioms activities that Mary's students completed were meaningful because the students wanted to interact with their peers and needed to understand these idioms in English. The assignment to create idiom posters engaged them because they used their creativity to illustrate the literal meanings of idioms and write the figurative meanings.

The final extended Future Unit shows how one high school teacher met several language arts standards working with students with different levels of English proficiency. Students wrote in a variety of genres, responded orally and in writing to authentic texts, and produced creative projects. Rather than having students study isolated vocabulary, read adapted texts that didn't interest them, and fill in worksheets, Mary made their classes meaningful, purposeful, and engaging while challenging students with complex content and concepts. As these examples show, effective teaching is meaningful and purposeful, it engages emergent bilinguals, and it helps them develop both academic language and knowledge of academic content.

APPLICATIONS

1. At the beginning of the chapter, we explained how students created a Culture Graffiti Wall. Try out this activity and some of the other activities Mary and Elizabeth used with your own students. Report back on how the activities worked and how you adapted them to your students.

2. For your content area, choose a topic you are working on with your students. Have your students draw a Venn diagram that reflects the concepts and fill it in. For example, students could do a Venn diagram comparing and contrasting conifers and deciduous tress, putting the facts within a drawing of each type of tree and overlapping the two drawings to show what they have in common.

3. Mary had students make idiom posters. Consider having your students make similar posters for similes, metaphors, and hyperbole. Share the results with colleagues.

4. Bring to class at least three books you consider to be culturally relevant. Be prepared to explain how these books fit the culturally relevant rubric.

5. Consider the different activities Mary's students engaged in during the Future Unit. Identify one of the activities, and be ready to discuss how it was meaningful and purposeful and how it engaged students. How could you adapt this activity for your class?

6

Teaching Should Include Interactions to Develop Both Oral and Written Language

THE IMPORTANCE OF INTERACTION

Researchers have pointed out the importance of interaction in learning. As Faltis and Hudelson (1998) state, "learning and language acquisition overlap to a great extent in the sense that both are social, contextual, and goal-oriented. That is, individuals learn both content and language as they engage with others in a variety of settings to accomplish specific purposes" (85). According to Faltis and Hudelson, "learning does not happen exclusively inside the heads of learners; it results from social interactions with others that enable learners to participate by drawing on past and present experiences and relating them to the specific context at hand in some meaningful way" (87). This social view of learning applies to all learning, including learning a language and learning academic content.

Research supports the importance of planning interactions among students to support their development of academic language and subject matter content. The Academic Language Development Network, a collaborative project cohoused at the University of California–Davis and Stanford University, focuses on research-based practices for developing the academic language and literacy skills needed to meet the demands of the Common Core State Standards. Researchers used a Delphi method research design to identify the essential practices for developing oral and written academic language. One practice that the panel identified as essential was fostering academic interactions. According to the researchers:

Fostering academic interactions focuses on structuring and strengthening student-to-student interaction that uses academic language. Interaction consists of students responding to one another, building and challenging ideas, and negotiating meaning. The teacher provides and scaffolds multiple opportunities for students to interact with original academic messages that require academic language. (O'Hara, Zwiers, and Pritchard 2014, 26)

The researchers explain the practices teachers can follow to foster interaction. Teachers should provide opportunities for students to engage in different kinds of interactions that require them to use academic language. For example, after completing a science experiment in which students alternate putting their hands in bowls with hot and cold water and then recording their reactions, they can work in small groups to discuss what they experienced and to form a hypothesis to account for their reactions. Then groups report out their results to other groups during a whole-class discussion.

A WONDERFILLED WAY OF LEARNING: KAREN'S FAST FOOD AND HEALTHY EATING UNIT

Karen's unit on fast food and healthy eating provides a good example of how a teacher can plan meaningful interactions to promote oral and written language development. Karen teaches a seventh-grade class that includes twelve emergent bilinguals and fifteen native English speakers. She has found that the techniques she uses to make lessons comprehensible for her English learners are important for all her students. She organizes her curriculum around big question units of inquiry and teaches academic language and content. As she plans her lessons, she thinks carefully about how she will group her students to promote interaction as they complete activities and projects.

The fast food unit activities described here are on the topic of health and nutrition. A controversy arose in the school district where Karen taught when some school cafeterias began to serve fast food from known restaurant chains. Students in her class were discussing the new food options and knew that this topic was on the local news and in the local newspaper. Karen saw this interest and student discussion as an opportunity to engage her students. The state health standards required seventh graders to be able to do several things related to nutrition: describe the short- and long-term impact of nutritional choices on health, differentiate between diets that are health-promoting and diets linked to disease, and analyze the caloric and nutritional value of foods and vegetables.

Karen's fast food and nutrition unit activities follow the steps of the Wonderfilled Way of Learning suggested by Don Howard (personal communication) when he was a teacher in Tucson, Arizona. Teachers can develop units by following Don's six steps, which we have modified slightly. The steps of the Wonderfilled Way of Learning include finding out what students know about a topic, asking what they wonder about the topic, and then brainstorming possible ways to find out about the topic. Then the teacher and students make an action plan to carry out their investigation and connect the plan to standards. After they have researched their topic, they present their findings in different ways. In the following sections, we describe Karen's unit, and then we show how the unit follows the steps of the Wonderfilled Way of Learning.

Throughout the various activities of Karen's unit, there were many opportunities for students to work together and learn from one another. The students did lots of talking, listening, reading, and writing, employing all four modes. In this chapter, we will discuss the importance of carefully planned interactions as students talk about the content they are studying, listen to each other as they investigate, read to gain more information, and write about what they are learning. Karen's unit engaged students from the beginning as she asked them to talk about fast food and what they knew about fast foods.

Fast Food

Karen started the lesson by announcing, "Today we're going to talk about a special kind of food, fast food. Do any of you know the names of some fast food restaurants?" As the students called out names of restaurants—including McDonald's, Wendy's, Subway, Pizza Hut, and Taco Bell—Karen wrote the names on the board. After a few minutes she had compiled a list of twenty different restaurants. Then she asked, "What kinds of food can you buy in these restaurants?" She worked through the list of restaurants with the class, writing down the kinds of food each restaurant serves. The students knew that they could get hamburgers and fries at McDonald's and that Pizza Hut had pizza and salad. This opening activity helped Karen assess what her students knew about fast foods. She paid particular attention to which students were volunteering answers, and she made a point of calling on some of her emergent bilinguals who were not participating as much as the native English speakers. As with many of the activities in this unit, Karen combined oral and written language so students could develop proficiency in all four language domains.

When the students had named several kinds of foods for each restaurant, Karen asked them to do a quick-write. "In the next two minutes, write down what you like and what you dislike about fast food." The students worked busily for the next two minutes, often glancing up at the board where the names of the restaurants and foods were listed. At the end of the time, Karen asked students to gather in groups of three and make one composite list. She grouped her English learners by home language so they could use their first language and English for this discussion. The students pushed their desks together and started compiling their lists. Karen circulated around the room, noting what the students were writing and answering their questions. After a few minutes, she asked the students to stop. "I'm going to start with what you like about fast food. I'll ask each group to give me one thing you wrote down, and I'll put it on the Smart Board."

Karen elicited first the likes and then the dislikes from the groups, projecting their responses so all the students could see them. Several of the likes and dislikes related to health matters. One group commented that they disliked fast food because it was high in fat. Another group stated that fast food was too salty. Karen continued, "You've said that in some ways fast food is not very healthy. What do you think? Is fast food healthy or not?" Some of the students stated that it was not healthy to eat fast food, but others pointed out that if you were careful you could find healthy food at a fast food restaurant by eating salads or low-calorie foods like some of the Subway sandwiches.

Healthy Eating and Fast Foods

Next, Karen asked the class how they could find out about fast food and healthy eating. The students brainstormed several ideas, including reading books, doing Internet searches, and asking experts. Karen summed up the students' responses and then said, "I'd like one person from each group to do a computer search for healthy fast food. Meanwhile, I'd like the other two students to discuss what makes a healthy meal and write down your ideas." Again, as the students discussed this question and conducted computer searches, Karen circulated around the room to answer questions and ensure that students stayed on task.

After about ten minutes, she came to the front of the room and asked the students who had been searching on the computer what they had found. Roberto reported that he had been directed to helpguide.org (retrieved from www.help guide.org/articles/healthy-eating/healthy-fast-food.htm). This website had quite a few tips for healthy eating at fast food restaurants, such as "try to keep your meal under 500 calories" and "watch your sodium intake." He went on, "It also has some good tips, like choosing grilled or roasted lean meats."

Anna said she had found some interesting information on the *Fitness* magazine website (retrieved from www.fitnessmagazine.com/recipes/healthy-eating /on-the-go/healthy-fast-foods/). This website had specific suggestions for different fast food restaurants. Anna reported, "The website recommends the Caesar salad with grilled chicken and low-fat balsamic vinaigrette dressing from McDonald's, the egg white veggie wake-up wrap from Dunkin' Donuts, and the half smoked-turkey breast on artisan whole grain loaf plus low-fat garden vegetable with pesto soup from Panera. It gives the calories and grams of fat for each item and has healthy suggestions for lots of the restaurants on our list."

After two more students reported what they had found, Karen asked the students who had listed their ideas for healthy eating to share what they had written down. The students in each group listed factors that make a healthy meal. They mentioned low fat, low sugar, and a balance of all the food groups. Next, Karen asked the class how the Internet suggestions for healthy fast food compared with what they had listed. This led to a good discussion. Karen also reminded the students to look back at what they had brainstormed earlier about what they liked and disliked about fast food since several students said it was not healthy.

Planning a Healthy Diet

At this point, Karen felt that all the students had enough background on the topic of healthy eating to explore in more depth the big question, "What makes a healthy diet that provides good nutrition?" She explained that the students would begin by looking at different print resources from the library and several Internet sites to determine what experts say is a healthy diet. They would use sources such as www.choosemyplate.gov/food-groups/, http://healthyeating.sfgate.com/four-basic-food-groups-kids-7043.html, and www.nutrition.gov/smart-nutrition-101/healthy-eating to find current information. Using this information, each group would write a report and also make an oral presentation to the class.

Different Views of Healthy Eating

During the unit, the students also studied how ideas about good nutrition have changed over time. One Wikipedia website Karen reviewed with them was http://en.wikipedia.org/wiki/History_of_USDA_nutrition_guides, which includes images of the various graphics that have been used to represent the food groups. For example, some images represented the food groups as a pyramid. Several students remembered seeing this on a cereal box. Other images showed the food groups using a pie chart. Karen and the students discussed how different visual representations were more or less effective for presenting the information. They also compared and contrasted current views of healthy eating with earlier views. These activities, designed to have students identify similarities and differences, helped her students develop both content knowledge and academic language. Marzano and his colleagues (Marzano, Pickering, and Pollock 2001) reviewed research showing that having students identify similarities and differences is one of the most effective strategies for increasing student achievement.

Since her students conducted Internet searches as they researched healthy eating, Karen also spent time discussing with them the different kinds of websites and the pros and cons of using each type. Most of her student realized that sites with URLs ending in .gov were government sites, such as the sites developed by the U.S. Department of Agriculture and other government entities. Some knew that .org, short for organization, was for groups such as the American Association of Retired Persons (AARP), the American Cancer Society, or Public Broadcasting Service (PBS), and that most of these are nonprofit organizations. Fewer students understood that websites with URLs ending in .com were commercial sites developed by for-profit organizations, such as the *Fitness* magazine site or any of the fast food company websites.

Karen asked her students to think about which of these sites was most reliable. Many of her students assumed that anything on the web must be true. They looked into how Wikipedia entries are created. Karen pointed out that some Wikipedia entries are well documented with current research while others are not clearly based on research. The class found examples of more reliable and less reliable entries and brought them in for class discussion. They also discussed the possible bias that some sites, especially .com sites, might have. Students agreed that a fast food restaurant web page, for example, would probably show that food from that restaurant is good for you, so that claim should be checked against other information.

Other activities during the unit included visits to local fast food restaurants, which included tours and free pamphlets, interviewing parents and friends about their eating habits, and surveying students from other classes about how often they ate fast food and which restaurants were their favorites. Perhaps the most important activity, however, was having students analyze their own eating habits. Students kept track of their diet over several days in a journal and then analyzed the results. This assignment provided an excellent opportunity to discuss the wide variety of foods that students from different cultural groups ate. The students also talked about what different cultures considered healthy or unhealthy eating. For example, in some cultures it is considered unhealthy to combine hot and cold food during a meal. Many cultures have very little meat or only certain meats in their diets. Some diets are high in carbohydrates and vegetables and low in meats. Online searches showed different food pyramids for different ethnic or regional groups, including an Asian food pyramid, a Japanese food pyramid, an African food pyramid, a Hispanic food pyramid, and regional U.S. food pyramids that included a southern U.S. food pyramid.

During these different activities, all of Karen's students developed the academic language and content associated with food and health through reading, writing, speaking, and listening. They worked individually, in pairs, and in small groups as they investigated questions about food and health. Some groups chose to look at the traditional food customs of their own culture and contrast those with typical

American dietary habits. Others investigated whether or not immigrants to the United States retain their own eating habits or adopt U.S. customs. Still others reviewed popular diets, like the Mediterranean diet, to see how these diets compared with recommendations from different organizations about good nutrition. What was important was that as they explored these questions, Karen's students increased their content area knowledge and also developed their oral and written language proficiency.

At the end of the unit students worked in small groups to make PowerPoint presentations on healthy eating and the pros and cons of eating fast food. Each group took a different aspect of what they had been studying. Some talked about how to determine the nutritional value of fast food meals at different restaurants; others talked about the older food pyramid and the new view of how we should look at our overall diet; and still others decided to compare and contrast healthy diets in different countries. When they were finished, the principal asked the student groups to present their PowerPoints to the whole school at an assembly. They rehearsed carefully and practiced in front of the class before making these presentations. Because the school community was interested in the topic of fast food being served at school, the students were also invited to present at a Parent-Teacher Association (PTA) meeting. In the end, their research and presentations benefited the entire school and the community.

A WONDERFILLED WAY OF LEARNING

As we mentioned earlier, this unit on healthy eating follows a unit plan model developed by Don Howard called The Wonderfilled Way of Learning. Teachers can develop units by following Don's six steps, which we have modified slightly:

Step 1: Ask the students: "What do we know about _____?"

Step 2: Ask the students: "What do we wonder about _____?"

Step 3: Ask the students: "How can we find out about _____?"

Step 4: With the students, work out a plan of action and, at the same time, ensure that the lessons teach the knowledge and skills required by federal and state standards.

Step 5: Plan some kind of celebration of what all of you have learned together.

Step 6: Learning is continuous. From any unit, more topics and questions come up. Begin the cycle again.

This model differs from the traditional K-W-L (What does the student **K**now? What does the student **W**ant to know? What has the student **L**earned?) approach in that it helps teachers focus in more depth on what students are interested in, and it involves the students in each step. This method of planning curriculum follows the principles we have discussed. The teaching is learner centered; it goes from the whole, the big question, to the parts; it involves teaching both language and content; it is meaningful for students; and it includes student interactions to develop both oral and written language.

The first step in this process is to choose a topic. The topic may arise naturally from student questions or from events that students find interesting. For example, students who see programs on TV about a water shortage and area drought might ask whether there will be enough water for people to drink or take baths. This could lead to answering a question like "Where does the water we use come from?" Or, having seen on TV the devastation of flooding in one part of the country and the problems of drought in another, students might ask, "How do weather patterns change, and what causes both droughts and floods?" Sometimes a topic comes directly from something that happens at school. In the case of Karen's topic on food and nutrition, students knew of a community controversy because the cafeteria was beginning to sell food from well-known fast food chains. The school claimed food sales increased dramatically, but concerned parents were not convinced that the sale of fast food was healthy. Since Karen's science standards connected to the topic of nutrition, she decided that fast food and nutrition might be a good unit of study.

After the topic is chosen, the teacher and students work together to combine their resources and discover what they already know about the topic. Bransford and colleagues (Bransford, Brown, and Cocking 2000) reviewed research showing the importance of building on students' current knowledge. As they state, "Teachers must draw out and work with the preexisting understandings that their students bring with them" (19). This can be done in a brainstorming session with the teacher writing on the board. Or, the teacher can put up butcher paper and ask students to list things they know over several days. As students list what they know, English learners naturally learn key vocabulary. During this time, teachers can also begin to assess students' background knowledge. Through brainstorming fast food restaurants and considering their likes and dislikes about fast food, Karen assessed what her students already knew and what would be good topics to continue to investigate.

After the students have reviewed what they know about a topic, they can begin to list their wonders. In Karen's case, students wondered whether or not fast food was healthy. In a discussion on water shortage or flooding, students might ask,

"Where does water come from?" "How much water is produced by melting snow?" "What would happen if there were no rain next year?" At this stage, teachers can help students focus on big questions. Again, these questions can be collected over several days. Students can talk with siblings and parents to find out what their questions are as well.

The third step, how to find out about a topic, is extremely important. It involves building background on the topic students want to learn about. Marzano (2004) has reviewed research on the importance of assessing and building background knowledge when teaching. Fisher and Frey (2009) have also shown the importance of building background, and they suggest a number of ways teachers build background to help students succeed. Karen's lesson shows how she draws on her students' background knowledge and also builds background they need.

The teacher does not need to provide all the answers to students' questions. Instead, the teacher works with the students to discover how they can find out the things they want to know. For example, they could read a book, watch a movie, browse the Internet, or invite in a guest speaker. During this step, students start to take responsibility for finding ways to answer their own questions. In Karen's lesson, students brainstormed ways to find out about fast food and decided they could read books, do Internet searches, tour fast-food restaurants, and ask experts.

When resources have been identified, the students and teacher work together to develop an action plan. What will they do and what will the timeline be? If the teacher has certain standards to meet, these can be worked into the action plan. Most teachers find that as they explore a topic, students go well beyond minimum standards. At the same time, teachers can be sure to include in the action plan any items the district requires. Since teachers are teaching both content and language, they also plan specific minilessons to present on certain language structures. For example, in some lessons Karen focused on comparative and superlative constructions as students compared and contrasted meals from different fast-food restaurants.

After students and teachers have completed their plan, it is important to have a clear closure, a celebration of learning. This might take the form of a book or a play presented to other classes. Karen's students presented the information they gathered to the whole school and the PTA.

As students finish answering one set of questions, they come up with new "wonders" that become the basis for beginning the cycle of "wonderfilled" lessons all over again. This method of organizing curriculum is very different from traditional methods because it starts and ends with topics and questions that have meaning for the students right now.

Using the steps of the Wonderfilled Way of Learning as a guide, teachers can apply all the principles for successful practice. Figure 6–1 shows how the lessons in Karen's healthy eating unit correspond to the Wonderfilled Way of Learning.

1. What do you know about fast food, and what do you know about healthy eating?

   a. Students brainstormed names of fast food restaurants and the food served in each restaurant.

   b. Students did a quick-write about what they liked and disliked about fast food. They shared their answers in small groups and with the class.

2. What do you wonder about how healthy fast food is?

   Based on student responses, Karen asked whether students thought that fast food was healthy or not. This led to a discussion of what made a healthy meal.

3. How can we find out?

   Karen had the students brainstorm ideas for finding answers to their questions.

4. Action plan

   a. Students conducted Internet searches on healthy fast food and compared the results with what they thought a healthy meal would be.

   b. Students read pamphlets, magazines, and other materials about fast food.

   c. They conducted Internet searches on healthy eating.

   d. They compared and contrasted different images for the basic food groups and the recommended servings from each one.

   e. They researched changes in the view of healthy eating over time.

   f. They researched the views of healthy eating of different cultural groups.

   g. They toured fast food restaurants and read the materials the restaurants provided.

   h. They interviewed friends and family members.

   i. They analyzed their own eating habits.

   j. Groups of students researched questions related to healthy eating.

5. Celebration

   Students prepared and presented PowerPoints on fast food and healthy eating to the entire school and the PTA.

FIGURE 6–1 *The Wonderfilled Way of Learning—Fast Food and Nutrition*

THE IMPORTANCE OF INTERACTION FOR LEARNING LANGUAGE

Second language and foreign language educators have debated the role that student interaction plays in language development. Krashen's (1992) theory of second language acquisition describes how individuals acquire language. He argues that language is acquired when students receive comprehensible input (messages they understand) that contains language structures that are slightly in advance of their present ability level. Social interaction plays only an indirect role in his theory. According to Krashen, social interactions help students manage conversations better and help students refine their ideas. In addition, these interactions can provide the comprehensible input needed for language acquisition. However, Krashen contends that language acquisition results from input, and the best sources of input come from teachers and others who can make the messages understandable or from reading interesting texts.

Input, Output, and Interaction

Other researchers have given importance to output as well as input. Ellis (1990) refers to theories such as Krashen's as reception based. He classifies theories that include attention to output as production based. According to Johnson (1995), "Reception-based theories contend that interaction contributes to second language acquisition via learners' reception and comprehension of the second language, whereas production-based theories credit this process to learners' attempts at actually producing the language" (82).

Long (1983) developed the interaction hypothesis, a theory of SLA that is reception based. Long claims that learners make conversational adjustments as they interact with others and that these adjustments help make the input comprehensible. As Johnson (1995) points out, "Like Krashen, Long stresses the importance of comprehensible input but places more emphasis on the interaction that takes place in two-way communication and the adjustments that are made as a result of the negotiation of meaning" (83).

Swain (1985) argues that language learners need opportunities for output. She noted that students in French immersion classes did not reach nativelike proficiency in French. These students were in classes where teachers did most of the talking. Peer interaction was limited, and when interaction occurred students spoke only with others learning French rather than with native speakers of French. Based on her observations of these students, Swain proposed that second language acquisition depends on output as well as input. According to Scarcella (1990), Swain's comprehensible output hypothesis:

suggests that students need tasks which elicit . . . talk at the student's i + 1, that is, a level of second language proficiency which is just a bit beyond the current second language proficiency level. She claims that such output provides opportunities for meaningful context-embedded use for the second language, which allows students to test out their hypotheses about the language and "move the learner from a purely semantic analysis of the language to a syntactic analysis of it." (70)

Swain's claim is that when we receive input that we understand, we focus on meaning—or the semantic level. However, in talking, we need to string sentences together and this requires attention to syntax. Our syntactic analysis is probably not conscious, but producing output requires us to access parts of the language system that are different from what we use to comprehend input.

One model of SLA that includes both input and output has been developed by Van Lier (1988) and our adaptation is shown in Figure 6–2. Van Lier claims that certain conditions are necessary for certain outcomes. According to this model, if learners are receptive during exposure to a new language, their attention will be focused. If attention is focused, the language becomes input. If learners invest some mental energy in the input, they will begin to comprehend it. Language that is comprehended changes from input to intake. If learners practice with intake, they can retain the language and access it later. Language that can be accessed is considered uptake. Finally, with authentic use, learners can extend their language and use it creatively. It is the ability to use language creatively that is a measure of proficiency.

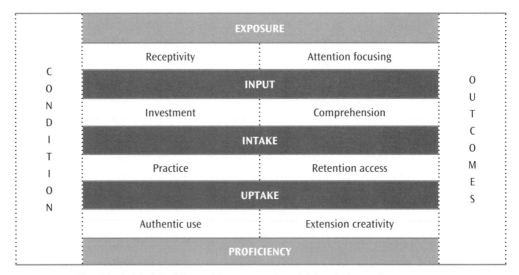

FIGURE 6–2 *Van Lier's Model of Second Language Acquisition* (adapted)

The Importance of Interaction

Several researchers have pointed out the importance of interaction for language acquisition. Grosjean (2010) refers to Wong-Fillmore's (1991) approach for learning a language. She reports that the successful second language learners she studied relied on three strategies. Grosjean explains the three steps.

1. Join a group and act as if you know what is going on, even if you don't
2. Give the impression, with a few well-chosen words, that you can speak the language
3. Count on your friends for help. (187)

By using these three general strategies, the good language learners were more fully involved with native speakers, and, in the process, they acquired both conversational and academic language.

In their review of the research on effective practices for emergent bilinguals, Goldenberg (2013) lists "active student engagement and participation" (5) as one effective practice and "providing hands-on, interactive activities" (7) as an additional support that emergent bilinguals need. Saunders and his colleagues (Saunders, Goldenberg, and Marcelletti 2013) list as one of their curricular guidelines for effective, research-based ELD instruction, "ELD instruction should include interactive activities among students, but they must be carefully planned and carried out" (23).

Emergent bilinguals need to develop communicative competence. Hymes (1970) defines communicative competence as knowing what to say to whom, when, and in what circumstances. Learning a language involves more than developing grammatical competence. Learners must also develop the knowledge of how to use the language appropriately in different situations. The norms for communicative competence vary from one linguistic and sociocultural group to another, and part of what we acquire when we acquire a language is the ability to function effectively in different settings. Often, second language learners have developed grammatical competence but still lack communicative competence. Emergent bilinguals can only develop communicative competence through interacting with native speakers socially or through carefully planned and structured classroom interactions.

Earlier we discussed how the TESOL organization has developed English language proficiency standards. The first standard is that "English language learners communicate for social, intercultural, and instructional purposes within the school setting" (3). This standard clearly points to the need to help ELs develop communicative competence as they interact in classroom contexts. Often, as teachers we focus on the academic content we are teaching, but when classes include emergent bilinguals it is also important to teach them how to use language in culturally appropriate ways in the classroom as they interact with their teacher and other students.

For example, communicative competence involves learning how to enter a conversation or to end one. In our native language, we seem to know instinctively the rules for contributing to an ongoing discussion. However, English language learners often have trouble knowing when to add to a classroom discussion. They may jump in at what seems to be an inappropriate time, or they may remain silent, even when called on. Classroom discussions may be particularly difficult if students have had previous schooling in other countries where the unwritten rules for discussion were quite different from the rules in their new country. Students benefit when teachers make the rules for classroom interactions explicit. In addition, teachers need to understand the importance of interaction for emergent bilinguals and know how to structure interaction in meaningful and engaging ways.

Organizing the Classroom for Interaction

The way a teacher organizes the classroom can either promote or inhibit student interaction. Figure 6–3 contrasts practices that encourage interaction with those that discourage students from talking and working together. English learners need opportunities for functional use of the language they are developing, and classroom organization plays an important role in determining the possible interactions students can have.

Unfortunately, the emphasis in American education has been on individual learning, not on social interaction. We see this individual emphasis in various

Restricts Social Interaction	Facilitates Social Interaction
• Seating is in straight rows.	• Desks are together in groups, or there are tables and chairs.
• Students do not move from seats.	• Students move freely and purposefully around the room.
• Only the teacher controls materials in the room.	• Students have ownership of the room, and they use and care for materials.
• The teacher works with reading groups while others read individually or complete worksheets.	• Students do shared reading, literature studies, and writer's workshop. They conduct research in inquiry groups.
• Students complete work for individual grades.	• Students work together on group projects for group grades.
• Silence is the golden rule.	• Students are encouraged to talk together to share ideas.

FIGURE 6–3 *Classroom Characteristics and Interaction*

traditional ways: Classrooms are set up with straight rows facing the teacher. In some math classes, students begin with five problems for the day. After the teacher introduces a new type of problem, students spend the rest of math time working individually to practice the skill that has been presented. In some traditional social studies classes, students spend the majority of their time silently reading chapters from the text and answering the end-of-chapter questions by themselves. As a result, emergent bilinguals in classes that follow this traditional pattern have little opportunity for social interaction.

The traditional, individual approach to education does not serve students well because learning is a social activity. This is true for any area of study, and it is particularly important for language study. Zwiers (2014) devotes a chapter in his book *Building Academic Language* to academic listening and speaking for students working in small groups and pairs. He begins by noting, "No matter how well we might engage the whole class in discussion, many students—often our diverse students—miss out on chances to talk" (151). He acknowledges that many challenges arise when having students work in small groups, such as behavior problems, high noise levels, and time wasted when students are off task. He points out that planning and carrying out effective group work takes time and careful attention to developing activities that produce academic talk. He goes on to give many good suggestions for ways teachers can use small-group and pair work to help students gain academic language proficiency.

Zwier's activities challenge students to think as they interact. For example, his Opinion Formation Cards Activity helps students interact as they build their opinion on a topic. Students are given different-colored cards on a topic of interest, such as the effects of watching TV. Different studies are summarized on the cards, including studies on how watching TV leads to violence and studies on how watching educational TV supports early reading. Students read their color-coded card to someone with another colored card and state their opinions. This activity can be scaffolded by giving the students a sentence frame, such as "In my opinion, _____ because _____."

As students interact and share their opinions, they build understanding, use language meaningfully, and develop academic language skills. In a related activity, Infer Themes from a Paragraph, students are given color-coded cards with a paragraph from a fiction text. They read these to one another and then predict what they think this paragraph tells them about the theme of the text. As they meet with others and listen to the different paragraphs, students work together to determine what the theme of the story might be (retrieved from www.jeffzwiers.org /oral-communication.html).

Cross-Age Tutoring

One activity that promotes social interaction is cross-age tutoring. Although there are different kinds of tutoring programs, all these programs create situations in which students can develop greater oral and written language proficiency as they interact with one another.

Cross-age tutoring programs link older students with younger students. For example, Charlene, a fourth-grade teacher who had many English language learners in her classroom, arranged for her students to read to first graders weekly. The fourth graders chose books they thought were appropriate for the first graders. They practiced reading them to one another in preparation for their visit to the first-grade buddies. Many of Charlene's fourth graders were emergent bilinguals themselves. Because the books written for the younger children often followed predictable patterns and had pictures that provided contextual support, Charlene's students were successful in reading them. Charlene was able to use these books to help her second language students develop reading proficiency in English without making them feel that they were reading "baby" books. Through the process of choosing books, practicing reading, and discussing the best ways to work with their reading buddies, the fourth graders had many chances to interact with one another and develop their oral skills as well as their reading ability.

Other teachers and teacher researchers have developed ideas for implementing cross-age tutoring in classes with English learners. Samway and her colleagues describe in detail the buddy reading system they set up in a multicultural school (Samway, Whang, and Pippitt 1995). In addition, a research project carried out in Canada on using seventh and eighth graders to teach reading to kindergartners showed that both the older students and the younger students benefited (Tiessen and Dust 2006). The buddy reading project:

> showed that partnerships between two unlikely groups of people can be beneficial for all involved. When the older students "helped" the kindergarten students, they realized that they were actually learning right along with their kindergarten partners. We felt that we were successful in creating a reading buddy program that met the needs of all students. (4)

Charlotte, a high school teacher, extended this idea of older learners sharing books. Charlotte's students were in her intervention reading class because they were considered to be low readers. Many were emergent bilinguals. She told her students they would be creating their own books and had the students read picture books so that they could find ideas to help them create their books. They spent a great deal of time discussing book ideas, writing the texts, and illustrating them.

Then students took the books they made home and read them to their younger siblings. The results were exciting for the students and their teacher. The students became much more confident readers, and the books they created were so beautifully written and illustrated that Charlotte was asked to share the project with other teachers throughout her school district. A number of websites, such as www .goodreads.com/shelf/show/picture-books-for-older-readers, list picture books for older learners.

Organizing Cross-Age Tutoring

Cross-age tutoring sessions can be conducted in different ways. Sometimes students read to two or three younger children together. More often the reading is one-to-one, with the older student reading first and then the younger one reading something he or she has written or has learned to read. The older students may work with the same student each time, or they may meet with different students in each session and read the same book to each of them.

More than reading is involved in tutoring sessions. Students talk together as they plan and practice their reading before going to read to their little buddies, and then there is more talk when they return to their class to debrief, to discuss the experience of working with the younger students. Labbo and Teale (1990) describe a successful cross-age tutoring program they were involved with. They list the four phases of that program:

1. *Preparation:* The teacher helps tutors, in this case fifth graders identified as low readers, select appropriate books from the library to read to kindergarten children. The fifth graders practice reading the books alone and in pairs to develop fluency. The teacher helps the tutors decide how to introduce the books to their kindergarten partners.

2. *Prereading collaboration:* Small-group collaboration time was established for the fifth graders to set personal goals, try out ideas, and receive and give feedback. They shared their books with other fifth graders and received feedback on the fluency of their oral reading and their expressiveness as well as on their use of questions and comments during discussion of the book. This time helped readers to prepare for successful sharing with the kindergarten students.

3. *Cross-age reading with the kindergartners:* The reading took place in the kindergarten room. Tutors from fifth grade chose their own partners and read to them. Some tutors read the same book to a different kindergarten child each day for a week, while others read a different book during each session.

4. *Postreading collaboration:* After their reading sessions, the tutors met with their teacher to reflect on the quality of the storybook reading interactions. During this time, the teacher also showed the fifth graders a number of strategies they could use with the kindergartners, such as asking them to predict what the story would be about or to make connections between the characters or events in the story and their own lives.

The success of this program rested on its careful organization. The older students were well prepared to work with the kindergartners. It is interesting that both groups of students learn through this kind of interaction. In fact, they learn not only reading skills but also social skills. One sixth-grade teacher whose students read every morning to younger children commented that her students were at their "most human" during that reading time.

Research and writing can also be involved in the cross-age tutoring projects. Heath and Mangiola (1991) describe a program that added a research dimension to a tutoring program. Older students were trained to take field notes and do a case study of their reading partner. These older students, who were labeled "at risk," became critical researchers as they analyzed their own work as tutors and their students' progress. In this way, the students became ethnographers. Heath and Mangiola's book contains many helpful suggestions for teachers wishing to implement a cross-age tutoring program.

Kay, a bilingual resource teacher in a small farming community, also showed that emergent bilinguals can benefit from a cross-age tutoring project. Seventh- and eighth-grade Spanish-speaking students read in Spanish to the monolingual Spanish-speaking kindergarten children at her school. The junior high school students who did this tutoring formed a Teachers of Tomorrow club. Several began to see themselves as future bilingual teachers. Their interest in doing well in English increased as these older students saw a need for both their native language and English in the future. The younger children they tutored were supported in their first language and also saw the older students as positive role models. All the students benefited from the social interaction of the tutoring.

All of these cross-age programs promoted student interaction and provided opportunities for students of different ages and language proficiencies to become better readers. Cross-age tutoring and reading programs have many benefits for emergent bilinguals. The English learners have a real meaning and purpose for reading and talking about books. They can read books that are below their grade level but are appropriate for their language level. They can learn and apply comprehension strategies. Extensions of the program, such as keeping a journal or conducting research, also help emergent bilinguals improve their writing skills.

Long and Porter's Study

Additional support for the importance of interaction in language learning comes from a study by Long and Porter (1985). They conducted research on group work for adult second language learners and found the following five benefits:

1. Group work increases language practice opportunities.
2. Group work improves the quality of student talk.
3. Group work helps individualize instruction.
4. Group work promotes a positive affective climate.
5. Group work motivates learners.

First, they discovered that in classes where teachers used collaborative group work, individual students had more chances to try out the language they were learning. In an hour-long class with one teacher and thirty students, each student only gets one or two minutes to talk, but when students discuss topics in groups, the talk opportunities are multiplied.

Not only does the quantity of student talk increase, so does the quality. This may seem strange at first because teachers might assume that students would make more mistakes when talking with each other since the teacher would not be there to correct errors. However, the researchers found that in small groups, students took risks and tried out more advanced structures and vocabulary than when they had to speak before the whole class. In the process of using more advanced language forms, the students increased their language proficiency.

Group work helps individualize instruction in two ways. For one, different groups can do different activities. This allows teachers to group students according to their interests or language proficiency levels. Not every student has to do the same assignment. In this way, grouping provides students with choice and makes assignments more meaningful. In addition, when students work in groups, teachers can move around the class and answer individual or small group questions.

The researchers also found that students enjoyed working in groups. The class atmosphere improved as students moved into groups. Students relaxed. At the same time, when students worked in groups, they were more motivated. They were motivated to help other group members. They realized that everyone's work was important to the success of the group.

Effective group work depends on careful organization, thoughtful selection of groups, and the active involvement of the teacher. The teacher has to think carefully through the task and give clear directions to avoid wasting time. Often groups are organized around student interests. Research has shown that students learn more in heterogeneous groups than in groups where the students are very similar in ability. On the other hand, at times teachers can group students homogeneously by home language, as Karen did during the unit on healthy eating, so that the students can draw on all their language resources.

When students begin to work in groups, teachers should circulate to check on progress and answer individual questions. It is also important to give groups an idea of how long they have to complete a task. Further, it is essential to have some sort of report-back period or group-produced product so that groups know that they are accountable for completing their work. As Long and Porter's research shows, when group work is well organized the increased social interaction has many benefits.

In addition to the benefits of group work for language acquisition, group work also aids in learning content. Marzano and colleagues (Marzano, Pickering, and Pollock 2001) reviewed the research on using cooperative groups and found that cooperative learning has a positive effect on student achievement. Dotson (2001) used cooperative learning structures in a study of students in sixth-grade social studies classes and found that cooperative learning resulted in higher scores on social studies curriculum assessments. Emergent bilinguals need many opportunities to work in groups with native English speakers as well as with other students who share the same home language.

THE IMPORTANCE OF DEVELOPING BOTH ORAL AND WRITTEN LANGUAGE

It is important for English learners to have many opportunities to speak, listen, read, and write as they did in Karen's health unit. Traditionally, however, most methods of teaching a second language begin with speaking and listening and only add reading and writing later. Grammar-Translation was an exception since this method typically includes little or no oral language teaching. The Natural Method and the Direct Method, in contrast, focused much more on oral language development.

The Audiolingual Method was based on insights from structural linguists who claimed that "Language is speech, not writing" (Diller 1978). ALM even proclaims the primacy of speech in its title. However, written language is also taught in ALM classes. In its original form the Natural Approach began with oral language and then added written language later. In later versions of the Natural Approach, written language was introduced at early stages. In professional materials, the four skill areas are also treated separately. Textbooks often discuss speaking, reading, writing, and listening in different chapters.

RESEARCH ON USING FOUR MODES

Even though some methods and materials emphasize oral language, researchers in second language acquisition have come to recognize the important contribution written language makes in the development of a new language. Krashen (2004) has found that reading for genuine interest with a focus on meaning provides language learners with written comprehensible input similar to oral comprehensible input. He argues that reading contributes to second language acquisition in the same way that listening contributes to oral language, and he proposes that reading contributes to competence in writing just as listening helps children develop the ability to speak.

Although earlier methods of teaching a second language emphasized teaching oral language first, with the increasing emphasis on testing and accountability, teachers often focus on written language since large-scale standardized tests require students to read and write and seldom measure oral language proficiency. This over-emphasis on written language is critiqued in the review of the research on English language development by Saunders and his colleagues (Saunders, Goldenberg, and Marcelletti 2013) who caution that "ELD instruction should incorporate reading and writing, but should emphasize listening and speaking" (23).

Research shows the importance of building oral language as well as literacy. In their review of research on literacy development for emergent bilinguals, the authors of the National Literacy Report (August and Shanahan 2006) found evidence that oral language development is important for growth in literacy. English learners with higher proficiency in oral language learn to read and write more easily than those with less ability in oral language. One of the major findings as reported in the executive summary is that "Instruction in the key components of reading is necessary—but not sufficient—for teaching language-minority students to read and write proficiently in English. Oral proficiency in English is critical as well" (4). The authors go on to say that "well-developed oral proficiency in English is associated with English reading comprehension and writing skills" (4). As this comprehensive review of the research on second language reading shows, it is important for teachers to integrate listening and speaking with reading and writing from the beginning.

DEVELOPING ALL FOUR MODES

Effective instruction for emergent bilinguals includes carefully planned interactions that develop oral and written language. Gibbons (2009) provides a model teachers can use to help develop academic language use as they learn content. The lesson sequence includes small-group work, teacher instruction, and student reading and writing.

Martin (1984, in Gibbons 2002) describes language use as ranging along a mode continuum. Martin observes that regardless of whether the language is oral or written, some language has the characteristics of spoken language and other language has characteristics of written language. At the spoken-like end of the continuum, we think of casual conversation as when discussing the weather or exchanging basic information. A text message to a friend would have characteristics of oral language even though it is written. On the other hand, an academic lecture would have some features of written language even though it is delivered orally. Both the lecture and text message might fall toward the middle of a spoken–written mode continuum. A newspaper article has syntax and vocabulary that is more written-like, and an academic journal article, such as an article from *TESOL Quarterly*, would have all the qualities associated with written language. Instruction designed to develop academic language proficiency builds on emergent bilinguals' oral language and moves them along the continuum from using language that is more spoken-like to language that is more written-like. Figure 6–4 shows some examples of language at different points on the continuum.

Gibbons (2002) provides an excellent model for teachers to use to help English learners move along the continuum and develop academic language through reading, writing, speaking, and listening. She begins by asking her readers to consider the differences between the following four texts:

- Look, it's making them move. Those don't stick.
- We found out the pins stuck on the magnet.
- Our experiments showed that magnets attract some metals.
- Magnetic attraction occurs only between ferrous metals. (40)

| | texting a friend | academic lecture | academic journal article |
| casual conversation | | academic discussion | newspaper article |

more spoken-like   **more written-like**

conversational language   **academic language**
fluency   **proficiency**
BICS   **CALP**

FIGURE 6–4 *Language Continuum*

The four texts represent the language students used in different contexts. The first three were produced as students first worked in small groups on a science experiment with magnets, then reported to the class, and finally wrote up the results. The first text was spoken by a girl during group work. The second was part of her oral report to the class. The third text is taken from her written report. The last text comes from a children's encyclopedia.

In analyzing the four texts, two things to note are that the reference becomes more explicit (the pronoun *them* is replaced by *pins*) and the vocabulary becomes more technical (*stuck* is replaced by *attract*). Explicit reference and technical vocabulary are features common to written academic language. During these activities students used oral language first and then applied what they had learned to writing a report.

The science experiment with magnets was a hands-on activity in which language was contextualized by the use of the manipulatives. In this part of the lesson, students used everyday expressions to comment on what they observed or to ask questions. They didn't need to name the objects because all the group members could see them. They could point and use gestures to convey meaning.

Next, the teacher briefly introduced the key concepts, *attract* and *repel*. She explained that these were more scientific terms that the students could use to explain what happened as they moved the magnets. Students understood the words because the teacher connected the meanings to the activity the students had just been involved in. She also bridged from oral to written academic terms by saying things like, "You said that the magnet pushes away. Another way to say that is to say that the magnet repels" (45). She accompanied her explanation with demonstrations of magnets attracting and repelling various items. She limited the number of technical terms that she introduced.

The third stage was to guide the students as they gave their oral reports. Here the teacher worked in what Vygotsky (1962) defined as the zone of proximal development (ZPD). Vygotsky stated that learning takes place in social interaction. We learn when we receive instruction that is just beyond our current ability level. With the help of an adult or more capable peer, we can do things we can't do on our own. Over time, we can do the same things independently. The key is for the teacher to build on what the students say or do, scaffolding instruction to extend their language and their understanding of academic concepts.

As the students reported on the results of the science experiment to the whole class, the teacher provided words and explained concepts the students needed. She affirmed their efforts and in some cases restated their language to include the scientific terms. For example, when one student said, "The two north poles are leaning together and the magnet on the bottom is repelling the magnet on top so that the magnet on the top is sort of . . . floating in the air," the teacher commented, "so these two magnets are *repelling* each other" (Gibbons 2002, 46). By repeating and emphasizing the key term *repelling*, the teacher helped all the students begin to acquire the term. Gibbons noted that the teacher contributed to the student talk during the reports, but the teacher always responded to what the students said, and the amount of teacher talk was about equal to the amount of student talk. This is different from typical classrooms where teachers do most of the talking.

After the students reported to the whole group, the teacher asked them to write what they had learned in their journals. Since they had worked in the small groups and listened to the teacher's introduction of key concepts and to the reports from each group, all the students were able to write an entry. This journal writing helped them bridge from oral to written language. Their entries show that they were beginning to include technical vocabulary and other features of academic language in their writing. Later, the teacher reminded students to refer to their journal entries as they read about magnets and wrote science reports. They were better prepared to read texts, such as the fourth example above from a children's encyclopedia, that contain technical explanations of magnetism.

The sequence that Gibbons describes—moving from small-group activities to teacher introduction of key terms, group reports, individual journal writing, and formal reports—is an excellent way to scaffold instruction for emergent bilinguals. During this sequence students speak, listen, read, and write. The different activities during the lesson help them develop academic language.

A GENRE-BASED APPROACH TO TEACHING LANGUAGE

The approach to teaching language that Gibbons describes is based on an analysis of genres. The Natural Approach and the different sheltered and content-based instructional methods are based on cognitive psychology and Chomsky's linguistic theory of generative grammar. A second theory of linguistics, systemic functional linguistics (SFL), developed by Halliday (1994), Martin (2001), and others, has been the basis of an approach to teaching language that focuses on teaching specific genres. A genre is a type of text, oral or written, such as a procedure, a report, or an analysis. Schleppegrell (2004), Schlepegrell and de Oliveira (2006), de Oliveira (2012), Gibbons (2002, 2009), Brisk (2015), and others have worked with teachers to show them how they can engage emergent bilinguals in carefully planned interactions to develop the oral and written academic genres that are used in schools.

As Gibbons (2009) points out, "The term *genre* is often used to refer to different forms of literary writing, such as poems, plays, or novels, or to describe different kinds of films or artwork" (108). She explains that each of these genres can be further divided. For example, a poem can be a sonnet or a haiku. According to Gibbons, "within functional grammar the notion of genre has been extended to describe all the language events, both spoken and written, that we participate in as members of a particular society and culture" (108).

Gibbons explains that every genre has specific characteristics. First, it serves a certain social purpose; that is, it allows people to get things done through language. For example, a teacher might explain how to carry out a procedure in science. A procedure is one genre commonly used in science. Second, a genre has a certain organization. The procedure, for example, is presented as a series of steps. Finally, each genre has certain language features. A procedure uses imperative forms of verbs, such as "*Turn on* the Bunsen burner." Genres are the expected types of texts that people in a culture use to interact effectively. English learners need to learn both the oral and written genres of a new culture to develop communicative competence. To communicate in school, they need to learn the academic genres used in the different disciplines.

Three general types of genres used in school are personal genres, factual genres, and analytical genres. Personal genres, such as personal recounts or accounts, are most often used in language arts/English classes. Using these genres, students describe their own experiences. Factual and analytical genres are more often used in science, social science, and math. These genres include reports, procedures, and analyses of different types. It is important for students to learn the genres used in different academic subjects.

One genre that students need to learn is oral presentations using visual media. We recently worked in a sixth-grade classroom where students were working together to create PowerPoint presentations on different features of the ocean. For example, one group was preparing a presentation on kelp forests and another on intertidal zones. Students began gathering information from their textbooks and then looked online to find additional information and images.

Each group member chose a different aspect of their topic and made two slides for a group PowerPoint. Students used a Google application to share slides and create one slideshow that combined the slides from each group member. This was a good interactive group activity through which students built science content knowledge.

In addition, the students developed academic language. An oral presentation using PowerPoint slides requires that students follow the conventions of this genre. In creating their slides, many students had a difficult time condensing their information to short, key ideas that could serve as bullet points. They also found it hard to locate appropriate images and insert them on the slides to illustrate their points.

Instead of bullet points, most of the students wrote long sentences and even paragraphs, leaving no room on the slide for an image. While the students could locate the content information, they struggled with the conventions of this genre, which was new to most of them.

Texts in different academic disciplines vary because of the differences in the field, tenor, or mode. The field is the content being presented, the tenor is the relationship between the speaker and listener or reader and writer, and the mode refers to the means of conveying the information. In this case, the mode was oral with visual media support. A written report on the same topic would be quite different. To communicate effectively in academic contexts, students need to learn the genres used in different academic disciplines. They need to understand that a lab report in science is different from a book report in language arts or a history report in social studies. They also need to learn that the written and oral forms of these reports are not the same.

The Teaching and Learning Cycle

The approach to teaching academic genres to emergent bilinguals developed by systemic functional linguists is referred to as the Teaching and Learning Cycle. As Gibbons suggests, this approach is "particularly relevant for content-based language teaching and is a very valuable way of integrating the development of curriculum knowledge with explicit language teaching. It also integrates listening, speaking, reading and writing" (114).

The Teaching and Learning Cycle consists of four stages: (1) building the field, (2) modeling the genre, (3) joint construction, and (4) independent writing. The field is the content or subject matter that students will talk, read, and write about. The first step, building up the field or drawing on and building background knowledge, can take different forms and includes all the strategies teachers normally use to teach subject matter content. Some examples Gibbons suggests would be to have students share what they know about a topic. For example, the class might start a KWL (**K**now, **W**ant to know, **L**earned) chart. Students or the teacher could read about the topic using different texts and activities, such as jigsaw or other cooperative learning structures. Sometimes teachers create word walls with key words from the subject area. Students can also conduct interviews with experts to find out more about a topic. In the example with the magnets, the teacher built up the field by engaging her students in a science experiment. During this building the field stage, students can read and talk in their home language as well as in English to build up their content knowledge.

Once students have built up knowledge about the field, the second stage of the Teaching and Learning Cycle is to model the genre. The teacher chooses a text of the type that he wants the students to read and write, and then he shares the model text with the students. Gibbons suggests that teachers might divide the class into groups and give each group a text from the genre. Students examine the texts to find key features. Then the groups compare their findings to discover typical features of the genre. In the example with the magnets, the teacher had already discussed with her students how to write a journal entry and had shown her students good examples of entries.

The teacher also works with students to analyze how the genre is organized. One activity to help students understand text organization is to break the model text into sections and then reassemble it. This enables students to determine both the parts of a text and the sequence of the parts. As students reconstruct a text, the teacher can introduce technical terms for the parts. For example, a narrative begins with an orientation that tells the *who*, *what*, and *where* of the account.

The third stage of the Teaching and Learning Cycle is called joint construction. The teacher and the students work together, using a modified language experience approach, to construct a text in the genre being studied. For example, a teacher might want students to write a historical recount. She begins by building students' general knowledge of a historical period through reading about the period, discussing it, and viewing a film on the period. Then she and the students work together to understand the purpose and organization of a historical recount. In this third stage, the teacher works with the students to construct a report similar to what the students will later write independently.

In this process of joint construction, then, the teacher might select a topic, such as the Jamestown Colony. The students suggest sentences for a report on the topic. The teacher guides the discussion, reminding them that a historical recount needs to begin by indicating the time and context in which the event takes place. Then comes a sequence of events in chronological order. Connectives—signal words/ phrases such as *in the beginning*, *during*, and *at the end*—need to show the order of events. Finally, there is a reorientation that summarizes the key events. This joint construction is an important stage and may be done over several days. The activity helps students clarify their content knowledge as well as their knowledge of the purpose and structure of the genre.

The last stage in the Teaching and Learning Cycle is for students to write independently using the same genre on a different topic. Throughout the cycle students learn both language and content as they interact with other students and with the teacher. They listen, speak, read, and write as they build up the field, study the model text, construct a text jointly, and then write a text independently. Figure 6–5 shows a model of the Teaching and Learning Cycle.

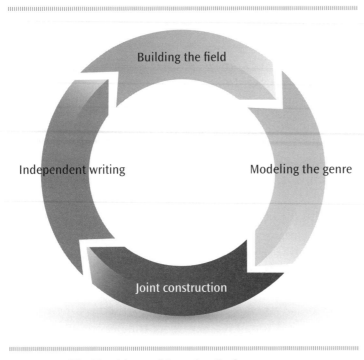

FIGURE 6–5 *The Teaching and Learning Cycle*

Language Objectives

In Chapter 4 we introduced language objectives and explained that language objectives should focus on the forms and functions students need to talk, read, and write about academic content. The genre-based approach expands the kinds of language objectives teachers can develop. As teachers teach the genres in their subject area or areas, they become more aware of the purpose of the genre, the organization of the genre, the technical vocabulary that occurs, and the language structures typical of each genre. Teachers can then use this knowledge to write language objectives for the genres students will use. Later, teachers can assess how students use the forms and functions of the genre. A language objective can target any aspect of the language used to discuss, read, or write about academic content. A general objective for each genre would be to teach the purpose or function of the genre.

After students understand the function of the genre (to compare, to analyze, to report, to explain), the teacher can develop language objectives in different ways. For example, objectives can focus on the organizational structure of a genre. According to Gibbons, the structure of a historical explanation, such as an explanation of why there was a general westward movement in the U.S., includes the identification of the issue with relevant information and possibly a brief review of relevant arguments. Following this comes a presentation of causes and consequences of the historical events. The conclusion sums up the significance of the events. Each genre has a typical organizational structure. A language objective for a historical explanation could be that students will include the expected components of the genre in the correct order.

Language objectives can also be based on the ways texts are made cohesive in different genres. For example, an objective could be that students would use pronouns that clearly refer to a preceding noun. In addition, texts are made cohesive by the use of particular types of conjunctions or signal words. For example, in a historical explanation, the connectives would be those that show cause and effect, such as *since*, as a *result*, or *consequently*. On the other hand, a procedural recount would use sequence connectives, such as *first*, *next*, and *last* to show the order of events. Each genre uses different kinds of signals to structure the information. A language objective for either a historical explanation or a procedural recount could be, "Students will use signal words to show the relationships among the ideas that are presented." Depending on the genre, students could meet this objective by using signal words that show cause and effect or signal words showing sequence.

A language objective can also focus on specific aspects of syntax. An objective can focus on word forms the genre calls for. A procedural recount describes the steps that were taken to complete a process, so a language objective could be to use past tense verb forms correctly. On the other hand, a procedure uses imperative forms, so a language objective could be to use imperative forms of verbs correctly. A math report describing the length of two objects by reference to a third object would use comparative and superlative forms of adjectives, such as, "The blue rod is shorter than the red rod, and the yellow rod is the shortest."

Academic language contains technical vocabulary, and teaching academic content requires teachers to use technical vocabulary as they teach key concepts. Consequently, teaching a word like *mitosis* is really teaching a scientific concept and should not be listed as a language objective although it should be a content objective. Instead of writing language objectives that list vocabulary, teachers should develop language objectives that relate to the purpose of a genre, the way the genre is structured, the kinds of words used to make the genre coherent and cohesive, and the specific kinds of syntax and word forms the genre requires. A teacher wouldn't list all these kinds of language objectives, but would normally choose one or two of them.

Teaching Students to Write Academic Genres

In her book *Engaging Students in Academic Literacies: Genre-Based Pedagogy for K–5 Classrooms* Brisk (2015) provides a detailed account of how the Teaching and Learning Cycle works in schools with many emergent bilinguals. Brisk worked with preservice and inservice teachers in two urban schools over a period of five years. During this time she helped them develop a genre-based pedagogy that involved students in reading and writing different academic genres.

Through intensive summer sessions, monthly professional development, and weekly in-classroom support, Brisk and her colleagues and graduate students worked with teachers to transform their writing instruction. After the first year, teachers met together and planned their writing curriculum. The teachers used a Teaching and Learning Cycle that was expanded to meet the needs of English learners. For example, the teachers provided a graphic organizer to aid students in understanding the structure of the genre. For English learners at lower levels of proficiency, their finished work could be a graphic that they created rather than a full piece of writing.

In the first three chapters of her book, Brisk explains the theory of the model of writing instruction and the steps teachers go through as they teach students to write different genres. Each of the following chapters describes in detail how teachers taught one genre unit and how that unit was adapted to different grade levels. For example, in the procedures unit in grade one teachers and students jointly constructed a text for a procedure students had seen demonstrated. The students used prepared sentence strips to present the procedure and then added images to the steps. In grade five, students wrote procedures to set up simple science experiments.

Each of the genre chapters provides "suggestions for unit preparation and teaching of purpose, stages of the genre (text structure), and aspects of language that would be most helpful to develop in order for children to write in that particular genre" (x). Each chapter also contains resources, such as charts and forms, that teachers can use as they teach the unit. The chapters include suggested texts that can be used as models for the genre. The chapters are ordered from least to most difficult. They include procedures, recounts and historical genres, reports, explanations, arguments, and fictional narratives. Brisk's book is a valuable resource for teachers because it explains how the Teaching and Learning Cycle can be used in classrooms to teach all students, including emergent bilinguals, to write the academic genres.

CAREFULLY PLANNED INTERACTIONS THAT BUILD ACADEMIC LANGUAGE

We visited a middle school for newcomer students in Fort Worth, Texas, where the teachers planned projects and had students work in groups that enabled these first- and second-year emergent bilinguals to learn academic content. The teachers were unified in their approach and made every effort to engage all their students in meaningful activities. The students were learning academic content that was quite advanced as they developed their academic language proficiency.

As we walked around the school, we saw a sign outside the math class that read, "When you enter this classroom you are mathematicians, problem solvers, responsible learners, important and loved, respected." Gee (2008) argues that all learning takes place in what he calls Discourses with a capital *D*. A Discourse is a way of thinking, believing, and acting that is typical of a certain group of people. By stating that when students enter this room they are mathematicians, the teacher is saying that students are becoming part of the math Discourse, the group of people who think, believe, and act like mathematicians.

This sign sets the tone for the math learning that goes on in the room. As in the other classes we visited, students in this room sit in desks grouped in fours. Together they work on math problems with a focus on building conceptual understanding through talking, reading, and writing about math. At times, the teacher introduced and explained a new math concept. Then she posed problems for the students to solve working together in their groups. The students were engaged, and they used both their home languages and English to solve math problems and to develop an understanding of math concepts and procedures. On a bulletin board, in Spanish and English, the teacher had posted key terms, such as *fraccíon* (fractions), *numerador* (numerator), and *denominador* (denominator), for the unit students were studying.

In another, more advanced chemistry/physics class students were studying the structure of atoms of different elements. Each group had a board with holes for marbles in concentric rings. In their groups of four, they were building atoms. Each group had been assigned a different element, and their task was to explain the structure of the atoms of the element. The teacher had posted a series of instructions:

> Use your colored paper to build an atom on the board.
>
> Use the green or red marbles for protons.
>
> Use the blue marbles for neutrons.
>
> Use the yellow marbles for electrons.
>
> Use the script on the colored paper to explain how you built the atom.

They used the board and the colored marbles to create a model showing the protons, neutrons, and electrons. When they finished, one student used the script to state what they had learned. The script was the following sentence frame: "A(n) _____ atom has ____ proton(s) and _____ neutron(s) in the nucleus, and ____ electron(s) that orbit(s) the nucleus."

We watched as one group modeled a hydrogen atom. They placed a red marble to show that there is one proton in the nucleus and a yellow marble to show that there is one electron in the orbit. Then, one student used sentence frames on the script to explain this atom to other group members: "A hydrogen atom has one proton in the nucleus, and one electron that orbits the nucleus." The other group members checked to confirm that the statement was correct.

Each group had a different element. When they finished, they drew a picture of their element and the atoms that make up that element to post on the bulletin board. In the halls near the class, there were also posters of different atoms and posters explaining the properties of matter. This teacher used the board with marbles and the script as scaffolds to help the students talk, read, and write about this important chemistry concept.

There were also posters from social studies classes in the halls. Rather than studying food, clothing, and weather in traditional ways, these students had developed vocabulary around these topics to compare and contrast their native country with their new country. For example, one poster showed similarities and differences between Burma and the U.S. Students had cut out or created pictures to illustrate clothing, food, and weather, and one student had written a short essay that began, "The difference between my home country and United States is very different. The language, culture, and schools are different." The student then went on to explain specific differences. Another student explained that, "Myanmar people eat rice and soup, meat and vegetable." These students were learning language through meaningful content as they described differences between their home and new countries.

One class had studied the Earth's climate zones. This was another example of students studying advanced academic content and building academic language. The class worked in groups. Each group created a poster telling about the Earth's tropical, temperate, and polar zones. One group, for example, wrote that the location of the tropical zone was between the Tropic of Cancer and the Tropic of Capricorn. Each poster included the location, temperature, humidity, and seasons of the zone.

As groups created posters, each student used a different colored marker. This allowed the teacher to see that all the group members had contributed to the final product. For example, a social studies class studying economics had created a poster by filling in a chart with factors of production, including natural resources, capital, and labor. The students used different colored markers to make their contribution to the finished chart.

Students in a language arts class had created posters depicting different characters from the novel they were reading, *The House on Mango Street* (Cisneros 1984). One student had drawn the face of Carmita, a character from the novel. The poster showed the setting and explained that Carmita is sad. The student included a sentence from the story to show why he thought Carmita was sad. After all the students finished their posters on *The House on Mango Street*, they put them up around the classroom. Then, the students walked around the room and read each other's posters and added sticky notes with their comments and reactions to their peers' posters.

This school provides an excellent example of teaching that uses carefully planned interactions to develop emergent bilinguals' oral and written language. All the classes we visited were organized in groups. Students worked busily on projects with their classmates. They were studying academic content that was advanced for their level of English proficiency but appropriate for their age. Even though many of the students had come with limited formal schooling, all the students were engaged in learning, and the teachers were making a unified effort to help their students develop academic English and content area knowledge.

CONCLUSION

This chapter began with a description of Karen's unit on fast food and healthy eating following the steps of the Wonderfilled Lessons. This unit is a good example of the fifth principle, that teaching should include carefully planned interactions to develop both oral and written language.

The next sections of the chapter reviewed the research on classroom interactions and on teaching both oral and written language. We also discussed ways to promote interactions, such as cross-age tutoring. We described a lesson on magnetism that scaffolded instruction, beginning with oral language and bridging to written language.

We outlined the Teaching and Learning Cycle, a method of teaching academic language based on helping students discuss, read, and write academic genres. We explained how this approach has been implemented in two urban schools in a comprehensive way to help emergent bilinguals write more effectively. We concluded with an example from an urban middle school that shows that even beginning students can be engaged in high-level academic content when teachers carefully plan interactions that help students develop oral and written language.

APPLICATIONS

1. We described a model of planning units called the Wonderfilled Way of Learning. Plan and teach a unit following the steps of this model. Take notes on how well this worked and any modifications you made. Be prepared to share your experience.

2. We reviewed the research on the importance of interaction for language acquisition. What is your view? Do students need both comprehensible input and comprehensible output to develop a high level of proficiency in a language? Write down your ideas and prepare to share them.

3. List some ways you use grouping in your class. Do you group students heterogeneously, homogeneously, or both? What have you found to be the keys for effective group work?

4. We described the Teaching and Learning Cycle. Try applying this model when you have students complete a writing project. Think about the genre they will write and the model text you will use to teach them the genre. Write language objectives based on the genre. Be prepared to share how this writing project worked.

7

Teaching Should Support Students' Languages and Cultures

It is April and the students in Gabriela's second-grade dual language class are going on a field trip to Central Park in New York City. They will travel from their school in the Bronx to picnic in the park and visit the zoo there. Approximately half of her students are native Spanish speakers and the other half are dominant English speakers although they may speak some Spanish, too. The class is preparing for their field trip by studying plants and animals. During Spanish time, the class has been discussing living things and read together *¿Qué son los seres vivos?* (What is a living thing?) (Kalman 2005) and *¿Esto es un ser vivo?* (Is it a living thing?) (Kalman 2008c). They talk about the plants and animals discussed in the books, and then they list things in their classroom that are living and things that are not. They identify *pupitres* (desks), *lápices* (pencils), and *libros* (books) as nonliving things and *una flor* (a flower), *una araña* (a spider), and even *¡nosotros mismos!* (ourselves!) as living things.

Gabriela knows that many of her students have lived in the Bronx all their lives and most have traveled a little, and that some of her Salvadoran, Dominican, and Puerto Rican students have traveled to their home countries or have memories of their homeland. Gabriela writes "The Bronx" on chart paper and asks students to name other places they have lived or visited. Some students have been to Long Island, others to the Jersey shore, and several to their home countries. She then asks the students to sit together in groups and think about the plants and animals that they remember seeing in the places they have been. Students talk together in Spanish and English and make lists of plants and animals they can name. Sometimes they know the words in Spanish and other times in English.

When their lists are completed the students call out the words and the teacher writes down the names of the plants and animals the students identify for each location—the Bronx, and different places the students mention. She puts words in Spanish on one side of the column and words in English on the other. As students name things in one language, she asks if students know the word in the other. For example, when students mention *las palmas*, *los aguacates*, and *los mangos* found in their home countries, she asks, "*Cómo se dice* las palmas, los aguacates, *y* los mangos *en inglés?*" ("How do you say *las palmas*, *los aguacates*, and *los mangos* in English?"). Some students call out *palm trees*, *avocados*, and *mangos*. Students who have visited Long Island and the Jersey shore name *pine trees, squirrels, crabs*, and *sea gulls*. When students don't know how to say those things in Spanish, she writes *los pinos*, *las ardillas*, *los cangrejos*, and *las gaviotas* next to the English words, and she and the students read the words together.

She then asks the students if one sees *las palmas* (palm trees) in New York. When the students tell her "no," she tells them they are going to be studying *los habitats de animales y plantas* (habitats of animals and plants). She asks her Puerto Rican students if they know what a *coquí* is and they tell her, "*Sí, se escucha los coquís en la noche.*" (Yes, you can hear los *coquis* at night.) Gabriela explains that "*el coquí, es una rana que vive en partes de Puerto Rico porque el habitat es perfecto para el coquí. No puede vivir en Nueva York.*" (The coqui is a frog that lives in parts of Puerto Rico because the habitat is perfect for the coqui. It cannot live in New York.) And she then asks them, "*¿Por qué no puede vivir en Nueva York?*" (Why can't it live in New York?) The students call out answers to her in Spanish, including telling her "*Hace frío aqui*" and "*Nieva aquí*" and "*No hay* árboles *cómo en Puerto Rico.*" (It's cold here. It snows here. There are not trees like in Puerto Rico.) Gabriela finds on YouTube a song entitled "*Coquí serenito*" (www.youtube.com/watch?v=4dcF9FYQ-9U) and plays it for the students. Some of her students had heard the song before and are excited to sing along when she plays it the second time.

Gabriela then reads three books to the class, *Habitats terrestes: Introducción a los habitats* (*Land Habitats: Introduction to Habitats*) (Kalman and Crossingham 2007, 2006), *¿Dónde viven los animales?* (*Where Do Animals Live?*) (Kalman 2010a, 2010b), and *¿Dónde crecen las plantas?* (*Where Do Plants Grow?*) (Spilsbury and Spilsbury 2006, 2005). After reading the books, the class discusses the plants and animals on the list they had brainstormed earlier and whether those plants and animals could live in different places and why or why not. During English/ESL time Gabriela shows students several books in English including the English versions of the three books she had read earlier in Spanish. She has the students use the classroom resource books she provides in both English and Spanish and work in groups to choose two different habitats and to make a Venn diagram comparing the plants and animals that live in each. Some of the books she provided in Spanish included *Animales de la selva Amazónica* (Animals of the Amazon forest) (Lopes da Silva 2013), *Explora tu mundo: La selva tropical* (Explore your world: The tropical rainforest) (Arlon 2013), *Las plantas son seres vivos* (*Plants Are Living Things*) (Kalman 2008d, 2007a), *Un habitat de desierto* (*A Desert Habitat*) (Macaulay and Kalman 2007b, 2006b), *Habitats acúaticos* (*Water Habitats*) (Aloian and Kaiman 2007c, 2006c), *Animales marinos* (Marine animals) (Lambilly-Bresson 2007), *Un habitat de bosque* (*A Forest Habitat*) (Kalman 2007b, 2006), *El habitat del Artico* (*The Artic Habitat*) (Aloian and Kalman 2007b, 2006b), and *El habitat de la Antártida* (*The Antarctic Habitat*) (Aloian and Kalman 2007a, 2006a). She has the English version of many of the books provided in Spanish.

The students choose their two habitats, and on their Venn diagram they label the habitats first. For example, students who chose *desert* and *rain forest* label each circle with these habitats. They look at animals and plants that only live in one of the habitats and put them in one of the two circles. Then they put the animals and plants that live in both habitats in the overlapping section. Students write *snakes* and *birds* in the center because both the desert and the rain forest have snakes and birds. The following day, the students in groups present their Venn diagrams to the rest of the class and show the books they used to get the information.

Gabriela then gives each student a small notebook, telling her students that on their field trip to Central Park they will be scientists and write in their notebook living things they see, both plants and animals, and what they notice about them. When in the zoo, they should read the information about the animals they see and notice their native habitat as well as what the animals are eating and doing.

The day following this field trip, Gabriela's students talk about their trip during both English and Spanish time and discuss what they observed. They talk about the feeding of the animals, including the sea lions at the entrance of the park zoo. They noticed the squirrels in the park picking up seeds and eating them, and they saw that some flowers were just blooming. Everything that they noticed helped her students understand habitats and what living organisms need to live in different environments, key concepts for the science standards. In the weeks that followed, students read books in English and Spanish and watch videos about different habitats, including water habitats, forest habitats, desert habitats, and backyard habitats. They learn in both Spanish and English about what animals eat and how they adapt to their environments. They read *Habitats de jardin* (Macaulay and Kalman 2007a) and the English version, *Backyard Habitats* (Macaulay and Kaiman 2006a); *¿Cómo se encuentran alimento los animals?* (Kalman 2008b) and the English version, *How Do Animals Find Food?* (Kalman 2000); and *¿Cómo se adaptan los animals?* (Kalman 2008a) and the English version, *How Do Animals Adapt?* (Kalman and Walker 2000). They then make a large class mural, cutting out pictures of animals and plants they drew and placing them in different habitats. As an end-of-the-unit celebration, they have a bilingual program for parents and other classes where they display their class mural and present what they learned about animal and plant habitats and adaptation.

Gabriela began her unit by drawing on what students knew about living things found in different environments and built on that knowledge as students learned concepts and the related vocabulary in two languages using books, videos, discussions, field trips, and projects. Figure 7–1 lists the books she used during the unit. Her bilingual classroom is one example of the power of drawing on students' background knowledge and home language in teaching academic content. While our opening example is from a bilingual classroom, in this chapter we discuss the importance of using students' home languages and background experiences in all teaching settings, not only in bilingual classrooms.

Aloian, Molly, and Bobbie Kalman. 2006a. *The Antarctic Habitat*. New York: Crabtree Publishing.

———. 2006b. *The Arctic Habitat*. New York: Crabtree Publishing.

———. 2006c. *Water Habitats*. New York: Crabtree Publishing.

———. 2007a. *El habitat de la Antártida*. New York: Crabtree Publishing.

———. 2007b. *El habitat del Artico*. New York: Crabtree Publishing.

———. 2007c. *Habitats acúaticos*. New York: Crabtree Publishing.

Arlon, Penelope. 2013. *Explora tu mundo: La selva tropical*. New York: Scholastic en español.

Kalman, Bobbie. 2000. *How Do Animals Find Food?* New York: Crabtree Publishing.

———. 2005. *¿Qué son los seres vivos?, La ciencia de los seres vivos*. New York: Crabtree Publishing.

———. 2006. *A Forest Habitat*. New York: Crabtree Publishing.

———. 2007a. *Plants Are Living Things*. New York: Crabtree Publishing.

———. 2007b. *Un habitat de bosque*. New York: Crabtree Publishing.

———. 2008a. *¿Cómo se adaptan los animales?* New York: Crabtree Publishing.

———. 2008b. *¿Cómo se encuentran alimento los animales?* New York: Crabtree Publishing.

———. 2008c. *¿Esto es un ser vivo?* New York: Crabtree Publishing.

———. 2008d. *Las plantas son seres vivos*. New York: Crabtree Publishing.

FIGURE 7–1 *Books for Gabriela's Second-Grade Environments Unit*

OPTIMAL USE OF EMERGENT BILINGUALS' HOME LANGUAGES

Decisions about using students' home languages are first made at the district and school levels. A number of large-scale studies and meta-analyses have shown that students in well-implemented, long-term bilingual education programs succeed at higher rates than students in transitional bilingual programs or ESL programs (Collier and Thomas 2009; Slavin and Cheung 2004; Greene 1998; Ramírez 1991; Rolstad, Mahoney, and Glass 2005). Despite this body of research, many emergent bilinguals are placed in programs that do not fully develop their home languages.

Various factors may keep schools from implementing bilingual programs. In some states, laws have been passed to block instruction in languages other than English. In some areas of the country, schools are not able to recruit bilingual teachers for the languages spoken by students in the district. For example, some schools have had an influx of students from Somalia or Myanmar, but there are no credentialed teachers available who speak the languages of these students. Further, in some schools there are emergent bilinguals with a variety of language backgrounds but

———. 2010a. ¿Dónde viven los animales? New York: Crabtree Publishing.

———. 2010b. *Where Do Animals Live?* New York: Crabtree Publishing.

Kalman, Bobbie, and John Crossingham. 2006. *Land Habitats*. New York: Crabtree Publishing.

———. 2007. *Habitats terrestes: Introducción a los habitats*. New York: Crabtree Publishing.

Kalman, Bobbie, and Niki Walker. 2000. *How Do Animals Adapt?* New York: Crabtree Publishing.

Lambilly-Bresson, Elisabeth de. 2007. *Animales marinos*. York, PA: Gareth Stevens Publishing.

Lopes da Silva, María Lourdes. 2013. *Animales de la selva Amazónica*. Charleston, SC: CreateSpace.

Macaulay, Kelley, and Bobbie Kalman. 2006a. *Backyard Habitats*. New York: Crabtree Publishing.

———. 2006b. *A Desert Habitat*. New York: Crabtree Publishing.

———. 2007a. *Habitats de jardin*. New York: Crabtree Publishing.

———. 2007b. *Un habitat de desierto*. New York: Crabtree Publishing.

Spilsbury, Louise, and Richard Spilsbury. 2005. *Where Do Plants Grow?* Mankato, MN: Heinemann.

———. *2006. ¿Dónde crecen las plantas?, El mundo de las plantas.* Mankato, MN: Heinemann.

not enough students from any one language background to implement a bilingual program for them. Although it may not be possible to establish a bilingual program in some schools or districts because of factors such as these, it is still important to draw on students' languages and cultures. We begin our discussion of instruction in students' home languages by looking at some common misconceptions about teaching emergent bilinguals using their home language. We then suggest ways to draw on students' home languages and cultures in ESL and bilingual contexts.

The Direct Instruction Misconception

Some ESL programs make no use of emergent bilinguals' home languages. Cummins (2007) argues that choosing to use methods that exclude the use of students' home languages is often based on what he calls the *direct instruction misconception*. This is the idea that the target language (TL) should be used exclusively for instructional purposes without recourse to the first language. The Direct Method, which we discussed earlier, was based on the exclusive use of the target language so that students would associate words in the target language with concepts without processing them through their first language. Within this direct instruction misconception fall several assumptions: that English is best taught monolingually; that the ideal teacher is always the native speaker; and that the more English is taught, the better. We will discuss each of these ideas briefly.

English Is Best Taught Monolingually

Although common sense seems to tell us that using only the target language would be the best approach to teaching the language, there are times when it is much more efficient to use the students' home language to explain an expression in the target language. For example, when David was teaching EFL to adults in Mexico, rather than spending a great deal of time trying to explain the idiomatic expression "by the way," meaning "incidentally," he asked if one of the students' could give an equivalent translation in Spanish, *por cierto* or *a propósito*. This quick translation ensured that all the students could understand "by the way" and, more importantly, David could continue the lesson without wasting valuable class time.

The Ideal Teacher Is a Native Speaker

A second assumption of the direct instruction misconception is that the ideal teacher is a native speaker of the target language. While a native speaker can model correct pronunciation (at least correct pronunciation of the dialect she speaks) and grammatical syntax, native speakers who are not trained in language teaching may prove to be ineffective teachers. Many native speakers can decide what sounds right in a language but can't explain grammatical rules because native speakers acquire rather than learn languages. In addition, native speakers may not understand how hard it is to develop proficiency in a new language, while a teacher who learned the target language as an additional language may be more empathetic.

More English Equals More English

A third assumption of the direct instruction misconception is the belief that more time spent teaching exclusively in the native language results in greater gains in proficiency in the language for students. While it is essential for students to have prolonged exposure to a language they are trying to learn, they also need to see a purpose in learning a language and have opportunities for meaningful use of the language. If the teaching is not effective, simply teaching for longer periods of time is not helpful. A student could listen to a Japanese radio station for hours without acquiring any proficiency in Japanese. It is the quality, not just the quantity, of instruction that counts.

The use of the first language to help make the second language understandable and accessible is often a much more efficient way to teach the second language than simply giving students lots of incomprehensible input in a second language. Krashen (1996) reviewed research on the importance of using the first language for instruction. He argues that we acquire language when we receive comprehensible input, messages that we understand. For second language learners, use of the home language is the best way to make input comprehensible. To learn a second language, students need to have an understanding of what they hear or read. If students enter school speaking languages other than English, and if English is the only language of instruction, then the students may simply not understand enough English to acquire the language or to learn any subjects taught in the language. This point leads into the second key misconception that Cummins discusses.

The No Translation Misconception

A second, related instructional practice that Cummins (2007) terms a misconception is the belief that translation has no place in the classroom. This practice runs counter to what happens in bilingual households and communities. Zentella's (2000) case studies of children in *el bloque* reveals example after example of how skilled the children were at translating back and forth between English and Spanish as they played with friends or interacted with the adult community. They often served as language brokers, helping adults with important business transactions.

Cummins (2007) suggests that using translation in the classroom recognizes skills children bring to school as language brokers, and it promotes the acquisition of English. Cummins is not referring to concurrent translation, in which the teacher translates each thing she says. Concurrent translation is ineffective because students only pay attention to the language they understand.

However, judicious use of students' home languages can enable students to better comprehend key concepts during activities such as the morning message. As students dictate their contributions to the morning message in their home languages, teachers can write in English what they are trying to say, or the teacher can have a more advanced bilingual translate the message if the teacher does not understand the students' home languages. Finally, students can read the English message together and, if necessary, students who are more bilingual can translate back to the home language so that a beginning English learner can understand all of what has been written in English.

Translation also promotes biliteracy development. For example, when students produce their own bilingual books, they develop both English and their home languages. When bilinguals share their bilingual books, they show monolingual peers their linguistic abilities, they are more valued by their classmates, and they develop a sense of self-esteem. Accessing and sharing their abilities in both their languages helps emergent bilinguals develop what Cummins has called "identities of competence" (2007, 228). Too often, emergent bilinguals are made to feel incompetent. Skutnabb-Kangas (1983) describes how newcomers to English feel when immersed in English-only instruction:

> [T]he child sits in a submersion classroom (where many of the students have L2, the language of instruction, as their mother tongue), listening to the teacher explaining something that the child is then supposed to use for problem solving . . . the child gets less information than a child listening to her mother tongue. (116)

Not only does the child learn less, the child may also come to view herself as not being competent in school tasks.

Ways to Draw on Students' Home Languages and Cultures

While bilingual education may not be possible in some schools for a variety of reasons, in ESL classes there are a number of ways that teachers can draw on their emergent bilinguals' home languages and cultures to promote academic success. These practices affirm students' identities, and they scaffold instruction in the target language. Figure 7–2 lists strategies used by teachers we have worked with to support emergent bilinguals' home languages.

1. Ensure that environmental print in the classroom reflects students' first languages.

2. Supply school and classroom libraries with books, magazines, and other resources in languages in addition to English.

3. Have emergent bilinguals read and write with paraprofessionals, parents, and other students who speak their home language.

4. Encourage emergent bilinguals to publish books and share their stories in languages other than English, or produce bilingual books in English and their home languages.

5. Allow bilingual students to respond in their home languages to demonstrate comprehension of content taught in English.

6. Use DVDs or videos in languages other than English, produced professionally or by the students, to support academic learning and raise self-esteem.

FIGURE 7–2 *Ways to Support Students' Home Languages*

Preview–View–Review

One other strategy that draws on emergent bilinguals' home languages is *preview–view–review* (PVR). This strategy allows teachers and/or students to make use of students' first languages to access content and enhance comprehension. Gutiérrez (2002) showed the importance of allowing students to use their primary language, Spanish, in high school math classes. She interviewed students allowed to use Spanish during class time. The students explained that they felt more comfortable discussing the content when allowed to use their first language. As one student said, "You know, we're all calm about [the math] that way. We all speak Spanish and we are comfortable" (1075). The teachers in the study were not fluent Spanish speakers and often did not understand their students, but they all agreed that allowing students to use Spanish was important. At the same time, the teachers "were keenly aware of the importance for students to negotiate the mathematics in English as well" (1076). The teachers in the Gutiérrez study encouraged the use of Spanish as a way for students to negotiate meaning about the content in English, but did not have a specific structure for when to use the language.

We suggest the preview–view–review structure. In his report of the research, Goldenberg (2008) writes, "another way to use the primary language but keep the focus on English instruction is to introduce new concepts in the primary language prior to the lesson in English, then afterward review the new content, again in the primary language" (19). This is the structure that preview–view–review provides. See Figure 7–3.

| PREVIEW |

home language

The teacher or a bilingual helper gives an overview of the lesson or activity in the students' home language. This could be giving an oral summary, reading a book, showing a film, asking a key question, or leading a short discussion.

| VIEW |

second or target language [English]

The teacher teaches the lesson or directs the activity in the target language using strategies for making the input comprehensible.

| REVIEW |

home language

Students work in the same language groups to summarize key ideas and raise questions about the lesson in their home language and report back in English.

FIGURE 7–3 *Preview–View–Review*

Preview

For the preview, the teacher, a bilingual peer, a bilingual cross-age tutor, a bilingual aide, or a parent can give the English learners a brief oral summary of key ideas for a lesson in their home language. There are several additional ways to provide the home language preview. The teacher could read a short picture book in the home language or show a video clip on the topic in the students' home language. In addition, especially in cases where emergent bilinguals in a class speak a variety of home languages, the teacher could ask a question in English and give students time working in same-language pairs or groups to list what they know about the topic. Then each group could report back in English. This allows a teacher to add to ideas students present and clarify any misconceptions they have about the topic.

View

During the view, the teacher conducts the lesson using strategies to make the input comprehensible. These include using gestures, tone of voice, pictures, and realia as well as having students work collaboratively on projects. During the view, the teacher teaches primarily in the target language but still may make judicious use of the emergent bilinguals' home languages to scaffold instruction.

Review

For the review, the teacher can have students return to their original same-language pairs or groups to list key ideas from the lesson and raise any questions they have. Again, students would report back in the target language since not all the students in the class may speak some of the home languages. With the help of the preview and the review, the students can follow the target language instruction more easily and acquire both the target language and academic content.

Mercuri (2015) conducted research with dual language teachers working in Texas who were implementing preview–view–review and found, among other conclusions, that PVR, when well planned and implemented, enhanced students' engagement in learning in two languages and scaffolded the students' learning of content. Mercuri interviewed teachers who told her: "P/V/R helps students become familiar with concepts, and review them" and "P/V/R allows the teacher to scaffold new concepts, particularly if the student has no background knowledge of the topic" (93). One teacher interviewed summarized the benefits well:

> PVR provides students with the opportunity to connect with background knowledge they may have in their native language; and, it also gives them the time to discuss/ share in their native language their thoughts, ideas, and questions. We need to keep in mind that ESL students are learning two things at once, language and content, so activities should be engaging. (99)

The PVR strategy provides a structured way to alternate English (or another target language) and home-language instruction. Using preview–view–review can help teachers avoid concurrent translation. PVR can also motivate students to stay engaged in the lesson. Listening to a second language is more tiring than listening to one's native language. Second language learners may appear to have shorter attention spans than native speakers, but in reality those students may be suffering from the fatigue of trying to make sense of their new language. Often teachers complain that their English learners misbehave and don't pay attention, or they think their second language learners may have some learning problems because they do not seem to be learning. The home language preview and review can help them understand and stay engaged in their lessons.

Yvonne recalls an experience she had in an elementary classroom when she was asked to give a demonstration lesson. The teachers in the school had little experience with English language learners. The principal had tried to explain to the teachers the importance of drawing on students' home languages and thought bringing in someone from the outside might help.

Yvonne taught a reading/science lesson on seed growth to a class of second graders with primarily native English speakers and five native Spanish speakers, one of whom, José, had been in the country only three months. She explained to the native English speakers that some of the lesson would be in Spanish but that she would do things to help them understand. She previewed the lesson in Spanish for the native Spanish speakers by showing some seeds and talking about them and then reading a very comprehensible big book in Spanish, *Una semilla nada más* (Just one seed) (Ada 1990).

The native English speakers got restless almost immediately and complained, "I don't understand!" and "Speak English!" However, the native Spanish speakers participated eagerly. Throughout the lesson, the newcomer José answered questions and commented so much that Yvonne had to tell him to let others talk. Yvonne followed the PVR model and did the view in English with lots of comprehensible input and a hands-on activity where students classified seeds according to shape, size, texture, and color. All the students, including the Spanish speakers, participated during the view. During the review, Spanish speakers participated again while English speakers were beginning to understand some and listened more carefully, but did not really participate.

At the end of the lesson Yvonne approached the classroom teacher, who had tears in her eyes. She told Yvonne:

> I thought José had serious learning and behavioral problems. Seeing him today helped me see that he wants to learn, he just doesn't understand! Look at how my English speakers responded! They were acting like José does when I teach in English all day long.

Allowing translation when it serves a pedagogical purpose, using preview–view– and review, and including different strategies to support students' first languages can promote academic success for emergent bilinguals. It is important to understand, however, that the most effective way for emergent bilinguals to develop both academic concepts and English language proficiency is through the full development of their first language (Thomas and Collier 2002; August and Shanahan 2006; Cummins 2001; Rolstad, Mahoney, and Glass 2005; Krashen 1999; Crawford 2007). Development of the first language supports both language and content learning in the second language.

VIEWS OF BILINGUALS

To benefit from instruction in the home language, emergent bilinguals need programs that reflect current views of bilinguals. Even in some bilingual programs that are long-term, such as one- and two-way immersion bilingual programs, current views of bilinguals and of bilingual education have not guided curricular practices. As O. García (2009) has argued, twentieth-century views of bilinguals have led to bilingual programs that attempt to keep the two languages separate.

The twentieth-century view was that the goal of bilingual education was to produce balanced bilinguals (Cummins 1989). A balanced bilingual is someone who is equally competent in two languages. This would mean that if a bilingual Spanish–English program did its job well, a student should be able to speak, read, and write both English and Spanish equally well in all settings.

However, research in sociolinguistics has led to the understanding that bilinguals are not balanced because "Bilinguals usually acquire and use their languages for different purposes, in different domains of life, with different people. Different aspects of life often require different languages" (Grosjean 2010, 29). Grosjean refers to this phenomenon as the *complementarity principle*. Rather than developing equal abilities in each language, bilinguals develop the languages they need to speak to different people in different settings or domains when discussing different subjects. Each language complements the others.

Grosjean points out three consequences of the complementarity principle. First, most bilinguals are more fluent in one language than the other. As Grosjean (2010) explains, "In general, if a language is spoken in a reduced number of domains and with a limited number of people, then it will not be developed as much as a language used in more domains with more people" (31). Many bilinguals report, for example, that they can do mental math more easily in one language than the other. To take a second example, someone teaching English as a foreign language may not acquire full fluency in the native language of the country simply because he spends most of the day speaking English to his students. This teacher may only develop proficiency in the local language in limited domains, such as speaking to clerks about purchases in stores or ordering food in restaurants. He may live in this country for several years without becoming equally fluent in his home language and the language of the country.

This leads to a second consequence. The language that bilinguals are more fluent in is their dominant language. Since bilinguals tend to use one language more often with more people in more situations than the other language, they don't use the two languages equally. For that reason, very few bilinguals are "balanced." For example, in the south Texas university where we taught, many students used Spanish with their peers, at home, at church, and in social settings with other Spanish speakers. Even though they studied almost exclusively in English, they were more dominant in oral Spanish. However, their academic Spanish was usually not nativelike because few of these bilingual students had been in bilingual education programs where they would have had opportunities to read and write academic Spanish.

The lack of balance shows up in a third consequence of the complementarity principle: the difficulty bilinguals have with translation. Since bilinguals develop fluency in different domains rather than an equal ability in each domain, they often find it difficult to translate. For example, a bilingual educator might be asked to explain in Spanish the rationale for bilingual education to parents or other community members. Even though this educator speaks Spanish, she may have studied bilingual theory in English and may not have developed the vocabulary needed to translate these complex concepts into Spanish.

Grosjean concludes his discussion of the complementarity principle by stating that most bilinguals "simply do not need to be equally competent in all their languages. The level of fluency they attain in a language . . . will depend on their need for that language and will be domain specific" (21). Because bilinguals develop their two languages differently, very few are completely balanced.

Our granddaughter, Maya, provides an example of a typical bilingual. When she was eight years old she almost always spoke in English with us. No one told her to speak English to us, she just figured out that English was our stronger language even though we spoke Spanish to others around her.

When Carmen, a monolingual Spanish speaker, came to the house, Yvonne spoke Spanish to her, and so did Maya. If Carmen and Yvonne were in conversation, Maya would often join the conversation in Spanish and speak in English for Yvonne to clarify something she had said in Spanish to be sure Yvonne understood. Even today, as a teenager, Maya speaks Spanish to her godparents from Argentina who do speak English but are native speakers of Spanish and who always make a point of speaking to her in Spanish.

At her tenth birthday party in south Texas, Maya called out in Spanish to one friend who was a newcomer to the country and then turned and spoke in English to another friend who only speaks English. Maya used her two languages with different people depending on their level of proficiency in either language.

Like most bilinguals, Maya is not completely balanced. She uses English more often than Spanish in more settings with more people. This is especially true now that she is in middle school. As a result, she is more fluent in English than in Spanish. However, her language dominance could change. If her parents moved to a Spanish-speaking country and Maya attended school where all the classes were taught in Spanish and if she developed Spanish-speaking friends, her language dominance would shift. Her fluency in Spanish would naturally increase as she used Spanish more often in more settings with more people.

Perhaps the reason that people assume that the ideal bilingual is balanced results from thinking of a bilingual as the sum of two fully developed monolinguals. However, Grosjean takes a holistic view of bilingualism. He argues that "the bilingual is an integrated whole who cannot easily be decomposed into two separate parts . . . he has a unique and specific linguistic configuration" (75). He compares a bilingual to a high hurdler in track and field. The hurdler has to jump high and run fast, but she combines these skills into a new and different skill. She does not have to be the highest jumper or the fastest sprinter to be a very proficient high hurdler. A problem with conceptualizing a bilingual as two monolinguals is that schools may isolate the two languages and teach and test them separately rather than drawing on the full language repertoire of emergent bilingual students. As a result, emergent bilinguals may be labeled as deficient in one or both of their languages.

VIEWS OF BILINGUAL EDUCATION

Traditionally, programs for bilingual students have been categorized in one of two ways: as subtractive when children go to school speaking a home language other than English and lose their home language in the process of learning English; or as additive when children go to school speaking a home language other than English, maintain and develop their home language, and learn English. The images used to depict these programs are of a unicycle and a bicycle. In subtractive programs, students begin and end school with just one language, so these students can be represented by the unicycle with just one wheel. Students in additive programs are like a bicycle with its two wheels. As we discussed earlier, the image of a balanced bilingual is often a bicycle with two equal wheels.

Rather than viewing programs for emergent bilinguals as additive or subtractive, García (2009, 2010) looks at bilingualism through a new lens. She argues that instead of picturing the languages of a bilingual as a unicycle or a bicycle, a better image is an all-terrain vehicle. The wheels may be of different sizes, they can move up and down independently, and they can move in different directions as the vehicle negotiates an uneven landscape. This perspective fits with Grosjean's (2010) contention that bilinguals use their different languages in different contexts and for different purposes.

García explains that programs labeled as additive, including dual-language and maintenance bilingual education, come from the view of a bilingual as two monolinguals because the goal of these programs is to develop a person who is equally proficient in two languages. In García's (2009) words, "bilinguals are expected to be and do with each of their languages the same thing as monolinguals" (52). For example, in a bilingual dual-language program students are expected to perform like English monolinguals during English time and like Spanish monolinguals during Spanish time. This view of bilinguals and of bilingual education programs has predominated in schools.

García discusses two models of bilingualism that are based on a holistic view of bilinguals: *recursive bilingualism* and *dynamic bilingualism*. Recursive bilingualism occurs when a community whose language is being lost makes an effort to revitalize that language. García uses the example of the Maori of New Zealand. The Maori language had been marginalized and was dying out, but now it is being taught in the schools. García explains that as they regain their language the Maori people are drawing on past knowledge. They move back and forth between Maori and English as they reconstitute the heritage language, using it for new functions as well as old. This reconstitution is not simply a new language being added; rather, it draws on the language knowledge already known, though not complete, to develop the language more fully to meet the present needs of the speakers.

Dynamic bilingualism for García is the appropriate term for bilingualism in a globalized society. From a dynamic perspective, bilinguals and multilinguals use their languages for a variety of purposes and in a variety of settings. They are more or less proficient in the various contexts where they use the languages and are more or less proficient in different modalities (visual, print, and sound). O. García (2009) draws on the Language Policy Division of the Council of Europe's definition of bilingualism to set a goal for students in U.S. schools: "the ability to use several languages to varying degrees and for distinct purposes" (54). The view of bilingualism as dynamic suggests different practices in bilingual programs rather than an additive or a subtractive view.

Consequences of Viewing Bilinguals as Two Monolinguals

The twentieth-century view that bilinguals are two monolinguals in one person has led to practices that Cummins (2007) argues are based on misconceptions. Earlier we discussed two misconceptions: first, that instruction should be conducted entirely in the target language, the direct instruction misconception; and second, that translation between students' home languages and the target language has no place in the teaching of language or literacy.

A third misconception applies to bilingual programs, which Cummins refers to as the *Two Solitudes assumption*. The idea is that in bilingual classrooms the two languages should be kept rigidly separated. In many dual language programs there is one teacher for each language; in others, different subjects are taught in each of the languages. For example, math might be in English and science in Spanish. In other programs the languages are distributed by time—mornings in English and afternoons in Spanish. Still other programs alternate languages on a daily or weekly basis. In all cases, there are specific times or subjects for each language with no overlap.

However, many effective practices are excluded when instruction is limited to one language at a time. For example, having students access cognates depends on using both languages simultaneously. When the languages are not separated students can carry out linguistic investigations and compare and contrast their languages. Students can also have exchanges with sister classes in other countries where one of their languages is spoken. All these practices build metalinguistic awareness as well as proficiency in the two languages. Cummins writes:

> It does seem reasonable to create largely separate spaces for each language within a bilingual or immersion program. However, there are also compelling arguments to be made for creating a shared or interdependent space for the promotion of language awareness and cross-language cognitive processing. The reality is that students are making cross-linguistic connections throughout the course of their learning in a bilingual or immersion program, so why not nurture this learning strategy and help students to apply it more efficiently? (229)

Cummins points out that there is theoretical support for using both languages for instruction. Research has shown that new knowledge is built on existing knowledge, and if that knowledge was developed in the home language, it can best be accessed through the home language (Bransford, Brown, and Cocking 2000). In addition, literacy skills are interdependent, so teaching should facilitate cross-language transfer.

He concludes his discussion of the Two Solitudes misconception by writing, "the empirical evidence is consistent both with an emphasis on extensive communicative interaction in the TL (ideally in both oral and written modes) and the utility of students' home language as a cognitive tool in learning the TL" (226–27).

CUMMINS' HYPOTHESES

Two hypotheses based on research Cummins conducted (1979) provide support for viewing bilingual students holistically and drawing on their full language repertoire: the Interdependence Hypothesis and the Common Underlying Proficiency (CUP) theory.

Interdependence Hypothesis and Common Underlying Proficiency

A commonsense assumption that is made in teaching emergent bilinguals in many places is that "more English equals more English." This idea, discussed earlier as the direct instruction misconception, seems logical. It is a variation of the time-on-task assumption that the more time spent on a task, the greater the proficiency a student develops. In this case, the idea is that the more time students spend studying English, the more proficient they will become in English. However, Cummins explains that this seemingly logical assumption fails to recognize that languages are interdependent, and the development of the first language has a positive effect on the development of a second language. As Cummins (1979) states:

> To the extent that instruction in L_X is effective in promoting proficiency in L_X, transfer of this proficiency to L_Y will occur provided there is adequate exposure to L_Y (either in school or the environment) and adequate motivation to learn L_Y. (29)

In other words, when students are taught in and develop proficiency in their home language, L_X, that proficiency will transfer to the second language, L_Y, assuming they are given enough exposure to the second language and are motivated to learn it. Cummins explains that the reason that proficiency transfers from one language to another is that a common proficiency underlies an emergent bilingual's languages. Because of this common underlying proficiency there is an "interdependence of concepts, skills, and linguistic knowledge that makes transfer possible" (191). Cummins cites extensive research showing that there is a common proficiency that underlies bilinguals' languages.

According to Cummins (2000) the common underlying proficiency can be thought of as "a central processing system comprising (1) attributes of the individual such as cognitive and linguistic abilities (memory, auditory discrimination, abstract reasoning, etc.) and (2) specific conceptual and linguistic knowledge derived from experience and learning (vocabulary knowledge)" (191). As a result of this interdependence, an emergent bilingual can draw on a common pool of cognitive and linguistic abilities and skills as she develops literacy and content knowledge in two languages. In addition, there is a transfer of background knowledge and related linguistic features, such as cognates or similar syntactic patterns.

To take a simple example of how CUP operates, young children learn how to distinguish different animals quite early. At first a young child might call a cat or a cow a dog, but soon the child begins to understand the different features of those three animals. When they begin to learn the names of these animals in another language, they simply learn the label. So, for example, they learn that *gato* is cat, *vaca* is cow, and *perro* is dog. However, they do not have to learn all over again the distinguishing features of these animals. They already understand the concepts of cat, cow, and dog. That is part of their background knowledge, their common underlying proficiency.

Cummins' CUP theory can help account for the difference in academic performance of students with similar levels of English proficiency. Consider José and Felipe, who arrived in Mrs. Enns' third-grade classroom in September. Both boys had just come from Mexico and did not speak any English. By April, Mrs. Enns wanted to refer Felipe to be tested for learning disabilities, as he was doing poorly in her class. José, on the other hand, was doing very well.

When the bilingual specialist conferred with Mrs. Enns, they looked at the previous schooling of the two boys. Felipe had lived in a rural area and had had interrupted schooling. He had never learned to read or write in Spanish and missed most of the content instruction of the early grades. José, in contrast, came from Monterrey, a large city, and had attended school since preschool. His report card from Mexico showed that he had received 8s, 9s, and 10s, high grades in the Mexican system. The difference in the boys' academic performance in English can be accounted for by the difference in their primary-language schooling and their native-language literacy, their underlying proficiency.

In another case, Claudia arrived in Mr. Bedrosian's class from Mexico City to attend sixth grade in a school that is 85 percent Latino. After eight months, Claudia was doing better academically than many of her classmates who entered elementary school speaking Spanish and had attended school in the United States all their lives. Mr. Bedrosian thought Claudia was more motivated and tried harder. However, when he began to study bilingual education, he investigated Claudia's past educational history. He discovered that Claudia had studied in Mexico City and was a top student in all subject areas there. Mr. Bedrosian could see that her schooling in Spanish in Mexico had provided the literacy and content-area knowledge she needed to succeed in English. She already knew how to read, and she knew the concepts in Spanish, so her literacy and academic knowledge transferred to her second language. In contrast, many of her U.S.–born classmates who had come to school speaking Spanish had never had instruction in their primary language to build the kind of knowledge base that Claudia had.

Cummins (2000) contrasts the idea of a common underlying proficiency with that of a separate underlying proficiency (SUP). Those who hold to the SUP theory must believe that what we learn in one language goes to one part of our brain and cannot be accessed when we are learning and speaking another language. This is a common assumption of opponents of bilingual education when they say that students learning in their first language are wasting time. They must believe that learning something in a home language does not influence what learners know in a second language and is completely separate from any knowledge or understandings gained in a second language. Therefore, those who hold the SUP perspective believe immigrant students should only be learning in English in order to achieve in English. However, research shows that students in programs that build students' home languages as they acquire English develop higher levels of academic proficiency in English than emergent bilinguals schooled only in English. They draw on their common underlying proficiency and apply their knowledge in the home language to English.

Cummins' Dual Iceberg Image

Cummins uses the image of a dual iceberg to characterize his CUP hypothesis. The two peaks of the iceberg that are above the waterline represent the surface features (the sounds or writing) of the two languages. The very compact ice core is relatively heavier and keeps a large percentage of the iceberg under water. When an iceberg tumbles over several times, its light snow layers on the surface are compacted. Thus, even more of the iceberg is submerged under water. As those who studied the *Titanic* disaster of 1912 discovered, what is seen on the surface is not the whole story. Figure 7–4 represents the dual iceberg.

If the two tips of the iceberg are thought of as the surface proficiency that speakers have in their first (L1) and second (L2) languages, then what is below the surface is the common underlying proficiency that has built up in the two languages and can transfer from one language to the other. Students who have more schooling in their home language can draw upon that knowledge as they are learning their second language. However, that proficiency may not always be apparent in the surface abilities they show in the second language. It is over time that students with greater total underlying proficiency show that proficiency in both their L1 and their L2. Students without the underlying academic proficiency in their home language, however, struggle because they have nothing to draw upon as they are learning academic content in a second language.

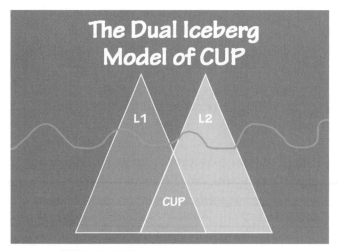

FIGURE 7–4 *The Dual Iceberg*

LANGUAGING AND TRANSLANGUAGING

O. García (2009) argues that "language" should be conceived of as a verb rather than a noun. She argues that people do not "have" one or more languages; instead, they *language* to carry out communicative functions. García's view is similar to Halliday's (1994). Halliday and other systemic functional linguists hold that language (or the ability to communicate using language) develops in the functional context of use. As we discussed in Chapter 6, systemic functional linguists analyze language use by considering the *field* (ideas being discussed), *tenor* (relation between speaker and listener or reader and writer), and *mode* (means of communication and devices used to make oral or written texts cohesive and coherent) of a spoken or written text. In this way, they determine the language functions that humans use systematically as they communicate. García's approach is consistent with functional linguistics because she also focuses on the ways humans communicate in social contexts to accomplish different functions, such as expressing ideas, apologizing, asking questions, and so on. García points out that since bilinguals can draw on two or more languages as they communicate, they translanguage and draw on their full linguistic repertoire. The examples from our granddaughter, Maya, described earlier show translanguaging well.

Like Grosjean (2010), O. García (2009, 2010) takes a holistic view of bilinguals. Earlier we discussed her concept of dynamic bilingualism that she represented with an all-terrain vehicle. García and Wei (2014) extend Cummins' ideas of a common underlying proficiency and the interdependence between languages in her concept of *translanguaging*. Cummins hypothesizes that there is a common proficiency that underlies the two or more distinct languages that a bilingual person has developed. The bilingual carries out certain functions in each of these languages, drawing on knowledge and skills developed in both languages. García, in contrast, sees monolinguals as drawing on their linguistic resources to language and bilinguals as drawing on all their language resources to translanguage through a dynamic process.

While Cummins suggests that a bilingual uses two linguistic systems, and that there is a common proficiency that underlies these systems and that the systems are interdependent, García and Wei state that "there is but one linguistic system . . . with features that are integrated" (15). Translanguaging, then, is a process of communicating by drawing on all the aspects of this one linguistic system. As García and Wei state, "Translanguaging is the discursive norm in bilingual families and communities" (23). Further, "bilinguals have one linguistic repertoire from which they select features strategically to communicate effectively" (22). *Code-switching* is a term that has been used to refer to the practice of switching between two languages. However, García and Wei use the term *translanguaging*. They argue that bilinguals do not switch between two linguistic codes. Rather, they have one linguistic system and use features of this single system as they communicate. As García and Wei state:

Translanguaging differs from the notion of code-switching in that it refers not simply to a shift or shuttle between two languages, but to the speakers' construction and use of original and complex interrelated discursive practices that cannot be easily assigned to one or another traditional definition of a language, but that make up the speakers' complete language repertoire. (22)

Bringing in words from both languages enriches the conversation in the same way that having a large vocabulary in one language allows a person to express herself more fully. For example, one of our daughters, Ann, is married to a Greek American. Most of his Greek American family members are dominant English speakers, but they use Greek expressions and words when appropriate to communicate. They greet each other and Greek friends the first day of every month with "Καλό μήνα" (*Kalo Mina*), which literally means "good month." Greeting one another in English would simply not convey the same meaning. Through exchanging this greeting and using other Greek words and expressions with Greek relatives, his family members translanguage and draw on their complete linguistic repertoire.

TRANSLANGUAGING IN THE CLASSROOM

The concept of dynamic bilingualism that views language as an action and translanguaging as the normal language use of bilingual individuals and communities has implications for teaching emergent bilinguals in ESL and bilingual programs. These practices involve drawing on the full linguistic system that emergent bilinguals bring to class rather than attempting to separate their linguistic system into two languages to be taught one at a time or by teaching only the English component of their system. Effective teaching involves the strategic use of students' language resources and the careful use of translanguaging.

The primary function of schools is to teach academic content, and teachers need to give students the language they need to read, write, and talk about that content. When planning instruction that includes translanguaging, it is important to keep in mind three goals for using translanguaging strategies: (1) to scaffold content, (2) to scaffold language, and (3) to affirm identity. Teachers can use translanguaging strategies, such as preview–view–review discussed earlier, to scaffold academic content by providing a preview and review in the students' home language. Accessing cognates is a translanguaging strategy that scaffolds language acquisition and builds metalinguistic awareness. Teachers who recognize the language abilities of their emergent bilinguals and allow translanguaging affirm students' bilingual identities. Students can translate when monolingual parents come to school, or students can give a preview in the home language of a lesson that will be taught in English. All of these are strategic uses of translanguaging that scaffold content and language and also affirm the identities of emergent bilinguals.

Translanguaging Examples

Teachers can use translanguaging in many settings. For example, in a social studies unit on immigration a teacher used interactive read-alouds and shared readings of books such as *Grandfather's Journey* (Say 1993, 1997), *Going Home* (Bunting 1998), and *My Diary from Here to There: Mi diario de aquí hasta allá* (Pérez 2002) to explore immigration experiences. As part of a final project for this unit, students interviewed a family member about the experience of immigration using their home language. Students translated a summary of the interview and wrote basic information about the person they interviewed and presented their report to the class using both English and their home language. Students then wrote in English about some of the difficulties of immigration.

During science, a teacher explained water cycle stages using English and supported the presentation with a clearly labeled visual. Then the teacher had the students work in home language groups or pairs and encouraged them to discuss their understanding of each stage using their home language or English. The students then worked in groups of students with different home languages. Each group drew and labeled the stages using English. The teacher called on different groups to explain each of the stages using English.

During math the teacher wanted to review measurement vocabulary. She gave students a short reading on measurement in English, but put a translation of the reading next to it in her students' home languages. Students first read the English version and then read the home language translation. They highlighted the words that looked similar in both languages. They found many cognates for measurement words, such as centimeter and *centimetro*, and added them to their list of math-related cognates. The teacher took the words students found and added them to a whole-class math cognate chart that was updated throughout the unit.

In other classes students read stories in their home language and retold the stories to other students in their class in English. They wrote drafts of papers in their home language and then wrote a final version in English. Students met in home language groups to discuss in the home language how to do homework in the target language. Students used the home language to discuss English homework with parents. As these examples show, there are many ways that teachers can make strategic use of students' home languages to scaffold both content and language learning and affirm students' identities.

Katie's Hmong Storyteller

A good example of the benefits of incorporating students' home languages comes from Katie. In her kindergarten class Katie had native English and Spanish speakers and several Hmong children. Her district provided books and music in Spanish, and she had access to Spanish-speaking paraprofessionals in her school. However, there were limited resources for her Hmong students who spoke little English and were often reluctant to participate in class. At a district workshop on Hmong culture, Katie learned a Hmong storyteller was available to come to classes to tell stories in Hmong, and "Three Billy Goats Gruff" was one of the stories in his repertoire.

Before the storyteller arrived, Katie read several versions of the folktale to her class in English. The students enjoyed the sound effects as Katie read how the goats trip-trapped across the bridge. She had the students act out the story as well. When the storyteller arrived, Katie insisted that he tell the story to the entire class in Hmong. She reasoned that the children knew the story so well that they would be able to follow along. She was right. When the storyteller arrived at the part of the story where the goats cross the bridge, the students shouted in delight when they recognized "Trip, trap, trip, trap" spoken in Hmong. All the children, no matter what their language background, enjoyed the story.

The storytelling in Hmong was a positive experience for all Katie's students, but her support for her Hmong students' language paid additional dividends in the days following the storytelling. Va John, a quiet Hmong boy, had seldom spoken in Katie's class in English or in Hmong, and he had not written anything even though Katie encouraged her students to draw and write in their journals each day. Va John proved to be a good learner and a good teacher. First, he wrote and drew in his journal about his favorite story, "Three Billy Goats Gruff" (see Figure 7–5). He copied the title and signed his name. His drawing showed a good understanding of the key elements of the story.

Katie responded to his journal as she did to all her students. She thanked Va John for writing and commented on how much she liked his goat's smile. This

FIGURE 7–5 *Billy Goat 1*

encouraged Va John to become a "teacher" of Hmong. In Figure 7–6 he writes that *Hon* is a boy's name (John) and *Mai Ja* is a girl's name. Katie thanked Va John for teaching her Hmong, so the next day (see Figure 7–7) Va John drew pictures of a rainbow, pants, a dress, and a skirt and labeled each one with invented-spelling Hmong. Below the pictures he wrote in English, "theys are mog log which theys are the thine to me." (These are Hmong language. These are the things to me.) Katie responded by telling him how much she liked reading his Hmong writing. Katie reported that from the time of the Hmong storyteller visit, Va John showed pride in his home language and culture and also showed an enthusiasm for school that had not been evident before.

Va John's response is a good example of translanguaging in a classroom. Katie encouraged the use of Hmong in her classroom when the Hmong storyteller told the story to all her students. Va John then felt free to draw on his full linguistic repertoire in Hmong and English to communicate with Katie. She affirmed his identity as a Hmong who was an emergent Hmong/English bilingual, and this had a positive impact on Va John's language and literacy development.

SUPPORTING STUDENTS' CULTURES

Effective teachers find many ways to support their students' cultural backgrounds

FIGURE 7–6 *Billy Goat 2*

FIGURE 7–7 *Billy Goat 3*

as well as their languages. We end this chapter with an example from Elaine, an exceptional teacher who found different ways to build on the cultural backgrounds of all the students in her diverse class.

Elaine taught fourth grade in an inner-city school. In her class she had Hispanic, Hmong, Laotian, Cambodian, and African American students. Most of her students were born in the U.S., and many had little understanding of their own cultural background or the backgrounds of their classmates. Elaine implemented several strategies each year to help her students learn about their own and their classmates' cultural backgrounds.

During the first week of school, students were asked to do a heritage investigation. They interviewed family members to find out about their own birthplace and those of their parents and grandparents. Then the class worked together to find these locations on a map of the world. They put a card with their name on the map and connected their name to their birthplace with one color of yarn and to the birthplace of their parents or grandparents with another color. When all the students had finished, they had created a colorful representation of the multiple origins of their class. This activity taught map-reading skills and much more—it validated each student's cultural heritage, provided opportunities for parents to communicate with their children about their family histories, ignited students' curiosity about their own cultural heritage and that of their classmates, and visibly showed students that together they had a rich cultural heritage.

Another strategy Elaine developed to encourage students to think about who they were was a culture share. For this activity students brought something from home that represented their culture. It could be an object, a picture, a piece of clothing, a recipe, or a piece of writing. Before and after students chose their own item to share, Elaine read stories about objects like those the students might bring to class or talk about. Elaine read books such as *The Whispering Cloth* (Shea 1995), the story of a young Hmong girl learning to make a Hmong story cloth; *Dia's Story Cloth* (Cha 1998), a story of the Hmong people told through different story cloths on each page; and *Chelsea's Chinese New Year* (Bullard 2012), a story about a family in the U.S. celebrating the customs of Chinese New Year. She also read *The Name Jar* (Choi 2003) in which the main character, Unhei, is hurt when classmates make fun of her name. She looks at her "name chop," an imprint in wood that when stamped in ink is her personal signature. It was a gift from her grandmother and represents the pride she realizes she has in her Korean background.

Elaine also read *A Perfect Season for Dreaming: Un tiempo perfecto para soñar* (Sáenz 2008), an imaginative and colorful counting book in which the grandfather, toward the end of his life, tells his granddaughter of his magical dreams of objects falling from a piñata—a magical guitar, coyotes dressed as mariachis, armadillos, cacti, and other artifacts of Mexican culture. Reading all of these books helped Elaine's students think about the importance of cultural objects in their own lives and gave them ideas for what they might bring to class.

Students shared the objects they brought to school in small groups and, if they were willing, with the whole class. This activity validated students' cultures, communicated Elaine's acceptance and celebration of multiculturalism to parents and students, and provided a casual environment that encouraged oral language development.

Elaine read many other culturally relevant books to her students, and they discussed and wrote about them. This helped them build appreciation for their own backgrounds and those of their classmates. She also encouraged her students to study their own cultures in more detail. One activity involved making cultural alphabet books.

Students were divided into groups by their background—there might be a Hmong group, a Cambodian group, a Mexican group, and an African American group depending upon the class makeup.

FIGURE 7–8 *Page from class Hmong book,* I *Is for* Invite

Each group worked with a paraprofessional from the same cultural background. In their groups, the students brainstormed things from their culture with English names that begin with each letter of the alphabet. One year the Hmong group, for example, chose objects (*A* is for *apron*), places (*L* is for *Laos*), family names (*V* is for *Vang*), and characteristics (*I* is for *invite* because Hmong people invite other Hmong into their homes). Figure 7–8 shows the page for *invite* and Figure 7–9 is the "*D* is for *dance*" page from the Cambodian book. The students illustrated each page, and then Elaine laminated the pages and assembled them into books for the class library.

FIGURE 7–9 *Page from class Cambodian book,* D *Is for* Dance

These cultural alphabet books were very popular. Students constantly checked them out. As they read the books from other groups, students realized they had many things in common. Elaine also used pages from the books to discuss and build her students' oral English proficiency.

Another activity that Elaine organized for her class was a cultural potluck. Held twice a year, these potlucks were designed to help students better understand and appreciate one another's cultures through food. Students wrote invitations to their families for this event. The families were asked to bring some food that was representative of their culture to the school. The day before the potluck, home language tutors called the homes to remind the families about the potluck and to answer any questions. Meanwhile, the class discussed what polite behavior is if you don't like the food from another culture. Elaine explained that one year, for example, she brought pickled okra, a food from her childhood in Louisiana that might seem strange to many of her students. She encouraged everyone to try at least a little of each dish, and if they did not like it to leave the rest on their plate without saying anything.

On the day of the potluck, parents brought food to the classroom around lunchtime. The cafeteria provided drinks, plates, silverware, and napkins. Parents and students organized the food on tables according to the culture and made signs that named each dish. Students described the food their parents brought and explained the ingredients. This led to discussion of similarities and differences among foods from different countries. After the meal, students performed dances typical of their cultural background and sang traditional songs. Elaine found that these student performances, which celebrated an important part of the cultures represented in her classroom, helped ensure that parents would not just bring in their food and leave early.

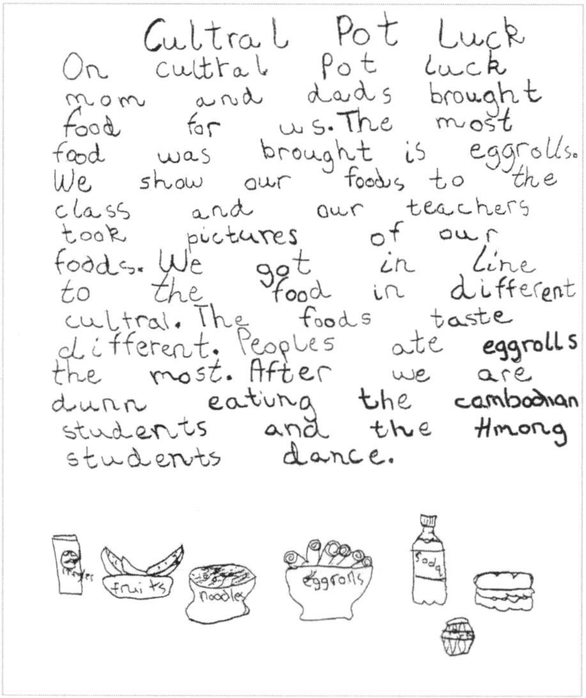

Elaine always used experiences like the cultural potluck to promote student writing. The day after the meal, students wrote their responses telling what happened and what they ate. Figure 7–10

FIGURE 7–10 *Cultural Potluck*

shows one student's response. Although this fourth-grade student is at an early stage of writing development in English, she was able to explain what went on, and she drew pictures of different foods and labeled them. Another student raised the question, "I wonder why do Hmong people food are almost the same as Cambodia culture?" Later, Elaine used these responses to discuss the similarities and differences among the cultures of the students in the class.

Elaine used activities such as the heritage investigation, the cultural share, the cultural alphabet books, and the cultural potluck to help her students understand their own cultural backgrounds and those of their classmates. This helped her build a class community from a very diverse group of students and enabled her students to see that they had many similarities despite their differences. These experiences helped them build the cultural competence they would need to succeed in a very diverse world.

CONCLUSION

The examples in this chapter from Gabriela, Katie, and Elaine all show the importance of drawing on the language and cultural backgrounds of emergent bilinguals. When teachers develop lessons that include students' languages and cultures, the students are more engaged. These lessons provide topics for oral language development and writing. Teachers can also include bilingual and culturally relevant books, as Gabriela and Elaine did, to extend the lessons.

In both ESL and bilingual programs, students' home languages can be used to scaffold both language and content learning and to affirm emergent bilinguals' identities. Cummins discusses three misconceptions that have led to the exclusion of first languages in programs for English learners. The first is the Direct Instruction misconception, which holds that the only language to be used in the classroom is the target language. This misconception results in English-only policies in many ESL classrooms. Cummins argues that students' first languages can be used effectively to promote second language acquisition.

The second misconception, which Cummins refers to as the No Translation misconception, is that teachers should never translate into students' home languages. However, there are many ways that teachers can use translation strategically to give students access to content and to develop language proficiency. The third misconception, the Two Solitudes misconception, applies to dual language and bilingual programs in which the two languages are kept strictly separate. Cummins points out that no empirical evidence supports this separation of languages. His theories of language interdependence and a common underlying proficiency show that concepts and skills transfer from the first language to the second. Teaching about cognates or using strategies like preview–view–review make use of the first language to build the second language of emergent bilinguals.

Grosjean and García argue that rather than viewing bilinguals as two monolinguals in one person, educators should view bilinguals holistically as unique individuals with a single linguistic system. Effective teaching allows emergent bilinguals to translanguage and draw on their full linguistic repertoire as they develop language and content knowledge. Translanguaging acknowledges the normal discursive practices of bilingual people and bilingual communities. This twenty-first-century holistic view of bilinguals has clear implications for teaching in both bilingual and ESL programs where teachers can make strategic use of students' home languages to promote learning.

APPLICATIONS

1. We began this chapter by describing how Gabriela used many books with her dual language class as they studied habitats. Choose a unit you have taught or plan to teach and develop a text set of books related to the theme. Bring some of the books and your bibliography to class to share.

2. Cummins describes three misconceptions, the Direct Instruction misconception, the No Translation misconception, and the Two Solitudes misconception. Based on your experience in either ESL or bilingual classes, would you agree that these misconceptions are influencing curricular decisions? Come with examples you could use for a discussion of these misconceptions.

3. Consider the two images of a bilingual person: a bicycle and an all-terrain vehicle. What assumptions about bilingual people and bilingual programs do each of these images support? Be prepared to explain.

4. We described several practices that involve the use of students' home languages to scaffold language and content instruction in a second language. List at least three additional activities you could use that draw on your students' home languages.

5. Elaine used a variety of activities to help her students understand their own cultural background and appreciate their classmates' backgrounds. List additional activities that promote students' pride in their home cultures and appreciation for the cultures of others.

8

Teaching and Assessment Should Reflect Faith in the Learner

FRANCISCO'S STORY

> I remember going to school and feeling like an outcast. I felt like I didn't belong here and that I was taking away something from someone else. I felt the negative attitude that some people have towards people from other countries. Before walking into a classroom, I would pray that the teacher or anyone wouldn't talk to me so I wouldn't have to say anything. I was afraid that I would say something wrong and everyone would laugh at me. Every time I remember those experiences, I feel nervous and insecure.

After living with his grandmother for eight years in El Salvador while his mother worked in the United States to make a home for Francisco and his younger brother, Francisco was finally able to join her in the United States when he was fourteen. Although he had been a good student in his rural school in El Salvador, he arrived speaking almost no English. He was overwhelmed in the large high school of more than 2,000 students that he attended. Teenagers often feel insecure in school and worry about what others think, but, as Francisco explained, insecurities can be even stronger when a student feels out of place and speaks a different language.

Francisco was fortunate. He found mentors who had faith in him. As a child he often played soccer in El Salvador, and this skill helped him when he came to the U.S. He was an excellent soccer player and qualified for the high school team. His soccer coach encouraged him to work hard in school and eventually helped him to get a scholarship at a local private college where the coach worked part time.

In college, Francisco was once again overwhelmed. Although his English was improving, and he had fairly good conversational English, he had been in this country only four years and was still acquiring academic English. Francisco found the reading and writing load in college extremely time consuming and considered dropping out. However, his soccer coach helped again. The coach went to his home and talked to Francisco and his mother, encouraging Francisco not to give up on college.

Francisco tried another semester. That semester he became friends with a Spanish-speaking Anglo who supported him and helped him edit papers. In addition, his bilingual advisor began to take an active interest in him and encouraged him to continue to study hard. By the time he graduated, Francisco had raised his grade point average to the B level required for entry to teacher education.

Then in the teacher education program, Francisco began to see what skills he had to contribute to the profession as a bilingual teacher. He wrote this entry in his journal after observing an elementary school bilingual classroom for the first time.

> *Ser bilingüe es como vivir en dos mundos. Uno puede hablar con personas en español y entrar en su mundo. Lo mismo pasa cuando hablas, escribes y lees en inglés. Ahora que empecé el programa de educación bilingüe, puedo ver que tan valioso es ser bilingüe porque hay tantos niños que puedo ayudar en su primer idioma.*

> To be bilingual is like living between two worlds. One can speak to people in Spanish and enter into their world. The same thing happens when you speak, you write, and you read in English. Now that I have begun the bilingual education program, I can see how valuable it is to be bilingual because there are so many children that I can help in their first language.

And helping students is exactly what Francisco saw as his role. In his first full-time teaching assignment as a third-grade bilingual teacher, he encountered Sergio, a student who at nine years old struggled with reading and writing in both English and Spanish and, in addition, constantly interrupted Francisco's class. Francisco talked to his mother, but she was at a loss as to how to control Sergio at home. Francisco suspected there were problems at home that also were affecting Sergio.

Francisco was determined to help Sergio. Francisco often played soccer with his students during recess and Sergio loved to play, but when he misbehaved Francisco wouldn't allow him to join in. Soon, Sergio's behavior improved. Francisco read one-on-one with Sergio every day and constantly encouraged him when he behaved well and tried hard. He told Sergio he believed he could be a reader and writer and celebrated when Sergio published his first limited-text bilingual book. By the end of the year, Sergio was a changed child. He participated appropriately in class, was reading almost at grade level, and enjoyed writing in writer's workshop. Francisco had done for Sergio what others had done for him: he showed Sergio that he had faith in him as a learner. Now, almost twenty years later, Francisco is still a dedicated teacher who loves to support all his students and makes it a point to provide extra help for students who are struggling in school. There have been many students like Sergio whose potential has been expanded by teachers like Francisco who show faith in their students.

SUPPORTING STUDENTS' FAITH IN THEMSELVES

Many emergent bilinguals never have the opportunities that Francisco had to work with people who believe in them. These students may come to believe that they cannot learn, that their first culture and language are not valuable, and that no place exists for them in American society. To use Goodman's (1991) term, these students need to "revalue" themselves as learners, and they need to revalue school as a place where important things can be learned.

Supporting Self-Efficacy

Bandura (1986) refers to students who fail to achieve their potential because they don't believe they can succeed academically as having low self-efficacy. He defines *self-efficacy* as "people's judgments of their capabilities to organize and execute courses of action required to attain designated types of performance" (391). Students with high self-efficacy view school tasks as challenges to be overcome and do the hard mental work required to learn new academic content, but students with low-self efficacy often give up. They have trouble picturing themselves as successful learners, so they don't put in the effort required to succeed. Then, when they fail at some academic task, their negative view of their ability is reinforced.

Self-efficacy may be equated with investment or motivation. Emergent bilinguals must be motivated to invest the effort needed to learn English and academic content. Guthrie has conducted research showing the importance of motivation for reading, and since reading is the primary source of academic language development, it is crucial to find ways to motivate English learners to read. In his discussion of reading Guthrie argues: "Motivational processes are the foundation for coordinating cognitive goals and strategies in reading. For example, if a person is intrinsically motivated to read and believes she is a capable reader, the person will persist in reading difficult texts and exert effort to resolve conflicts and integrate text with prior knowledge" (www.readingonline.org/articles/handbook/guthrie/#author).

Guthrie points out several instructional practices that foster motivation and engagement in reading and result in students' having higher self-efficacy. The first is that teachers should have learning goals for their students. When teachers have clear learning goals, students recognize that it is more important for them to learn the content than to get a correct answer. Francisco believed that Sergio would become a reader and writer and worked with him to value reading as something worthwhile and enjoyable. He didn't test him but talked with him about the books they read together and responded to Sergio's writing with interest.

A second instructional practice that increases student self-efficacy is for teachers to include real-world interactions. When teachers connect what students are learning to the world beyond school, students are more motivated to learn. For example, instead of relying on a textbook account of the Vietnam War, a teacher can invite veterans to come to the class and share their experiences. The teacher and the students conduct research on the war and develop questions for the veterans. After the veterans visit the class, students can compare what they read with what they learned when they asked the veterans questions. This can lead to further research on the war. In this process, the students learn much more than they would have by merely reading the section on the Vietnam War in a textbook.

A third instructional practice to increase self-efficacy is what Guthrie calls autonomy support. As he explains, "Autonomy support refers to the teacher's guidance in helping students make choices among meaningful alternatives in texts and tasks to attain knowledge and learning goals" (www.readingonline.org/articles /handbook/guthrie/#author).

Choice motivates students, but teachers need to provide guidance to help them make good choices. For example, Ann, a bilingual teacher in a rural community, showed her emergent bilingual second and third graders three books and asked, "Which of these is the hardest one to read, and which do you think is the easiest?" The students all thought the book with the most pages would be hardest and the book with the fewest would be easiest. Then Ann opened the book with many pages to show the students that it had large text and many pictures. After that, she showed them that the book with fewer pages had small print and no pictures.

Ann and the class discussed the importance of looking carefully when choosing books to read. The class started a list of characteristics of books that made them hard or easy to read. In addition to pictures, the students realized that books are easier to read if they are on topics the students already know about. Over time, Ann worked to help her students make good choices. She also followed up with individual students to provide additional help in choosing appropriate books. Through this process of autonomy support, Ann enabled her students to choose books at a level they could read.

Another example of the importance of autonomy support comes from Jason, a high school teacher. One of his Hmong students, Kaub, had come to America at age six. At age thirteen, Kaub was extremely shy and quiet. Jason wrote, "When called on in class he would not say anything and only shake his head from side to side, the mute 'no.'"

Jason had his students write an I-Search paper instead of the traditional research report. Students researched a topic of their choice and wrote about it. Jason gave this assignment to all his students, including his emergent bilinguals, because he wanted to demonstrate his belief that all his students could succeed. Jason also guided students as they made their choices, and he encouraged them to choose topics related to their backgrounds and interests. For his I-Search, Kaub chose to write about the Hmong New Year. Jason commented:

> When it came time for him to present orally to the class his research, I was surprised when he pulled authentic celebration clothing, complete with intricate sewing, from his backpack. He also pulled a number of hand-drawn pictures of Laos from his backpack. I had expected him to again decline talking in public, and although his English was not perfect, he gave an excellent oral report.

Jason provided his students with autonomy support by giving them choices and guiding them to choose appropriate topics, and this enabled Kaub to choose a topic that related to his background and interests. The usually shy student spoke up confidently when explaining a topic he really knew about. By giving Kaub a choice, Jason demonstrated his faith in his student and helped Kaub build self-efficacy.

Additional instructional practices that foster student self-efficacy include providing many different texts as Ann did, teaching strategies such as predicting and visualizing to use during reading, having students collaborate on projects, and praising students for their efforts. Teachers who combine these practices provide instruction that shows their faith in their students' ability to learn and helps students build confidence in their own capabilities.

TEACHERS SHOW FAITH IN THEIR STUDENTS

Teachers can show faith in their students in different ways. They can advocate for their students with other teachers, they can develop curriculum that will help their students build self-confidence, and they can create a classroom community that supports learners. Mary, Connie, and Rhoda provide examples of teachers showing faith in their students.

Mary

In some cases, ESL or bilingual teachers can serve the role of advocates for their students when other teachers fail to recognize the strengths of emergent bilinguals. Mary, who was teaching ELD classes at a high school, describes how she helped a mainstream teacher come to have more faith in one student:

When Jorge was in my ELD 4 class, he was a top student. He worked hard on all of his assignments and did a good job. This year I had him put into regular English 12. A few weeks into the school year I asked the twelfth-grade English teacher how he was doing. She told me that from what she could see of his performance, he was a student who did not care about school because he did not even try in class.

I expressed my surprise at her evaluation and explained that he had been one of my top students who worked hard on every assignment. The English 12 teacher had a talk with Jorge and asked why he was not doing any work. Jorge explained that he was confused about what was going on because he had entered the class about a week late. He had never received a textbook and was having a hard time finding other students who would share their book with him.

This gave the teacher a whole new perspective on Jorge. She spent time helping him catch up, made sure he got a textbook, and showed more faith in him overall. Because of this, Jorge's performance began to improve.

Mary's talk with the English 12 teacher helped her reevaluate Jorge. Once she realized that he wasn't clear on what the assignments were and that he was having trouble getting access to the textbook, she was able to get him involved in class, and Jorge started to work up to his potential.

Connie

At times, it is not just individual students but whole groups that need to feel a teacher's faith. Connie worked with a class that had been labeled "out of control." Connie recognized that their problem was a lack of self-confidence. She commented, "The feelings of not being good enough are seen in their actions. In the beginning many of my students were afraid to take risks. They would give up before they even started. This made it difficult to do group activities because they were afraid to work as a group."

As Connie engaged her students in interesting activities that they could complete successfully, she built their confidence and the atmosphere changed. Connie observed, "As the trust grew and they felt more comfortable, this barrier was taken down." The class was no longer out of control once they had a teacher who helped them develop confidence in their ability to complete their work successfully. As Connie concluded, "This tells me that beyond the curriculum, building self-confidence is essential to learning."

Rhoda

Teachers who show faith in their students can produce amazing individual results. Rhoda, a fifth-grade teacher, was concerned about one of her students, Surjit, a

Punjabi from India. He was twelve years old with no literacy in his first language. Surjit had been in the United States for just five months and had attended school in this country for only the last two months of the previous school year. He was entering Rhoda's classroom having already established a reputation for disturbing classmates and having little potential. The previous teacher had recommended that Surjit be tested for a learning disability.

The first month with Surjit was discouraging. His lack of previous schooling and English kept him from participating. Because he could not understand, he often wandered around the room disturbing the other students as they worked together on projects. Rhoda, however, decided she would not give up. Each time he wandered, she found a way to involve him in some kind of project. She tried to find activities that provided enough nonlinguistic context so that he could participate at least minimally. She set a goal for herself and Surjit—to get him to participate with other students in their group work by the end of the year.

Because Rhoda stressed the importance of community, the students in her classroom also took responsibility for Surjit. In October, two girls asked if they could be Surjit's ESL teachers during writer's workshop. This was the beginning of Surjit's real integration into the classroom. He was encouraged by his peer teachers and the entire class. By Christmas he was speaking enough English for the students to communicate with him. When he wrote his first coherent story, the whole class applauded. By the end of the year, Surjit was participating in a class project and even made a travel brochure for a state report.

Rather than being singled out as a student with learning disabilities, Surjit was viewed by his teacher and his classmates as having real learning potential, and he showed incredible growth. Rhoda, in fact, concluded at the end of the year that he not only had potential and could achieve and participate if encouraged but that he succeeded beyond her wildest dreams: "I think I could have expected even *more* of him!" The most important lesson we can learn as teachers is that our students have unlimited potential and that we, their teachers, must show our faith in them to allow them to show us that potential.

CUMMINS' CONVERSATIONAL AND ACADEMIC LANGUAGE DISTINCTION

Sometimes teachers conclude that emergent bilinguals who speak English but struggle academically are unmotivated or have learning disabilities. Cummins (1984) observed that English language learners were overrepresented in the special education population of schools in Canada. As he researched reasons for the high number of ELLs who were placed in special education classes, he discovered that although these students appeared to have developed the ability to use English for daily communication, they had difficulty understanding lectures in school, reading textbooks, and writing school papers. In other words, these students spoke and comprehended everyday conversational English quite well, but they lacked the academic English needed to complete school tasks.

Cummins' observations were consistent with studies of Finnish children in Sweden conducted by Skutnabb-Kangas and Toukomaa (1976). These researchers reported that the Finnish immigrants in Sweden appeared to be quite fluent in Swedish. However, when they were given tests in Swedish that involved complex cognitive operations, the Finnish children were not able to score at expected grade-level standards.

Cummins' own research in Canada supported Skutnabb-Kangas and Toukomaa's findings. Cummins analyzed the teacher referral forms and psychological assessments of more than four hundred English language learners. He found a consistent pattern of results: The students were perceived as having good oral English fluency, but they scored low on academic tests. For example, one referral read, "Arrived from Portugal at age 10 and was placed in a second-grade class; three years later in fifth grade, her teacher commented that 'her oral answering and comprehension is so much better than her written work that we feel a severe learning problem is involved, not just her non-English background'" (34). Another referral stated, "He speaks Italian fluently and English well. He is having a great deal of difficulty with the Grade One program. His attention span is very short. He is always very easily distracted" (33).

Since students appeared to speak English well, teachers and administrators assumed that their low scores on academic tasks reflected limited cognitive ability. This perspective led to the misplacement of many emergent bilinguals into special education. This distinction between conversational and academic language is important. Previously, large numbers of ELLs were placed in special education classes because many of the tests used to measure English language proficiency only tapped their conversational fluency. The results of the oral proficiency tests and teachers' daily conversations with the students led teachers to believe that some of their emergent bilinguals had developed the English they needed for school. However, since the students did poorly on written tests that measured academic knowledge and problem-solving ability, it was assumed that their low scores reflected a cognitive deficit, so they were placed in special education classes.

Based on this research, Cummins concluded that language proficiency is not a unitary construct. Instead, he argued that there are two types of language proficiency, conversational fluency and academic language proficiency. There are significant differences between the everyday language students use outside school and the academic language students are expected to use in school. A student can have a high level of conversational proficiency in a language and still have a low level of academic language proficiency.

Most students, like those described on the referral forms, develop oral fluency in a language much more quickly than they acquire academic language proficiency. Estimates are that it takes about two years to develop conversational fluency in a new language. Academic language proficiency, which Cummins (2000) defines as "the extent to which an individual has access to and command of the oral and written academic registers of schooling" (67) takes longer, from five to seven years (Cummins 1981a; Collier 1989). Francisco, whose story began this chapter, had only been in this country four years and did not have the academic language proficiency he needed to do the reading and writing required of him at the college level. Teachers can support their emergent bilinguals when they understand the two types of language proficiency because they avoid using their English learners' conversational fluency as a measure of their academic language proficiency.

Cummins' Quadrants

Cummins represents the difference between conversational fluency and academic language proficiency with a model that consists of a horizontal and a vertical line that cross to form four quadrants. The horizontal line extends from context-embedded communication to context-reduced communication, and the vertical line goes from cognitively undemanding to cognitively demanding tasks. Figure 8–1 provides a visual of Cummins' Quadrant model.

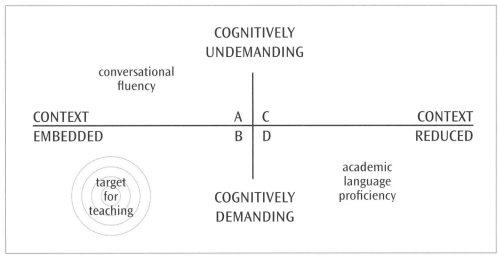

FIGURE 8–1 *Cummins' Quadrant*

All language occurs in some context. However, the amount of nonlinguistic support can vary greatly. For example, when talking with someone face to face we pick up much of the message from tone of voice, facial expression, gestures, and so on. If the conversation is about something we know well, our background knowledge supplies extra context. In addition, if we can see what we are discussing or if we have pictures or other visual cues, it is easier to follow the conversation, even if we lack a high level of language proficiency. A good example of context-embedded language would be a discussion about the weather with a friend as we stand in the rain under our umbrellas waiting for a ride to school. Even if some of the words or sentences are not clear, we can follow the thread of the conversation quite well and also contribute to it.

At the other end of the horizontal axis is language that is context reduced. Here, we have to depend much more on the words than on any other cues. An example might be reading a test question on a standardized test. Often test questions are not related to one another, so other sections of the test do not provide extra clues. In addition, there are no visual cues. The test taker has to rely on knowledge of the language. Context-reduced language is not limited to written language. Many ELs have trouble following lectures in school if the teacher simply talks. On the other hand, the teacher can make the lecture more context embedded by using a PowerPoint, a graphic organizer, or a video clip. While these scaffolds are helpful for all students, they are especially beneficial for emergent bilinguals because the visuals reduce the students' dependency on linguistic cues for making sense of the lecture.

The vertical scale on Cummins' diagram goes from cognitively undemanding to cognitively demanding. In describing this continuum, Cummins (1981b) comments, "Cognitive involvement can be conceptualized in terms of the amount of information that must be processed simultaneously or in close succession by the individual in order to carry out the activity" (12–13). Cognitive demand does not depend on the subject as much as it does on a person's background knowledge. The conversation about the weather is cognitively undemanding for most people because they know a great deal about weather—they don't need to expend a great deal of mental energy to understand whether it is raining or not. On the other hand, learning a new math concept could be very demanding. A young child learning how to multiply two numbers would have to devote a great deal of attention and memory to the task. Of course, most older students would find multiplication quite easy and not very demanding cognitively. This continuum, then, represents a developmental sequence. As students become more familiar with a procedure or task, the cognitive demand is reduced.

The two continuums form four quadrants. Quadrant A contains language that is context embedded and cognitively undemanding. The example of the weather would fall into this quadrant. The teachers and administrators in Canada who referred children for special education assessed students' English proficiency by using evidence from Quadrant A. They assumed that if students demonstrated conversational fluency, they were fully proficient in English.

However, an emergent bilingual who has developed conversational fluency may still lack academic language proficiency. The same student who does well in settings in which English is context embedded and cognitively undemanding (Quadrant A) may struggle listening to a lecture or taking a test, because in those settings the language is context reduced and cognitively demanding (Quadrant D). When school administrators ask teachers to prepare students for standardized tests by giving them benchmark tests frequently or by reading passages similar to those on the test and answering questions, the teaching falls into Quadrant D. These tasks are cognitively demanding and context reduced.

Although many tests and school tasks fall into Quadrant D, teaching should not be targeted to Quadrant D. What emergent bilinguals need is instruction that is cognitively demanding but also context embedded. They need scaffolded instruction to make difficult academic concepts comprehensible. When teachers use graphic organizers, have students work in cooperative groups, and engage them in hands-on activities to teach important concepts, they are teaching in Quadrant B. They are providing contextual support while still maintaining high cognitive demand. We would say that Quadrant B should be the target for teaching emergent bilinguals. When teaching occurs in Quadrant B, students develop the academic language they need to perform well on Quadrant D–types of tasks that are cognitively demanding and context reduced.

Teaching in the Challenge Zone

Gibbons (2009) also describes language proficiency using a quadrant model similar to Cummins' model. Figure 8–2 shows our adaptation of Gibbons' model.

As Figure 8–2 shows, any school assignment can be placed on a continuum from high to low challenge. For an English learner, repeating after the teacher would be a low-challenge activity. On the other hand, being assigned to conduct research and write a history report would be a high-challenge assignment for most ELs. The horizontal continuum in Figure 8–2 goes from high support to low support. If a teacher models how to solve a math problem and writes the steps on the board, then has students work in pairs to solve similar problems, and finally gives students additional problems of the same kind to complete individually, she is providing high support. On the other hand, if a teacher merely assigns students to solve a series of math problems on a worksheet and then has them work individually, the teacher is providing low support.

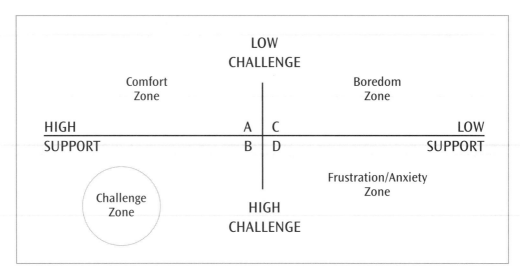

FIGURE 8–2 *Gibbons' Challenge Zone*

Figure 8–2 has four quadrants. Quadrant A, high support and low challenge, is what Gibbons calls the Comfort Zone. For example, if intermediate English learners are reviewing some basic commands using Total Physical Response in an activity in which the teacher models a series of commands, such as "stand up," "sit down," or "raise your hand," and the students respond to each command by performing the action without speaking, this is a low-challenge/high-support activity. Students like working in the Comfort Zone because success is easy, but they don't learn anything new.

Quadrant B is the Challenge Zone because there is high challenge and high support. An example of an activity in this zone for low-intermediate English learners would be for the teacher to give a short PowerPoint on the differences between ocean fish and marine mammals, have students work in pairs to read through an article on the differences between ocean fish and marine mammals, and then have each pair complete a Venn diagram showing the similarities and differences.

Quadrant C, low challenge and low support, is the Boredom Zone. For example, a teacher may give advanced English learners a worksheet that requires them to correct subject-verb agreement errors in sentences such as "Bill run to work every day." Then, if she has them work on these individually with no help from her, the students become bored. They may complete the assignment to earn a grade but, again, they do not learn anything new.

Sometimes teachers attempt to prepare students to pass difficult tests by teaching in Quadrant D, high challenge and low support. For example, the teacher might give students a benchmark test before teaching the concepts on the test. Or a teacher might assign beginning English learners to read a chapter in a grade-level science text and answer questions at the end of the chapter working alone. Quadrant D is what Gibbons calls the Frustration/Anxiety Zone. Krashen (1982) argues that when students are anxious and frustrated, their affective filter prevents them from acquiring new language.

Gibbons bases her model on Vygotsky's theory of learning. Vygotsky holds that learning is a social process that takes place when a person receives help to accomplish something they cannot do individually. For example, a student might not be able to solve a math problem alone, but she might be able to solve it while working with a more knowledgeable partner who can guide her and point out aspects of the problem that she should attend to. Vygotsky refers to this process as "working in the zone of proximal development." When teachers provide challenging lessons and support for English learners, they are teaching in the zone of proximal development. They show faith in the learner by teaching challenging curriculum and expand student potential by giving them the support they need to succeed.

MARY'S TONE UNIT

A good example of teaching in the Challenge Zone comes from Mary, the high school ELD teacher we mentioned earlier. Mary taught ELD classes to newcomers and second-year emergent bilinguals and also taught language arts to mainstream students. All her English learners spoke Spanish as their home language. She taught the same units to all her students because she knew that with carefully scaffolded instruction all of them could achieve academically (Soto 2014).

One especially challenging unit that Mary taught focused on tone, a difficult language arts concept. Mary's goal was to involve her students in activities that would help them analyze the tone in a story. Her students needed both the concept of tone and the vocabulary to describe tone. Mary knew that the state exam her students would have to pass included tone. She looked at release tests to find words used to describe the tone of literary pieces or that could be used to describe the tone of voice characters used. These included words like *poignant*, *giddy*, *vexed*, and *condescending*.

Mary gave her students a word list taken from the release exam, and they discussed the words. Then she asked each student to create a tone dictionary with some of the words. Each entry included the word, a translation into Spanish, a synonym, an antonym, what the word reminded the student of, and a drawing. She had her newcomers work in groups of four and her second-year students work in pairs to complete their entries. As the students worked Mary circulated to give them needed support, especially to the newcomer students. Students used colored paper to create a cover and stapled their finished tone dictionaries into small books that were displayed in the classroom.

Next, Mary formed groups of students and assigned each group one word. Students were asked to use words and drawings to represent the meaning of the word on a poster. One group demonstrated their understanding of the word *condescending* very well. They drew a picture of two small people standing on either side of a large person. They labeled this "what he thinks." Then they added a second picture with two tall people standing on either side of a small person. They labeled this picture "the reality." Students enjoyed this activity. Figure 8–3 shows one group's poster for the word *giddy*. The posters were also put up around the room.

When students began to develop the concept of tone and the vocabulary to describe tone, Mary gave them short passages from literature and asked them to identify the tone. One source Mary used for the passages was the website www .eastoftheweb.com. Students had to identify the tone and then support their choice with words or phrases from the text. For example, students chose *bitter* to describe the tone of a passage about a man who had grown up in an orphanage. They supported their choice with phrases like "the orphanage turned me into an old man."

To extend the students' understanding of tone and to prepare them to study Greek myths, Mary brought in a series of urban legends for students to read and discuss. Then the class decided on the tone of each legend. Following this, students chose or invented an urban legend of their own and made a poster with the tone and key words that supported their choice. One student chose a legend with a "suspenseful, scary, creepy tone" and identified words such as *evil*, *blood*, *angry*, and *revenge* to

FIGURE 8–3 *Tone Poster for the Word* Giddy

support his choice. As a final assignment, Mary asked students to write a story and identify the tone of the story.

By including drawings, posters, and urban legends, Mary was able to engage all her students in this study of tone. She scaffolded the instruction carefully. Her newcomers wrote group stories while her second-year students worked in pairs to create their tone stories. Student work was posted around the room to serve as models for other students. Although this tone unit was challenging, Mary had faith that her students could complete the assignments if she provided high levels of support.

DEVELOPING ACADEMIC LANGUAGE

Francisco, Jason, Connie, Rhoda, Mary, and the other teachers highlighted in this book provide teaching that demonstrates faith in their students and expands their potential. One of the biggest challenges teachers of emergent bilinguals face is to accelerate the development of academic language. We mentioned earlier that despite research that consistently shows that it takes from five to seven years for English learners to achieve academically at the levels of native English speakers (Cummins 1981a; Collier 1989; Thomas and Collier 2002) second language students are required to take standardized tests in English after only one year in U.S. schools. While it is not reasonable to expect teachers to bring students from beginning to advanced levels of English proficiency and to teach them grade-level content in so short a time, it is important for teachers to help English learners develop the academic language they need to succeed in school.

In previous chapters we described programs such as SIOP, CALLA, GLAD, and QTEL, which are designed to promote academic language acquisition. We have also reviewed the research on effective practices for teaching ELs and described a series of principles to help emergent bilinguals develop the academic language they need for school success. We conclude this section by outlining a six-step plan for teaching academic language. As the research demonstrates, it takes time for students to develop academic language, and it is important that teachers present challenging curriculum and organize their instruction to maximize student potential.

A Six-Step Plan

In the following sections we describe a six-step plan for developing academic language. Our example comes from a government class that Denise teaches in a large urban school. Many of her students are long-term English learners who have been reclassified as fully English proficient but still struggle academically. She also has intermediate and advanced emergent bilinguals, most of whom had adequate formal schooling in their home country. Figure 8–4 lists the six steps.

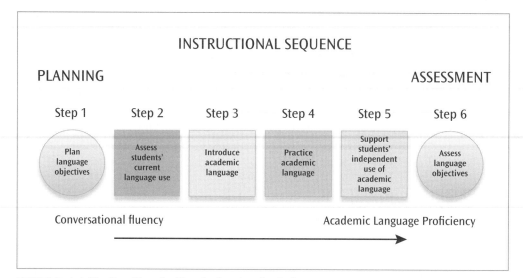

FIGURE 8–4 *A Six-Step Plan for Developing Academic Language*

Step One: Plan Language Objectives

Denise was teaching a unit designed to meet different state standards. Her content objective for a series of related lessons was that her students should understand the contributions of different people in creating the U.S. Constitution. Since Denise was teaching emergent bilinguals, she also wanted to teach academic language. For each lesson, she developed both content objectives and language objectives. Language objectives should be based on content objectives, so Denise asked herself, what language forms and functions will my students need to discuss, read, and write about the people who contributed to the creation of the Constitution? Although Denise knew that her students would need to develop academic vocabulary such as *revolution*, *preamble*, and *separation of powers* as they studied the events that led to writing the Constitution, she recognized that these words and phrases represented concepts that were part of her content objectives and not her language objectives. Academic vocabulary is an important part of academic language, but language objectives should focus on aspects of language beyond vocabulary.

Denise also thought about the specific genres she would ask her students to read and write. One genre would be a history report that would include a series of paragraphs about the different people instrumental in forming the Constitution. She knew that her students had difficulty writing cohesive paragraphs when they wrote reports. Often one sentence didn't seem to relate to another one, and many of her students included information that was not related to the rest of the paragraph. She decided that her language objectives would be to teach students how to write cohesive paragraphs in a history report.

Step Two: Assess Students' Current Language Use

It is important for teachers to have good information about their students' current level of language use in order to provide instruction that is challenging but not too far beyond their current ability. Denise wanted to assess her students' ability to write a cohesive paragraph.

Denise decided to use an on-demand writing sample to determine her students' current language use. She assigned a short section of the government textbook for her students to read. This was an important section for them to understand in their study of the people who created the Constitution. Then the class discussed the reading. When Denise felt that her students had a good understanding of this section, she told them to close their books and write a summary of the section. She gave them twenty minutes to write. She explained that she would not help them as they were writing, but students could use print or electronic bilingual dictionaries.

At the end of twenty minutes, Denise collected her students' papers. She had prepared a checklist for assessing their writing. She read each student's paper and recorded the results on the checklist. Figure 8–5 shows her assessment of some of the students. The results confirmed her general impression that all her students wrote paragraphs that included sentences unrelated to the main topic of the paragraph. Several students did not divide their paper into paragraphs, indent the first line, begin with a thesis statement, or include several details. Denise wanted to work on all these aspects of their writing. She decided to focus on having them write cohesive paragraphs by teaching them to maintain a constant topic.

Step Three: Introduce Academic Language

In step three, teachers introduce new academic language. One way to do this is by providing a model. Denise projected the following paragraph on the screen at the front of the class:

> One of America's political leaders had not played a part in drafting the Constitution. During the debates over the Constitution, Thomas Jefferson, one of the most brilliant thinkers of his day, was in Paris where he served as America's ambassador to

Name	Writes paragraphs	Indents first line	Begins with a thesis statement	Includes details	Maintains a constant topic
Juan	✓	✓	✓		
Doua				✓	
Alberto	✓	✓			
Alicia	✓			✓	

FIGURE 8–5 *Denise's Checklist for Assessing Writing*

France. He had written the Declaration of Independence and the Virginia law that protected religious freedom. Although Jefferson did not help draft the Constitution, he still had an impact on the issue of a bill of rights.

Denise read the first sentence and then asked, "Who do you think *one of America's political leaders* refers to?"

Carlos volunteered, "Thomas Jefferson."

"That's right," responded Denise. "How did you know?"

"I read the next sentence, and it names Thomas Jefferson," Carlos responded.

"That's a good strategy," Denise replied. "One way writers make paragraphs cohesive is by having something in one sentence connect or refer to something in another sentence." Denise reminded her students that many sentences in academic texts have more than one clause. "Remember that academic writing contains sentences with more than one clause. A clause always has a subject or topic and a verb. Let's look now at the sentences one by one and decide on the subject of each clause." Together, the class read through the paragraph and underlined the subjects of the clauses. When they had finished, Denise drew a chart on the board and copied the subject of each clause on the chart. The finished chart looked like this:

Subject or topic
One of America's political leaders
Thomas Jefferson
he
He
Jefferson
he

"What do you notice about the clauses in this paragraph?" asked Denise.

"They all have the same subject," said Veronica.

"That's right," Denise said, "and this is called a *constant topic*. One way to be sure all the sentences in a paragraph are related to the same topic or idea is to check that each sentence has the same subject." Denise also discussed with her students that if every sentence started with "Thomas Jefferson" the writing would seem repetitive. She reviewed the paragraph with the students to show them the different ways the author kept the same subject but varied the writing. For example, in some cases the author used a pronoun. In others, he used a synonym phrase, "One of America's political leaders."

Step Four: Practice Academic Language

The fifth step is to practice using the new language. Over the next few days, Denise gave the students key passages from their text to read and discuss. The students wrote a summary of each passage. By doing this, Denise combined content and language teaching. Students underlined the topic of each clause in their summaries to be sure that they all referred to the same person, place, or idea. They also practiced varying their sentences by using pronouns and synonyms.

Denise had her students work in pairs. They exchanged their summaries with a partner. They read one another's papers to be sure that all the sentences in each paragraph related to the main idea. Together, each pair marked any sentence that was not clearly related to the topic. They discussed their summaries and rewrote them to make them more cohesive.

Step Five: Support Independent Use of Academic Language

The fifth step is to have students use academic language independently. When Denise felt that most of her students were writing cohesive summary paragraphs, she assigned the students to write a report on one of the important figures involved in creating the Constitution. Her students used their textbook, supplementary texts, and Internet resources to gather information about the subject of their reports. They included pictures taken from the Internet in their completed report. Finally, they presented the reports to the whole class and posted them on the bulletin board. All the students learned about the important historical figures involved in writing the Constitution, and they also became more proficient in writing cohesive paragraphs with a constant topic.

Step Six: Assess Language Objectives

Denise used the final reports to assess both her content and language objectives. To determine whether her students could write cohesive paragraphs, Denise used a rating scale. As she read the students' papers, she marked each paragraph to indicate whether all, most, some, or none of the sentences had the same subject. This gave her a quick measure of how well her students had learned to write cohesive paragraphs. She used this information to guide her teaching.

As the semester progressed, Denise introduced other ways to write cohesive paragraphs. For example, rather than using a constant topic, students can write using what Brown (2009) refers to as a *derived topic*. Derived topics are subtopics or examples of the main topic of a sentence. For example, if the main topic is the writers of the Constitution, the following sentences in the paragraph could each include one of the writers as the subject. Each sentence has a topic that is derived from the main idea of the paragraph.

Academic writing often uses a third cohesive device, *chained topics*. Systemic functional linguists divide sentences (or clauses) into two parts, the topic and the comment. These correspond to the subject and the predicate of a clause. Take, for example, the sentence "Emergent bilinguals can write cohesive paragraphs." The topic is "emergent bilinguals," and the comment is "can write cohesive paragraphs." Speakers and writers introduce a topic and then add a comment about that topic. In a paragraph that uses chaining, the comment of one sentence is connected to the topic of the following sentence.

The following paragraph shows how chaining works:

> Thomas Jefferson wrote the <u>Declaration of Independence</u>. <u>This document</u> provided a justification for declaring independence from <u>Great Britain</u>. <u>Great Britain</u> had imposed <u>burdensome taxes</u> on the colonists. <u>One of these</u> was a <u>tax on tea</u>. <u>This tax</u> led the colonists to stage the Boston Tea Party.

Students practiced using different combinations of constant, derived, and chained topics as they wrote reports and analyses during the semester. As she introduced these different ways of writing cohesive paragraphs, Denise followed the six-step plan. She planned language objectives, assessed students' current language, introduced academic language, devised activities so students could practice the new language, supported their independent use of academic language, and then assessed her language objectives. This approach helped her students build academic language as they learned important social studies content.

ADVOCACY IN ASSESSMENT

Teachers can show faith in their students and expand student potential by taking what Cummins' (2001) calls an *intercultural orientation*. He contrasts an intercultural orientation with an *assimilationist orientation*. Figure 8–6 shows the four components of these two orientations.

As Figure 8–6 illustrates, these two orientations differ in four areas: use of students' primary languages and cultures in the curriculum, relationships with minority community members, approach to teaching, and methods of assessment. When schools take an intercultural orientation, they include their students' primary languages and cultures, they involve minority parents in school activities, they encourage the use of current methods of collaborative critical inquiry, and they design assessments that allow students to demonstrate their competence. In

	Intercultural Orientation	Assimilationist Orientation
Students' languages and cultures	Add them to the curriculum	Exclude them from the curriculum
Minority community members	Involve them in the school	Exclude them from the school
Teaching	Use transformative methods	Use traditional methods
Assessment	Help students show what they know	Use measures to justify grades

FIGURE 8–6 *Intercultural and Assimilationist Orientations*

other words, in schools with an intercultural orientation, teachers employ assessments that enable them to advocate for their students. This is the approach Denise took when she assessed her students' ability to write cohesive paragraphs.

In contrast, when schools take an assimilationist orientation, they exclude students' primary languages and pay little attention to students' cultures, they discourage minority community members from active involvement in the schools, they teach using traditional methods, and they use forms of assessment that help teachers justify student placement or grades.

Schools that take an intercultural orientation see student diversity as an asset. Such schools find ways to incorporate diverse students into the institution and to provide programs that promote their success. On the other hand, some schools have as their goal the assimilation of diverse students into the mainstream. In the attempt to assimilate students, such schools operate programs that disempower and marginalize second language students and the minority communities they come from. Punitive assessment systems, especially in this era of high-stakes tests, serve to disempower English learners. However, teachers who see themselves as advocates for their emergent bilinguals use assessment to help shape effective instruction, as Denise did when she assessed her students' ability to write cohesive paragraphs.

USING FORMATIVE ASSESSMENT

Teachers like Denise who take an intercultural orientation show faith in their students and expand their students' potential by relying on formative assessment to guide their teaching rather than by putting too much emphasis on summative assessments to make decisions about their students' abilities. Emergent bilinguals generally score low on state and national summative tests. This has become even more evident in the tests designed to assess the Common Core standards. The danger is that scores on these tests are often interpreted as showing that emergent bilinguals are academically deficient.

In contrast, formative assessments are designed to help teachers determine students' current ability in order to plan the next steps in instruction. MacDonald and her colleagues (2015) state that formative assessment "occurs in the midst of instruction and compares students' ongoing progress to possible trajectories of learning. It can help identify the most productive next steps in instruction" (xi). Formative assessment is an integral part of teaching and learning rather than something added on. It is one component of an overall assessment system that also includes interim and summative assessments. Teachers who advocate for their students use formative assessments to guide day-to-day instruction and ensure that English learners develop the knowledge and skills they need to show progress on interim and summative assessments.

Four-Stage Process for Integrating Formative Assessment

MacDonald and her coauthors describe a four-stage process they use to integrate formative assessment into teaching. The first step is to design and teach lessons that have a consistent focus on developing both academic content knowledge and academic language. These lessons have clear language learning targets. The second step is to sample students' language. This requires that teachers plan lessons during which students will produce language in oral or written form that can be collected. In the third step teachers analyze student language samples. They use different tools to conduct their analyses and use this information to plan further instruction. The final step is to provide formative feedback. As MacDonald and her colleagues comment, this stage is designed to:

> give students clear, progress-oriented, and actionable information about their language use—both what they're doing well and what they can do to become more effective users of English—and to adjust instruction to meet students' needs. (xix)

The four steps form a cycle. The teacher plans instruction, gathers language samples, analyzes the samples, and provides formative feedback. The teacher assumes that with the proper feedback, emergent bilinguals will continually improve. Feedback is designed to affirm students' achievements and then outline clear next steps that students can attain. Through this process, teachers use formative assessment to continually scaffold instruction.

In their book on formative assessment, MacDonald and her colleagues provide extended examples from three different students to show how the four steps can be implemented. Their approach to conducting systematic language analysis is key. They consider four elements in student writing or oral presentations: (1) the genre components, (2) text structure, (3) grammatical forms, and (4) vocabulary usage. In analyzing a writing sample or an oral report, a teacher should consider each of these components, as we describe next, although when providing feedback a teacher would normally only focus on one or two of them.

Language Analysis: Genre

As discussed in Chapter 6, genres are specific types of texts, such as procedures, reports, recounts, and analyses. Each genre is widely used in academic writing, and the form for the genre has been established by convention. Genres are composed of different sections. For example, a procedure includes an orientation that may include the purpose, the materials needed, a sequence of steps, and an outcome. A recount also has an orientation. This is followed by a retellling of the events and may include an explanation followed by a conclusion. In analyzing student writing, a teacher would look to see that all the parts expected of the genre are included.

Language Analysis: Text Structure

Text structure refers to making sure that the different parts of the text are clearly connected so that a reader can follow the writing easily. This involves using pronouns with clear referents and ensuring that all the sentences in each paragraph are connected to the main topic. In addition, the paragraphs should be linked by appropriate conjunctions. For example, in a recount, the paragraphs would be connected by words indicating the sequence, such as *first*, *next*, and *finally*.

Language Analysis: Grammatical Structure and Vocabulary

The last two elements for analysis are grammatical structure and vocabulary. Grammatical structure can refer to things like use of complex sentences or subject-verb agreement. Vocabulary includes technical words related to the discipline as well as general academic terms such as *synthesis* and *explanation*. Teachers often focus on grammatical structures and vocabulary, but it is just as important to follow the conventions of the genre and make the writing cohesive.

Language Learning Targets

Based on the analysis of the four components of the language sample, a teacher develops language learning targets for the student. This is best done working with the student. It is important that students have a clear understanding of what they have done well and what the next steps are in making improvements. In the example that follows, MacDonald and her colleagues explain the process the teacher used to set language learning targets with Jorge.

Jorge wrote a procedure for solving a two-step equation in math. Based on her analysis, his teacher wrote the following language learning targets:

1. Make your descriptions clear to readers who can't see your computations. Think carefully every time you use a pronoun (it, that one, the other one) and ask yourself whether the reader will know what you are referring to.

2. Remove any details that aren't part of the genre components for a procedure. (29)

The teacher went over these language learning targets with Jorge, and he added one more: "Make sure the reader can see when you move from one step to another (Check your sentence markers)" (47). What is important here is that Jorge understood what he should do as he revised his paper. With these clear goals in mind, he was able to improve his writing. His teacher used formative assessment to scaffold her feedback.

Assessment Tools

Teachers who use formative feedback to help English learners become more proficient in their use of academic language develop different tools to assess language for formative purposes. Three useful tools are checklists, rating scales, and rubrics. Checklists contain items that students or teachers can respond to with a simple "yes" or "no." For example, for a checklist, Jorge could check whether or not he included an orientation and whether or not he organized the steps in order. The next tool, a rating scale, moves beyond "yes" and "no" to indicate how well something was done. For example, Jorge could judge whether what he wrote was very clear, somewhat clear, or not clear. Rating scales could also indicate student performance on a scale from "most of the time" to "not at all." Rubrics, the final tool, are more detailed and outline the criteria students should meet in various areas. For emergent bilinguals, rubrics can indicate goals for students at different proficiency levels. Developing checklists, rating scales, and rubrics helps teachers make expectations clear and allows students to know exactly what they need to do to succeed.

Teachers show faith in their students and expand their potential by using assessments that help English learners increase their academic content knowledge and their academic language proficiency. Formative assessments are designed to help teachers identify students' strengths and weaknesses and to determine next steps in instruction. The cycle for formative assessment begins with designing and teaching lessons. Then it moves to sampling student performance, analyzing the samples, and providing feedback. Teachers can use checklists, rating scales, and rubrics as tools for analysis of student work. Throughout this process, teachers can involve students to ensure that they understand how they can continually improve their work.

CONCLUSION

Emergent bilinguals face double the work of native English speakers since they have to learn English and learn in English (Short and Fitzsimmons 2007). As a result, they may have low self-efficacy. Teachers can motivate students by teaching in the Challenge Zone (Gibbons 2009) and providing feedback based on formative assessments. When teachers show faith in their students, they adopt practices that expand student potential.

The principles we have outlined in this book are based on current research and best practice for second language teaching. These principles are closely interrelated. They include making lessons learner centered, moving from whole to part, teaching both language and content, making lessons meaningful and purposeful to engage students, carefully planning interactions that help students develop both oral and written language, supporting students' home languages and cultures, and showing faith in English learners' ability to succeed. When teachers follow these principles, they increase emergent bilinguals' potential for success. We conclude this book with one last extended unit, one we believe represents all the principles we have promoted throughout the book.

IF THE WORLD WERE A VILLAGE

> As of 2012, the world's population was around 7 billion 50 million . . . Numbers this big are hard to understand, but what if we imagined the whole population of the world as a village of just 100 people? (Smith 2011, 7)

This information comes from *If the World Were a Village,* a fascinating book telling readers about what proportion of people in the world speak different languages, come from different countries, are different ages, have different levels of education, and own the world's wealth. The book is an excellent starting place for the development of a unit of study about geography, economics, science, math, and the social studies concept of interdependence. A study of the world as a global village is particularly relevant to English learners whose first languages are some of those 6,000 world languages Smith describes in his book. Through a thematic study about the interdependence of people, animals, and nature around the world, second language learners acquire English as they study academic content.

Ricardo teaches third grade to a group of diverse students. He chose the unit on interdependence because he wanted to draw on his students' backgrounds and experiences. About half of his students are English learners. Most of the emergent bilinguals are Latinos, several of whom began school speaking only Spanish.

However, he also has two students whose first language is Punjabi, one student who is Vietnamese, and another who speaks Arabic. The native speakers of English include several African American students who add to the rich diversity of his classroom.

Ricardo planned his interdependence theme to meet state standards in different content areas. For example, in math students are expected to learn place value, and they should be able to read a bar graph. In social studies third-grade students are expected to be able to locate areas on maps and globes. And in science they should understand how the components of a system relate to each other and to the whole. Ricardo's daily routine includes an extended language arts block in the morning. In the afternoon he teaches social studies, science, math, and enrichment areas such as music and art. He stresses language development and academic content development for all his students throughout the day. Ricardo shows his faith in his English learners by providing challenging instruction and carefully scaffolding assignments to accommodate the different levels of English proficiency among his students.

Ricardo introduced the unit with the book *If the World Were a Village* (Smith 2011) during shared reading in the language arts block. He showed the students the classroom globe, and they talked about where they or their ancestors had come from. Then Ricardo read to the students about how many people are in the world and how many are in the imaginary, reduced global village of 100 people. He read sections of the book telling the number of people in the global village who would come from different countries, the languages they would speak, their age ranges, and their religions.

Next, Ricardo showed the students a video updated with 2013 data posted on YouTube that summarizes much of the same data found in the book (www.you tube.com/watch?v=QrcOdLYBIw0). He asked the students to turn and talk to each other about what information they found most interesting and what information was new for them in the video. Students were especially interested in the different languages spoken since seven of the people in the village of 100 spoke Spanish and nine spoke English!

After the class read the book and watched the video, Ricardo asked his students how the author of the book had decided how many people of each type should be in the global village. "Why did the author say that twenty-one people out of the 100 would speak Chinese?" With careful scaffolding, he showed the students how the author had used percentages to determine the number of Chinese speakers and the other numbers in the 100-person village. The video showed the numbers in percentages, and the class talked about the difference between the 22 percent shown in the video and twenty-one people in the book and discussed why that might be.

Then Ricardo surveyed the class to find out how many students spoke English as their first language, how many spoke Spanish, and how many spoke other languages. He wrote the languages and the number of speakers on the board. He reviewed with the students how they could represent information in a bar graph and a pie chart. Then he asked students to work in pairs to convert the numbers from the class into a graph and a chart. The students posted their finished charts and graphs on the bulletin board.

For language arts, Ricardo had his students write about their class statistics in a paragraph. First, he taught a minilesson on capitalizing names since names of languages in some languages aren't capitalized. Then students wrote their paragraphs. For his beginners, Ricardo provided a sentence frame, "In our class _____ speak _____." When students finished their paragraphs, the class discussed the importance of speaking different languages and being bilingual. Students who spoke Spanish were proud that so many people in the world spoke Spanish and interested that English was also an important language. However, some students pointed out that it would be good to learn Chinese since so many people in the world speak Chinese.

The next day, Ricardo brought in another book that the students found even more interesting, *If America Were a Village* (Smith 2009). This book was like the *If the World Were a Village* in that the data on the entire population of America quoted in the book as 306 million is also reduced to a village of 100 people. The book celebrates the diversity of America, and in the opening pages the author talks about how the country changes so frequently. He points out that there is one birth every eight seconds, one death every twelve seconds, and a new immigrant arrives every twenty-seven seconds. The next pages talk about the "rainbow of colors" (7) in our nation. The book states that "In our village of 100 about 13 are foreign-born. . . . Of the 13, 7 were born in Latin America" (7). The book tells readers that although eighty-two people in the village are English speakers, ten are Spanish speakers. This book gives information about the country's past, present, and future. Topics explored include family make-up, religions, jobs, ages, wealth, items owned, energy and water use, and health.

Ricardo also found a video posted on YouTube about data (www.youtube.com /watch?v=zZPtWsTNo2Q), similar to the book about America as a village, which was produced by a Vernon Township High School class in New Jersey. After he finished this book and showed the video, he asked students to write in their journal what they remembered from the book and video and how what was discussed was the same as and different from them and their families.

Later that day, during social studies, Ricardo read *Me on the Map* (Sweeney 1998). In this book a young girl shows a series of colorful maps of different types. She shows herself on a map of her room, her room on the map of her house, her house on the map of her street, and she keeps zooming out to show her country on a map of the world. She demonstrates how readers can find their own country, state, and city and keep zooming in all the way to their house. The students also read *Our Book of Maps* (2004), which shows how to make different kinds of maps and ends with a discussion of the globe. Students then used the classroom globe to locate the countries they had read about in *If the World Were a Village*. They found the countries with the largest populations and those with the largest number of speakers of the world's eight major languages. They also located the native countries of each child's family on a large world map and marked the countries with pushpins.

In math the class was studying place value and learning to count by tens, hundreds, and thousands. So, during math time the next day Ricardo read some of the statistics again from *If the World Were a Village* and *If America Were a Village*. He repeated the numbers of 7 billion, 50 million people living in the world, and 306 million people living in America. He then asked students to write out those numbers and other statistics from the books and identify the place values. In small groups the students also made graphs showing the number of people in the countries with the largest populations.

Over the next few days, to introduce the idea of how everyone in the world has some connection to one another, Ricardo read the students several books about children all over the world who, though different in some ways, have similar interests, needs, and goals. These included *Whoever You Are* (Fox 2006); *Children Around the World* (Montanari 2004); and for his Spanish speakers, *Niños alrededor del mundo* (Rice 2012) and *Ninos del mundo* (Vidard 2008).

During language arts, students wrote paragraphs comparing and contrasting themselves with other children in the world. Since the language arts standards include poetry, Ricardo read *I Am of Two Places* and *Soy de dos lugares* (Carden and Cappellini 1997a, 1997b). The Spanish version served as a preview and review for his Spanish speakers. In *I Am of Two Places* and *Soy de dos lugares*, immigrant children write poems about family traditions and their immigrant experiences. Ricardo's students talked about their native countries and traditions of their ancestors. Working in small groups, they wrote interview questions to ask family members about their family traditions and immigrant experiences. Students then used the results of the interviews to write their own poems for a class poetry book. Figure 8–7 contains a bibliography of the books Ricardo used during this unit.

2004. *Our Book of Maps, On Our Way to English*. Barrington, IL: Rigby.

Carden, Mary, and Mary Cappellini. 1997a. *I Am of Two Places*. Crystal Lake, IL: Rigby.

Carden, Mary, and Mary Cappellini. 1997b. *Soy de dos lugares, Saludos*. Crystal Lake, IL: Rigby.

Fox, Mem. 2006. *Whoever You Are*. Boston: HMH Books for Young Readers.

Montanari, Donata. 2004. *Children Around the World*. Tonawanda, NY: Kids Can Press.

Rice, Dona. 2012. *Niños alrededor del mundo*. Huntington Beach, CA: Teacher Created Materials.

Smith, David J. 2009. *If America Were a Village*. Tonawanda, NY: Kids Can Press.

Smith, David J. 2011. *If the World Were a Village*. 2nd edition. Tonawanda, NY: Kids Can Press.

Sweeney, Joan. 1998. *Me on the Map*. New York: Dragonfly Books.

Vidard, Estelle. 2008. *Niños del mundo*. Barcelona, Spain: Molino.

FIGURE 8–7 *"If the World Were a Village" Unit Bibliography*

Demonstrating Faith in Emergent Bilinguals

Ricardo's global village unit followed the principles for effective teaching that we have discussed in this book. The English learners in Ricardo's class were able to engage in the activities because their teacher carefully scaffolded the instruction. He developed the unit because he had faith that he could engage all his students in the different activities, and their success helped his students develop faith in themselves as learners. Ultimately, teachers who incorporate the principles we have suggested in each chapter of this book show faith in their students and expand their potential. This is a goal of all teachers for their students.

APPLICATIONS

1. Guthrie suggests several practices to motivate and engage students. Analyze your own teaching or the lessons of a teacher you have observed to determine how many of these practices are incorporated. List examples, and prepare to share them.

2. We described Ricardo's global village and Mary's tone units. Consider a unit of study you have taught. Describe the unit and then use the principles for effective practice to analyze the unit.

3. We described a six-step plan to teach academic language and content. Review the six steps. How could you adopt or modify this approach for units you teach?

4. MacDonald and her colleagues explain the cycle for formative language assessment. Consider a lesson or series of lessons you have taught. How could you use the four steps of formative language assessment to help your students improve their academic language? List some specific ideas and prepare to share them.

References

Asher, James. 1977. *Learning Another Language Through Actions: The Complete Teacher's Guide.* Los Gatos, CA: Sky Oaks.

Auerbach, Elsa, and Nina Wallerstein. 2004. *Problem-Posing at Work: English for Action.* Edmonton, Canada: Grass Roots Press.

August, Diane, and Timothy Shanahan. 2006. *Developing Literacy in Second-Language Learners: Report of the National Literacy Panel on Language Minority Children and Youth.* Mahwah, NJ: Lawrence Erlbaum Associates.

Bandura, Albert. 1986. *Social Foundations of Thought and Action: A Social Cognitive Theory.* Englewood Cliffs, NJ: Prentice-Hall.

Barnes, Douglas. 1990. "Oral Language and Learning." In *Perspectives on Talk and Learning,* edited by Susan Hynds and Donald Rubin, 41–54. Urbana, IL: National Council of Teachers of English.

———. 2008. "Exploratory Talk for Learning." In *Exploring Talk in Schools,* edited by Neil Mercer and Steve Hodgkinson, 1–12. London, UK: Sage.

Batalova, Jeanne, Sarah Hooker, and Randy Capps. 2013. *Deferred Action for Childhood Arrivals at the One-Year Mark.* Washington, DC: Migration Policy Institute.

Bartalova, Jeanne, and Margie McHugh. 2010. *Number and Growth of Students in U.S. Schools in Need of English Instruction.* Washington, DC: Migration Policy Institute.

Boyd-Batstone, Paul. 2013. *Helping English Language Learners Meet the Common Core: Assessment and Instructional Strategies K–12.* New York: Taylor & Francis.

Bransford, John, Ann Brown, and Rodney Cocking. 2000. *How People Learn: Brain, Mind, Experience, and School.* Washington, DC: National Academy Press.

Bridges, Andrew, and Janet Raloff. 2015. "Most Students Wrong on Risks of Smoking Occasionally." In *Student Science: A Resource of the Society for Science and the Public.* Washington, DC: Society for Science and the Public.

Brinton, Donna, Marguerite Snow, and Marjorie Wesche. 1989. *Content-Based Second Language Instruction.* Boston: Heinle and Heinle.

Brisk, María. 2015. *Engaging Students in Academic Literacies: Genre-Based Pedagogy for K–5 Classrooms.* New York: Routledge.

Brown, David. 2009. *In Other Words: Grammar Lessons for Code-Switching, Composition, and Language Study*. Portsmouth, NH: Heinemann.

Brown, H. Douglas. 2007. *Principles of Language Learning and Teaching*. 5th ed. White Plains, NY: Pearson Education.

Brozo, William, Gerry Shiel, and Keith Topping. 2007/2008. "Engagement in Reading: Lessons Learned from Three PISA Countries." *Journal of Adolescent & Adult Literacy* 51 (4): 304–17.

Chamot, Anna. 2005. "The Cognitive Academic Language Learning Approach (CALLA): An Update." In *Academic Success for English Language Learners: Strategies for K–12 Mainstream Teachers*, edited by Patricia Richard-Amato and Marguerite Snow, 87–102. White Plains, NY: Pearson.

———. 2009. *The CALLA Handbook*. 2nd edition. New York: Pearson Longman.

Chamot, Anna, Sarah Barnhardt, Pamela Beard-El-Dinary, and Jill Robbins. 1999. *Learning Strategies Handbook*. New York: Longman.

Chamot, Anna, and Michael O'Malley. 1989. "The Cognitive Academic Language Learning Approach." In *When They Don't All Speak English: Integrating the ESL Student into the Regular Classroom*, edited by P. Rigg and V. Allen, 108–25. Urbana, IL: NCTE.

———. 1994. *The CALLA Handbook*. Boston: Addison-Wesley.

Chomsky, Noam. 1959. "Review of Verbal Learning." *Language* 35: 26–58.

Collier, Virginia. 1989. "How Long? A Synthesis of Research on Academic Achievement in a Second Language." *TESOL Quarterly* 23 (3): 509–32.

Collier, Virginia, and Wayne Thomas. 2009. *Educating English Learners for a Transformed World*. Albuquerque: Dual Language Education of New Mexico Fuente Press.

Comenius, Johannes. 1728. *Orbis Sensualium Pictus*. 11th ed. London: John and Benjamin Sprint.

Crawford, James. 1999. *Bilingual Education: History, Politics, Theory and Practice*. 4th edition. Los Angeles: Bilingual Educational Services.

———. 2007. "The Decline of Bilingual Education: How to Reverse a Troubling Trend?" *International Multilingual Research Journal* 1 (1): 33–37. www.elladvocates.org/.

Crawford, James, and Sharon Reyes. 2015. *The Trouble with SIOP®: How a Behaviorist Framework, Flawed Research, and Clever Marketing Have Come to Define—and Diminish—Sheltered Instruction for English Language Learners*. Portland, OR: Institute for Language and Education Policy.

Cummins, Jim. 1979. "Linguistic Interdependence and the Educational Development of Bilingual Children." *Review of Educational Research* 49 (2): 222–51.

Cummins, Jim. 1981a. "Age on Arrival and Immigrant Second Language Learning in Canada: A Reassessment." *Applied Linguistics* 1: 132–49.

———. 1981b. *The Role of Primary Language Development in Promoting Educational Success for Language Minority Students Schooling and Language Minority Students: A Theoretical Framework* (pp. 3–49). Los Angeles: Evaluation, Dissemination and Assessment Center, California State University.

———. 1984. *Bilingualism and Special Education: Issues in Assessment and Pedagogy*. Clevedon, UK: Multilingual Matters.

———. 1989. *Empowering Minority Students*. Sacramento: CABE.

———. 2000. *Language, Power and Pedagogy: Bilingual Children in the Crossfire*. Tonawanda, NY: Multilingual Matters.

———. 2001. *Negotiating Identities: Education for Empowerment in a Diverse Society*. 2d ed. Ontario, CA: California Assocation of Bilingual Education.

———. 2007. "Rethinking Monolingual Instructional Strategies in Multilingual Classrooms." *Canadian Journal of Applied Linguistics* 10 (2): 221–40.

———. 2011. "Literacy Engagement: Fueling Academic Growth for English Learners." *The Reading Teacher* 65 (2): 142–46.

Daniels, Harvey, and Steven Zemelman. 2014. *Subjects Matter: Exceeding Standards Through Powerful Content-Area Reading*. Portsmouth, NH: Heinemann.

de Oliveira, Luciana. 2012. "What History Teachers Need to Know about Academic Language to Teach English Language Learners." *The Social Studies Review* 51 (1): 76–79.

Diller, Karl. 1978. *The Language Teaching Controversy*. Rowley, MA: Newbury House.

Dotson, Jeanie M. 2001. "Cooperative Learning Structures Can Increase Student Achievement." *Kagan Online Magazine*. www.kaganonline.com/free_articles/research _and_rationale/increase_achievement.php.

Ebe, Ann. 2010. "Culturally Relevant Texts and Reading Assessment for English Language Learners." *Reading Horizons* 50 (3): 193–210.

———. 2011. "Culturally Relevant Books: Bridges to Reading Engagement for English Language Learners." *Insights on Learning Disabilities* 8 (2): 31–45.

———. 2015. "The Power of Culturally Relevant Texts: What Teachers Learn About Their Emergent Bilingual Students." In *Research on Preparing Inservice Teachers to Work Effectively with Emergent Bilinguals*, edited by Yvonne S. Freeman and David E. Freeman. Bingley, UK: Emerald Books.

———. 2016. "Student Voices Shining Through: Exploring Translanguaging as a Literary Device." In *Making Meaning of Translanguaging Learning from Classroom Moments*, edited by Ofelia García and Tatyana Kleyn. New York: Routledge.

Echevarria, Jana, and Deborah Short. 2010. "Programs and Practices for Effective Sheltered Content Instruction." In *Improving Education for English Learners: Research-Based Approaches*, 251–322. Sacramento: California Department of Education.

Echevarria, Jana, Mary Ellen Vogt, and Deborah Short. 2010. *The SIOP Model for Teaching Mathematics to English Learners*. Boston: Allyn & Bacon.

———. 2012. *Making Content Comprehensible for English Learners: The SIOP Model*. 4th edition. New York: Pearson.

Ellis, Rod. 1990. *Instructed Second Language Acquisition*. Oxford, UK: Blackwell.

English Master Plan. 2012. "English Learner Master Plan." Los Angeles: Los Angeles Unified School District.

Espinosa, Linda M. 2013. "PreK–3rd: Challenging Common Myths About Dual Language Learners." *PreK–3rd Policy to Action Brief* (Vol. Policy Action Brief 10, pp. 1–23). New York: Foundation for Child Development.

Faltis, Christian, and Sarah Hudelson. 1998. *Bilingual Education in Elementary and Secondary School Communities*. Boston: Allyn and Bacon.

Feger, Mary Virginia. 2006. "'I want to read': How Culturally Relevant Texts Increase Student Engagement in Reading." *Multicultural Education* 13 (3): 18–19.

Fisher, Douglas, and Nancy Frey. 2009. *Background Knowledge: The Missing Piece of the Comprehension Puzzle*. Portsmouth, NH: Heinemann.

Fix, Michael, and Randy Capps. 2005. *Immigrant Children, Urban Schools, and the No Child Left Behind Act*. www.migrationalinformation.org/feature/display.cfm?ID=347.

Flores, Stella, Jeanne Bartalova, and Michael Fix. 2012. *The Educational Trajectories of English Language Learners in Texas*. Washington, DC: Migration Policy Institute.

Freeman, David E., and Yvonne S. Freeman. 1994. *Between Worlds: Access to Second Language Acquisition*. Portsmouth, NH: Heinemann.

———. 2007. *English Language Learners: The Essential Guide*. New York: Scholastic.

———. 2009. *Academic Language for English Language Learners and Struggling Readers: How to Help Students Succeed Across Content Areas*. Portsmouth, NH: Heinemann.

———. 2011. *Between Worlds: Access to Second Language Acquisition*. 3rd edition. Portsmouth, NH: Heinemann.

Freeman, Yvonne, Ann Freeman, and David Freeman. 2003. "Home Run Books: Connecting Students to Culturally Relevant Texts." *NABE News* 26 (3): 5–8, 11–12.

Freeman, Yvonne S., and David E. Freeman. 1998. *ESL/EFL Teaching: Principles for Success*. Portsmouth, NH: Heinemann.

Freeman, Yvonne S., and Alma Rodriguez. 2015. "Promoting Exploratory Talk with Emergent Bilinguals." In *Research on Preparing Inservice Teachers to Work Effectively with Emergent Bilinguals*, edited by Yvonne S. Freeman and David E. Freeman, 55-80. Bingley, UK: Emerald Books.

Freire, Paulo. 1970. *Pedagogy of the Oppressed*. Translated by Myra Ramos. New York: Continuum.

Freire, Paulo, and Donaldo Macedo. 1987. *Literacy: Reading the Word and the World*. South Hadley, MA: Bergin and Garvey.

Fries, Charles. 1945. *Teaching and Learning English as a Foreign Language*. Ann Arbor: University of Michigan Press.

García, Eugene. 2002. *Student Cultural Diversity: Understanding and Meeting the Challenge*. 2d ed. Boston: Houghton Mifflin.

———. 2012. *Language Development and the Education of Hispanic Children in the United States*. New York: Teachers College Press.

García, Gilbert. 2000. *Lessons from Research: What Is the Length of Time It Takes Limited English Proficient Students to Acquire English and Succeed in an All-English Classroom?* Washington, DC: National Clearinghouse for Bilingual Education.

García, Ofelia. 2009. *Bilingual Education in the 21st Century: A Global Perspective*. Malden, MA: Wiley-Blackwell.

———. 2010. "Misconstructions of Bilingualism in U.S. Education." *NYSABE News* 1 (1): 2–7.

García, Ofelia, and Jo Anne Kleifgen. 2010. *Educating Emergent Bilinguals: Policies, Programs, and Practices for English Language Learners*. New York: Teachers College Press.

García, Ofelia, Jo Anne Kleifgen, and Lorraine Flachi. 2008. *From English Language Learners to Emergent Bilinguals*. New York: Teachers College Press.

García, Ofelia, and Li Wei. 2014. *Translanguaging: Language, Bilingualism, and Education*. New York: Palgrave Macmillan.

Gee, James. 2008. *Social Linguistics and Literacies: Ideology in Discourses*. 3rd edition. New York: Routledge.

Gibbons, Pauline. 2002. *Scaffolding Language, Scaffolding Learning*. Portsmouth, NH: Heinemann.

———. 2009. *English Learners, Academic Literacy, and Thinking: Learning in the Challenge Zone*. Portsmouth, NH: Heinemann.

Goldenberg, Claude. 2008. "Teaching English Language Learners: What the Research Does—and Does Not—Say." *American Educator* (Summer): 8–44.

———. 2013. "Unlocking the Research on English Learners; What We Know—And Don't Yet Know—About Effective Instruction." *American Educator* 37 (2): 4–11.

Goldenberg, Claude, Judy Hicks, and Ira Lit. 2013. "Dual Language Learners." *American Educator* 17 (2): 26–29.

Goldenberg, Claude, Karen Nemeth, Judy Hicks, Marlene Zepeda, and Luz Marina Cardona. 2013. "Program Elements and Teaching Practices to Support Young Dual Language Learners." In *California's Best Practices for Young Dual Language Learners*, edited by Faye Ong and John McLean. Sacramento: California State Department of Education.

Goodman, Ken. 1991. "Revaluing Readers and Reading." In *With Promise: Redefining Reading and Writing for "Special" Students*, edited by S. Stires, 127–33. Portsmouth, NH: Heinemann.

Goodman, Yetta. 1982. "Retellings of Literature and the Comprehension Process." *Theory into Practice: Children's Literature* 21 (4): 301–307.

———. 1985. "Kidwatching: Observing Children in the Classroom." In *Observing the Language Learner*, edited by A. Jaggar and M. T. Smith-Burke, 9–18. Newark, DE, and Urbana, IL: International Reading Association and the National Council of Teachers of English.

Goulah, Jason, and Sonia W. Soltero. In press. "Reshaping the Mainstream Education Climate through Bilingual-Bicultural Education." In *Research on Preparing Inservice Teachers to Work Effectively with Emergent Bilinguals* (Vol. 2), ed. Stefinee Pinnegar. Bingley, UK: Emerald Books.

Gramigna, Susana. 2005. "Estrategias y estilos para promover las interpretaciones literarias: Una investigación en el nivel inicial." *Lectura y Vida* 26 (2): 30–38.

Graves, Donald. 1994. "Inviting Diversity Through Writing." In *4th Annual Meeting of the Whole Language Umbrella*. San Diego, CA.

Greene, Jay. 1998. *A Meta-Analysis of the Effectiveness of Bilingual Education*. Claremont, CA: Tomas Rivera Policy Institute.

Grosjean, Francois. 2010. *Bilingual: Life and Reality*. Cambridge, MA: Harvard University Press.

Guthrie, John, and Marcia Davis. 2003. "Motivating Struggling Readers in Middle School Through an Engagement Model of Classroom Practice." *Reading & Writing Quarterly* 19: 59–85.

Gutiérrez, Rochelle. 2002. "Beyond Essentialism: The Complexity of Language in Teaching Mathematics to Latina/o Students." *American Educational Research Journal* 39 (4): 1047–88.

Halliday, M. A. K. 1994. *An Introduction to Functional Grammar*. 2d ed. London: Edward Arnold.

Hay, Denys. 1977. *The Italian Renaissance in its Historical Background*. 2d ed. Cambridge, UK: Cambridge University Press.

Heath, Shirley Brice, and Leslie Mangiola. 1991. *Children of Promise: Literate Activity in Linguistically and Culturally Diverse Classrooms*. Washington, DC: National Education Association.

Horwitz, Amanda Rose, Gabriela Uro, Ricki Price-Baugh, Candance Simon, Renata Uzzell, Sharon Lewis, and Michael Casserly. 2009. *Succeeding with English Language Learners: Lessons Learned from the Great City Schools*. Washington, DC: Council of the Great City Schools.

Hymes, Del. 1970. "On Communicative Competence." In *Directions in Sociolinguistics*, edited by J. Gumperz and D. Hymes, 35–71. New York: Holt, Rinehart and Winston.

Jiménez, Robert. 1997. "The Strategic Reading Abilities and Potential of Five Low-Literacy Latina/o Readers in Middle School." *Reading Research Quarterly* 32 (2): 224–43.

Johnson, Karen E. 1995. "Understanding Communication in Second Language Classrooms." In *Cambridge Language Education*, edited by Jack Richards. New York: Cambridge University Press.

Kaplan, Karen Cadiero, Magaly Lavandez, and G. Elvira Armas. 2011. "Essential Elements of Effective Practices for English Learners." Long Beach: Californians Together.

Kelly, Louis. 1969. *25 Centuries of Language Teaching: 500 BC–1969*. Rowley, MA: Newbury House.

Krashen, Stephen D. 1982. *Principles and Practice in Second Language Acquisition*. New York: Pergamon Press.

———. 1985. *Inquiries and Insights*. Haywood, CA: Alemany Press.

———. 1992. *Fundamentals of Language Education*. Torrance, CA: Laredo.

———. 1996. *Under Attack: The Case Against Bilingual Education*. Culver City, CA: Language Education Associates.

———. 1999. *Condemned Without a Trial: Bogus Arguments Against Bilingual Education*. Portsmouth, NH: Heinemann.

———. 2004. *The Power of Reading: Insights from the Research*. 2d ed. Portsmouth, NH: Heinemann.

———. 2013. "Does SIOP Research Support SIOP Claims?" *International Journal of Foreign Language Teaching* 8 (1): 11–24.

Krashen, Stephen, and Tracy Terrell. 1983. *The Natural Approach: Language Acquisition in the Classroom*. Hayward, CA: Alemany Press.

Kucer, Stephen, and Cecilia Silva. 2006. *Teaching the Dimensions of Literacy*. Mahwah, NJ: Lawrence Erlbaum Associates.

LAUSD. 2012. *English Learner Master Plan*. Los Angeles: Los Angeles Unified School District.

Labbo, Linda D., and William H. Teale. 1990. "Cross-Age Reading: A Strategy for Helping Poor Readers." *The Reading Teacher* 43 (6): 362–69.

Larsen-Freeman, Diane. 1986. *Techniques and Principles in Language Teaching*, edited by W. Rutherford. Oxford, UK: Oxford University Press.

Lindholm-Leary, Kathryn, and Fred Genesee. 2010. "Alternative Educational Programs for English Language Learners." In *Research on English Language Learners*, edited by California Department of Education. Sacramento, CA: California Department of Education Press.

Long, Michael. 1983. "Does Second Language Instruction Make a Difference? A Review of the Research." *TESOL Quarterly* 14: 378–90.

Long, Michael, and Patricia Porter. 1985. "Group Work, Interlanguage Talk, and Second Language Acquisition." *TESOL Quarterly* 19 (1): 207–28.

Lozanov, Georgi. 1982. "Suggestology and Suggestopedy." In *Innovative Approaches to Language Teaching*, edited by R. Blair. Rowley, MA: Newbury House.

Lucas, Tamara, Ana M. Villegas, and Margaret Freedson-González. 2008. "Linguistically Responsive Teacher Education: Preparing Classroom Teachers to Teach English Language Learners." *Journal of Teacher Education* 59 (4): 361–73.

MacDonald, Rita, Timothy Boals, Mariana Castro, Gary Cook, Todd Lundberg, and Paula White. 2015. *Formative Language Assessment for English Learners*. Portsmouth, NH: Heinemann.

MacQuarrie, Brian. 2009. "Fear Envelops a Refuge of Immigrants in Maine." *The Boston Globe*, July 13, 1–2.

Majumdar, Archita Datta. 2014. "Survey Results Show Teachers Need More Professional Development." *ESOL English Language Bulletin* (July 25). Available at http://exclusive.multibriefs.com/content/survey-shows-teachers-need-more-professional-development/education.

Martin, Jim. 2001. "Language, Register, and Genre." In *Analysing English in a Global Context: A Reader*, edited by A. Burns and C. Coffin, 149–66. London: Routledge.

Martini, Martha, Evelyn Marino, Consuelo Raley, and Tracy Terrell. 1984. *The Rainbow Collection: Teachers' Guide*. Northvale, NJ: Santillana.

Marzano, Robert. 2004. *Building Background Knowledge for Academic Achievement: Research on What Works in Schools*. Alexandria, VA: Association for Supervision and Curriculum Development.

Marzano, Robert, Debra Pickering, and Jane Pollock. 2001. *Classroom Instruction That Works: Research-Based Strategies for Increasing Student Achievement*. Alexandria, VA: Association for Curriculum Development and Supervision.

Maxwell, Leslie. 2014a. "A Long Journey from Honduras to Middle School in the U.S." *Education Week* 34: 6.

———. 2014b. "U.S. School Enrollment Hits Majority-Minority Milestone." *Education Week* 34: 1, 12, 14–15.

McNeil, Linda, Eileen Coppola, and Judy Radigan. 2008. "Avoidable Losses: High-Stakes Accountability and the Dropout Crisis." *Education Policy Analysis Archives* 16 (3): 1–45.

Menken, Kate, and Tatyana Kleyn. 2009. "The Difficult Road for Long Term English Learners." *Educational Leadership* 66 (7): 1–3.

Menken, Kate, Tatyana Kleyn, and Nabin Chae. 2007. "Meeting the Needs of Long-Term English Language Learners in High School." New York: Research Institute for the Study of Language in an Urban Society.

———. 2012. "Spotlight on Long-Term English Language Learners: Characteristics and Prior Schooling of an Invisible Population." *International Multilingual Research Journal* 6: 121–42.

Mercuri, Sandra. 2015. "Teachers' Understanding of Practice: Planning and Implementing Preview/View/Review in the Dual Language Classroom." In *Research on Preparing Inservice Teachers to Work Effectively with Emergent Bilinguals*, edited by Yvonne Freeman and David Freeman. Bingley, UK: Emerald Books.

Miles, Heidi. 2014. *Teaching Content and Literacy Across the Curriculum*. Portsmouth, NH: Heinemann.

Moll, Luis. 1994. "Literacy Research in Homes and Classrooms: A Sociocultural Approach." In *Theoretical Models and Processes of Reading*, edited by R. B. Ruddell, M. R. Ruddell, and H. Singer. Newark, DE: International Reading Association.

New York State Education Dept. 2014. *Blueprint for ELLs' Success*, 1–5. New York: New York State Education Department.

No Child Left Behind (NCLB). 2001. "No Child Left Behind Act of 2001," Pub. L. No. 107–110, 20 USC §6319. 2002.

Nwosu, Chiamaka, Jeanne Bartalova, and Gregory Auclai. 2014. *Frequently Requested Statistics on Immigrants and Immigration in the United States*. Washington, DC: Migration Policy Institute.

O'Hara, Susan, Jeff Zwiers, and Robert Pritchard. 2014. "Cutting to the Common Core: Academic Language Development Network." *Language Magazine* (January): 24–27.

Olsen, Laurie. 2010a. "Changing Course for Long-Term English Learners." *Leadership* 40 (2): 30–33.

———. 2010b. *Reparable Harm: Fulfilling the Unkept Promise of Educational Opportunity for California's Long-Term English Learners*. Long Beach, CA: Californians Together.

———. 2014. *Meeting the Unique Needs of Long Term English Language Learners: A Guide for Educators*, 1–41. Washington, DC: National Education Association.

Ramírez, J. David. 1991. *Final Report: Longitudinal Study of Structured English Immersion Strategy, Early-Exit and Late-Exit Bilingual Education Programs*. Washington, DC: U.S. Department of Education.

Richards, Jack, and Theodore Rodgers. 1986. *Approaches and Methods in Language Teaching: A Description and Analysis*. New York: Cambridge University Press.

Rigby. 2004. *Our Book of Maps*. On Our Way to English. Barrington, IL: Rigby.

Rivers, Wilga, and Mary Temperley. 1978. *A Practical Guide to the Teaching of English as a Second or Foreign Langauge*. New York: Oxford University Press.

Rodriguez, Alma. 2009. "Culturally Relevant Books: Connecting Hispanic Students to the Curriculum." *GiST Colombian Journal of Bilingual Education* 3: 11–29.

Rogers, Carl. 1951. *Client-Centered Therapy*. Boston: Houghton Mifflin.

Rolstad, Kellie, Kate Mahoney, and Gene Glass. 2005. "A Meta-Analysis of Program Effectiveness Research on English Language Learners." *Educational Policy* 19 (4): 572–94.

Romijn, Elizabeth, and Contee Seely. 1979. *Live Action English*. San Francisco: Alemany Press.

Rosario, Vanessa Pérez, and Vivien Cao. 2015. *The CUNY–NYSIEB Guide to Translanguaging in Latino/a Literature*. New York: CUNY–NYSIEB Graduate Center.

Rosenblum, Marc R. 2015. "Unaccompanied Child Migration to the United States: The Tension Between Protection and Prevention." *Translatlantic Council on Migration*. Washington, DC: Migration Policy Institute.

Samson, Jennifer F., and Brian A. Collins. 2012. *Preparing All Teachers to Meet the Needs of English Language Learners*. Washington, DC: Center for American Progress.

Samway, Katherine, Gail Whang, and Mary Pippitt. 1995. *Buddy Reading: Cross-Age Tutoring in a Multicultural School*. Portsmouth, NH: Heinemann.

Sánchez, María Teresa, Ivana Espinet, and Kate Seltzer. 2014. *Supporting Emergent Bilinguals in New York: Understanding Successful School Practices*. New York: CUNY–NYSIEB.

Saunders, William, Claude Goldenberg, and David Marcelletti. 2013. "English Language Development: Guidelines for Instruction." *American Educator* 37 (2): 13–25.

Scarcella, Robin. 1990. *Teaching Language Minority Students in the Multicultural Classroom*. Englewood Cliffs, NJ: Prentice-Hall Regents.

Schifini, Alfredo. 1985. "Sheltered English: Content-Area Instruction for Limited English Proficiency Students." Los Angeles: Los Angeles County Office of Education.

Schleppegrell, Mary J. 2004. *The Language of Schooling: A Functional Linguistics Perspective*. Mahwah, NJ: Lawrence Erlbaum.

Schleppegrell, Mary, and Luciana de Oliveira. 2006. "An Integrated Language and Content Approach for History Teachers." *Journal of English for Academic Purposes* 5: 254–68.

Seely, Contee, and Elizabeth Romjin. 2006. *TPR Is More Than Commands at All Levels*. Berkeley, CA: Command Performance Language Institute.

Segal, Bertha. 1983. *Teaching English Through Action*. Brea, CA: Berty Segal, Inc.

Severns, Maggie. 2012. *Starting Early with English Language Learners: First Lesson from Illinois*. Washington, DC: New American Foundation.

Short, Deborah. 1999. "The Sheltered Instruction Observation Protocol: A Tool for Teacher-Researcher Collaboration and Professional Development." Washington, DC: Center for Research on Education, Diversity, and Excellence.

Short, Deborah, and Shannon Fitzsimmons. 2007. *Double the Work: Challenges and Solutions to Acquiring Language and Academic Literacy for Adolescent English Language Learners—A Report to Carnegie Corporation of New York*. Washington, DC: Alliance for Excellent Education.

Short, Deborah, Mary Ellen Vogt, and Jana Echevarria. 2011. *The SIOP Model for Teaching Science to English Learners*. Boston: Allyn & Bacon.

Short, Kathy, Jerome Harste, and Carolyn Burke. 1996. *Creating Classrooms for Authors and Inquirers*. Portsmouth, NH: Heinemann.

Skinner, B. F. 1957. *Verbal Behavior*. New York: Appleton.

Skutnabb-Kangas, Tove. 1983. *Bilingualism or Not: The Education of Minorities*. Clevedon, UK: Multilingual Matters.

Skutnabb-Kangas, Tove, and P. Toukomaa. 1976. *Teaching Migrant Children's Mother Tongue and Learning the Language of the Host Country in the Context of the Socio-cultural Situation of the Migrant Family*. Helsinki: The Finnish National Commission for UNESCO.

Slavin, Robert, and A. Cheung. 2004. *Effective Reading Programs for English Language Learners: A Best-Evidence Synthesis*. www.csos.jhu.edu/crespar/techReports/Report66.pdf.

Smith, Karl, Sheri D. Shappard, David W. Johnson, and Roger T. Johnson. 2005. "Pedagogies of Engagement: Classroom-Based Practices." *Journal of Engineering Education* 94 (1): 87–101.

Snow, Marguerite, and Donna Brinton. 1997. *The Content-Based Classroom: Perspectives on Integrating Language and Content*. White Plains, NY: Longman.

Soto, Mary. 2014. "A Self-Study of Teacher Educator Practice: Strategies and Activities to Use with Authentic Texts." In *Research on Preparing Preservice Teachers to Work Effectively with Emergent Bilinguals*, edited by Yvonne Freeman and David Freeman. Bingley, UK: Emerald Books.

Stevick, Earl W. 1976. *Memory, Meaning and Method*. Rowley, MA: Newbury House.

Strong, Richard, Harvey Silver, and Amy Robinson. 1995. "Strengthening Student Engagement: What Do Students Want?" *Educational Leadership* 53 (1): 8–12.

Swain, Merril. 1985. "Communicative Competence: Some Roles of Comprehensible Output in its Development." In *Input in Second Language Acquisition*, edited by S. Gass and C. Madden, 235–53. Rowley, MA: Newbury House.

TESOL. 2006. *PreK–12 English Language Proficiency Standards*. Alexandria, VA: Teachers of English to Speakers of Other Languages.

Texas Education Agency (TEA). 2013. *Texas Essential Knowledge and Skills for Health: Subchapter A. Elementary*, Chapter 115, edited by TEA. Austin: Texas Education Agency.

Thomas, Wayne P., and Virigina P. Collier. 1995. "Acquiring a Second Language for School." In *Language Minority Student Achievement and Program Effectiveness*. Washington, DC: National Clearinghouse for Bilingual Education (NCBE).

Thomas, Wayne P., and Virginia P. Collier. 2002. "A National Study of School Effectiveness for Language Minority Students' Long-Term Academic Achievement." www.crede.usc.edu/research/llaa/1.1_es.html.

Tiessen, Jasmin, and Dawn Dust. 2006. *Building Literacy Skills Through Buddy Reading*. Saskatoon, SK: McDowell Foundation.

Van Lier, Leo. 1988. *The Classroom and the Language Learner*. New York: Longman.

Vogt, Mary Ellen, Jana Echavarría, and Deborah Short. 2010. *The SIOP Model for Teaching English-Language Arts to English Learners*. Boston: Allyn & Bacon.

Vygotsky, L. 1962. *Thought and Language*. Translated by Eugenia Hanfmann Gertrude Vakar. Cambridge, MA: MIT Press.

Ward, Daniel. 2010. "Scaffolding Success: Five Principles for Succeeding with Adolescent English Learners." *Language* (February): 24–29.

Walter, Teresa, Maryann Cucchiara, Rebecca Blum-Martínez, Lily Wong-Fillmore, Gabriela Uro, Lynne Rosen, and Michael Casserly. 2014. *A Framework for Raising Expectations and Instructional Rigor for English Language Learners*, 1–29. Washington, DC: Council of the Great City Schools.

Widdowson, Henry. 1978. *Teaching Language as Communication*. Oxford, UK: Oxford University Press.

Wiggins, Grant, and Jay McTighe. 2005. *Understanding by Design*. Alexandria, VA: ASCD.

Wiley, Terrance G., David R. Garcia, Arnold B. Danzig, and Monica L. Stigler. 2013. "Language Policy, Politics, and Diversity in Education." *Review of Research in Education* 38 (1): vii–xxiii.

Wilkins, D. A. 1976. *Notional Syllabuses*. Oxford, UK: Oxford University Press.

Wong-Fillmore, Lily. 1991. "Second-Language Learning in Children: A Model of Language Learning in Context." In *Language Processing in Bilingual Children*, edited by Ellen Bialystok, 49–69. Cambridge, MA: Cambridge University Press.

Zwiers, Jeff. 2007. *Building Academic Language: Essential Practices for Content Classrooms*. Hoboken, NJ: Jossey-Bass.

———. 2014. *Building Academic Language: Meeting Common Core Standards Across the Disciplines, Grades 5–12*. 2nd edition. San Francisco: Jossey-Bass.

Children's and Adolescent Literature Cited

Abraham, Susan Gonzales, and Denise Gonzales Abraham. 2004. *Cecilia's Year*. El Paso, TX: Cinco Puntos Press.

Ada, Alma Flor. 1990a. *Just One Seed*. Carmel, CA: Hampton-Brown.

———. 1990b. *Una semilla nada más*. Carmel, CA: Hampton-Brown.

———. 1991. *Días y días de poesía*. Carmel, CA: Hampton-Brown.

———. 2003. *A Magical Encounter: Latino Children's Literature in the Classroom*. Boston: Pearson.

Aloian, Molly, and Bobbie Kalman. 2006a. *The Antarctic Habitat*. New York: Crabtree Publishing.

———. 2006b. *The Arctic Habitat*. New York: Crabtree Publishing.

———. 2006c. *Water Habitats*. New York: Crabtree Publishing.

———. 2007a. *El habitat de la Antártida*. New York: Crabtree Publishing.

———. 2007b. *El habitat del Artico*. New York: Crabtree Publishing.

———. 2007c. *Habitats acúaticos*. New York: Crabtree Publishing.

Ancona, George. 2004. *Mi familia: My Family*. New York: Children's Book Press.

Anzaldúa, Gloria. 1993. *Friends from the Other Side: Amigos del otro lado*. San Francisco: Children's Book Press.

Arlon, Penelope. 2013. *Explora tu mundo: La selva tropical*. New York: Scholastic en Español.

Bertrand, Diane. 2007. *Somos primos: We Are Cousins*. Houston, TX: Piñata Books.

Blackaby, Susan. 2003. *Plant Packages: A Book About Seeds*. North Mankato, MN: Capstone.

Bradbury, Ray. 2014. "The Pedestrian." In *The Golden Apples of the Sun*. New York: HarperCollins.

Brown, Monica. 2011. *Waiting for Biblioburro*. Berkeley, CA: Tricycle Press.

Browne, Anthony. 2000. *My Dad*. London, UK: Doubleday.

———. 2002. *Mi papá*. México, DF: Fondo de Cultura Económica.

———. 2005a. *Mi mamá*. México, DF: Fondo de Cultura Económica.

———. 2005b. *My Mom*. London, UK: Doubleday.

———. 2007a. *Mi hermano*. México, DF: Fondo de Cultura Económica.

———. 2007b. *My Brother*. London, UK: Doubleday.

Browne, Mónica. 2011. *Marisol McDonald Doesn't Match: Marisol McDonald no combina*. New York: Children's Book Press.

Bullard, Lisa. 2012. *Chelsea's Chinese New Year*. New York: Millbrook Press Trade.

Bunting, Eve. 1996. *Sunflower House*. New York: Trumpet.

———. 1998. *Going Home*. New York: HarperTrophy.

Canizares, Susan, and Pamela Chanko. 2003. *What Do Insects Do? ¿Qué hacen los insectos?* New York: Scholastic.

Canizares, Susan, and Mary Reid. 2003. *Where Do Insects Live? ¿Dónde viven los insectos?* New York: Scholastic.

Carden, Mary, and Mary Cappellini. 1997a. *I Am of Two Places*. Crystal Lake, IL: Rigby.

———. 1997b. *Soy de dos lugares*. Crystal Lake, IL: Rigby.

Carle, Eric. 2006. *The Very Busy Spider*. New York: Scholastic.

Carle, Eric. 2009. *The Tiny Seed*. New York: Little Simon.

Cha, Dia. 1998. *Dia's Story Cloth: The Hmong People's Journey of Freedom*. New York: Lee and Low Books.

Cheng, Andrea. 2013. *The Year of the Book*. Boston: HMH Books for Young Readers.

Choi, Yangsook. 2001. *The Name Jar*. New York: Knopf.

Cisneros, Sandra. 1984. *The House on Mango Street*. New York: Vintage Contemporaries.

Claes, Esther. 2015. *The Star*. Available at www.eastoftheweb.com/short-stories/UBooks /Star717.shtml.

Colato Laínez, René. 2004. *Waiting for Papá: Esperando a papá*. Houston: Arte Público Press.

———. 2009. *René Has Two Last Names/René tiene dos apellidos*. Houston, TX: Arte Público.

Collins, Suzanne. 2008. *The Hunger Games*. New York: Scholastic Press.

Dorros, Arthur. 1997. *Abuela*. New York: Penguin Putnam Books.

Fox, Mem. 2006. *Whoever You Are*. Boston: HMH Books for Young Readers.

Garza, Carmen Lomas. 1990. *Family Pictures: Cuadros de familia*. San Francisco: Children's Book Press.

———. 1996. *In My Family: En mi familia*. San Francisco: Children's Book Press.

———. 2005. *Family Pictures: Cuadros de familia*. 15th anniversary edition. San Francisco: Children's Book Press.

Garza, Xavier. 2005. *Lucha libre: The Man in the Silver Mask*. El Paso, TX: Cinco Puntos Press.

———. 2011. *Maximillian: The Mystery of the Guardian Angel: A Bilingual Lucha Libre Thriller*. El Paso, TX: Cinco Puntos Press.

———. 2013. *Maximillian and the Bingo Rematch: A Lucha Libre Sequel/Maximiliano y la Revancha de lotería: La Continuación de la Lucha Libre*. El Paso: Cinco Puntos Press.

———. 2015. *The Great and Mighty Nikko!: ¡El gran y poderoso Nikko!* El Paso, TX: Cinco Puntos Press.

Grande-Tabor, Nancy María. 2004. *Celebrations/Celebraciones: Holidays of the United States and Mexico/Días feriado de los Estados Unidos y México*. Watertown, MA: Charlesbridge.

Heller, Ruth. 1983. *La razón de ser una flor*. New York: Scholastic.

Heller, Ruth. 1992. *How to Hide a Butterfly and Other Insects*. New York: Grosset and Dunlap.

———. 1999. *The Reason for a Flower: A Book About Flowers, Pollen, and Seeds*. New York: Penguin Putnam Books for Young Readers.

Hussain, Asim. 2015. *Khadijah Goes to School—A Story About You*. 2d ed. Self-published (LogixPlayer Inc.).

Hutts Aston, Dianna, and Sylvia Long. 2014. *A Seed Is Sleepy*. San Francisco: Chronicle Books.

Jackson, Ian. 1998. *The Big Bug Search*. New York: Scholastic.

Jiménez, Francisco. 1997. *The Circuit: Stories from the Life of a Migrant Child*. Albuquerque: University of New Mexico Press.

———. 1998. *La mariposa*. Boston: Houghton Mifflin.

———. 2000. *La mariposa*. Spanish edition. Boston: Houghton Mifflin.

Jordan, Helene J. 1996. *Cómo crece una semilla*. Translated by María A. Fiol, *Harper Arco Iris*. New York: HarperCollins.

———. 2000. *How a Seed Grows*. New York: HarperCollins.

Kalman, Bobbie. 2000. *How Do Animals Find Food?* New York: Crabtree Publishing.

———. 2005. *¿Qué son los seres vivos?* New York: Crabtree Publishing.

———. 2006. *A Forest Habitat*. New York: Crabtree Publishing.

———. 2007a. *Plants Are Living Things*. New York: Crabtree Publishing.

———. 2007b. *Un habitat de bosque*. New York: Crabtree Publishing.

———. 2008a. *¿Cómo se adaptan los animales?* New York: Crabtree Publishing.

———. 2008b. *¿Cómo se encuentran alimento los animales?* New York: Crabtree Publishing.

———. 2008c. *¿Esto es un ser vivo?* New York: Crabtree Publishing.

———. 2008d. *Las plantas son seres vivos*. New York: Crabtree Publishing.

———. 2010a. *¿Dónde viven los animales?* New York: Crabtree Publishing.

———. 2010b. *Where Do Animals Live?* New York: Crabtree Publishing.

Kalman, Bobbie, and John Crossingham. 2006. *Land Habitats*. New York: Crabtree Publishing.

———. 2007. *Habitats terrestes: Introducción a los habitats*. New York: Crabtree Publishing.

Kalman, Bobbie, and Niki Walker. 2000. *How Do Animals Adapt?* New York: Crabtree Publishing.

Katz, Karen. 2012. *My First Chinese New Year*. New York: Square Fish.

Khan, Hena. 2012. *Golden Domes and Silver Lanterns: A Muslim Book of Colors*. San Francisco: Chronicle Books.

Krauss, Ruth. 1945. *The Carrot Seed*. New York: HarperTrophy.

———. 1978. *La semilla de zanahoria*. Translated by A. Palacios. New York: Scholastic.

Lai, Thanhha. 2013. *Inside Out and Back Again*. Brisbane, AU: University of Queensland Press.

Lambilly-Bresson, Elisabeth de. 2007. *Animales marinos*. York, PA: Gareth Stevens Publishing.

Latour, David, and Melissa Latour. 2014. *I Spy a Bug*. Self-published (Books with a Purpose).

Lin, Grace. 2013. *Bringing in the New Year*. New York: Knopf Books for Young Readers.

Lopes da Silva, María Lourdes. 2013. *Animales de la selva Amazónica*. Charleston, SC: CreateSpace.

Lucca, Mario. 2001. *Plants Grow from Seeds*. Washington, DC: National Geographic Society.

Macaulay, Kelley, and Bobbie Kalman. 2006a. *Backyard Habitats*. New York: Crabtree Publishing.

———. 2006b. *A Desert Habitat*. New York: Crabtree Publishing.

———. 2007a. *Habitats de jardin*. New York: Crabtree Publishing.

———. 2007b. *Un habitat de desierto*. New York: Crabtree Publishing.

———. 2003. *De las semillas nacen las plantas*. Washington, DC: National Geographic Society.

Marzollo, Jean. 1996. *I'm a Seed*. Carmel, CA: Hampton-Brown.

Mascareli, Amanda Leigh. 2014. "The Dangerous Rise of Electronic Cigarettes." In *Student Science: A Resource for the Society for Science and the Public*. Washington, DC: Society for Science and the Public.

McMillan, Bruce. 1994. *Growing Colors*. New York: William Morrow & Co.

Montanari, Donata. 2004. *Children Around the World*. Tonawanda, NY: Kids Can Press.

Myers, Walter Dean. 2015. *145th Street*. New York: Scholastic.

Nazario, Sonia. 2014. *Enrique's Journey* (YA version). New York: Delacourt Press.

———. 2015. "The Refugees at Our Door." New York Times, October 10. www.nytimes.com/2015/10/11/opinion/sunday/the-refugees-at-our-door.html?emc=eta1&_r=0.

Nelson, Kadir. 2015. *If You Plant a Seed*. New York: HarperCollins.

Oppenheim, Joanne. 1996. *Have You Seen Bugs?* New York: Scholastic.

Pérez, Amada Irma. 2002. *My Diary from Here to There: Mi diario de aquí hasta allá*. San Francisco: Children's Book Press.

Rajczak, Kristen. 2011. *Watch Corn Grow*. New York: Gareth Stevens.

Raloff, Janet. 2013. "Many Teens Try Alternatives to Cigarettes." In *Student Science: A Resource of the Society for Science and the Public*. Washington, DC: Society for Science and the Public.

Rattini, Kristin Baird. 2014. *Seed to Plant*. Washington, DC: National Geographic.

Reid, Mary, and Betsey Chessen. 1998. *Bugs, Bugs, Bugs*. New York: Scholastic.

Reiser, Lynn. 1998. *Tortillas and Lullabies/Tortillas y cancioncitas*. New York: Greenwillow Books.

Rice, Dona. 2012. *Niños alrededor del mundo*. Huntington Beach, CA: Teacher Created Materials.

Rivera-Ashford, Roni Capin. 2015. *My Tata's Remedios/Los remedios de mi tata*. El Paso, TX: Cinco Puntos Press.

Robbins, Ken. 2005. *Seeds*. New York: Atheneum.

Rodríguez, Luis. 1998. *América Is Her Name*. Willimantic, CT: Curbstone Press.

Ryan, Pam Muñoz. 2000. *Esperanza Rising*. New York: Scholastic.

Sáenz, Benjamin Alire. 2008. *A Perfect Season for Dreaming: Un tiempo perfecto para soñar*. El Paso, TX: Cinco Puntos Press.

Say, Allen. 1993. *Grandfather's Journey*. Boston: Houghton Mifflin.

———. 1997. *La jornada de abuelo*. Boston: Houghton Mifflin.

Shea, Pegi. 1995. *The Whispering Cloth: A Refugee's Story*. Honesdale, PA: Boyds Mills Press.

Smith, David J. 2009. *If America Were a Village*. Tonawanda, NY: Kids Can Press.

———. 2011. *If the World Were a Village*. 2d ed. Tonawanda, NY: Kids Can Press.

Soto, Gary. 2006. *Buried Onions*. Wilmington, MA: Houghton Mifflin Harcourt.

Spilsbury, Louise, and Richard Spilsbury. 2005. *Where Do Plants Grow?* Mankato, MN: Heinemann.

———. 2006. *¿Dónde crecen las plantas?* Mankato, MN: Heinemann.

Sweeney, Joan. 1998. *Me on the Map.* New York: Dragonfly Books.

Trapani, Iza. 1996. *The Itsy Bitsy Spider.* Boston: Houghton Mifflin.

Vidard, Estelle. 2008. *Niños del mundo.* Barcelona, Spain: Molino.

Waber, Bernard. 1972. *Ira Sleeps Over.* Boston: Houghton Mifflin.

Wainman, Margaret. 1982. *One Elephant, Two Elephants.* Port Coquitlam, BC: Class Size Books.

Young, Caroline. 2010. *The Big Bug Search.* Glasgow, UK: Usborne.

Zentella, Ana Celia. 2000. *Growing Up Bilingual.* Malden, MA: Blackwell Publishers.

Index

More best-selling resources from David and Yvonne Freeman

Essential Linguistics, Second Edition
What Teachers Need to Know to Teach ESL, Reading, Spelling, and Grammar
Grades K–12 / 978-0-325-05093-5 / 2014 / 312pp

Between Worlds, Third Edition
Access to Second Language Acquisition
Grades K–12 / 978-0-325-03088-3 / 2011 / 296pp

Academic Language for English Language Learners and Struggling Readers
How to Help Students Succeed Across Content Areas
Grades 6–12 / 978-0-325-01136-3 / 2008 / 232pp

Diverse Learners in the Mainstream Classroom
(with co-editor Reynaldo Ramírez)
Strategies for Supporting ALL Students Across Content Areas—English Language Learners, Students with Disabilities, Gifted/Talented Students
Grades PreK–12 / 978-0-325-01313-8 / 2008 / 272pp

For more information or to place an order, visit **Heinemann.com**.

 @HeinemannPub

WEB Heinemann.com • **CALL 800.225.5800** • **FAX 877.231.6980**

Houghton Mifflin Harcourt

Heinemann
DEDICATED TO TEACHERS